EMERGING MARKET ECONOMIES

Transition and Development

Series Editor: Professor Ken Morita
Faculty of Economics, Hiroshima University, Japan

The Transition and Development series aims to provide high quality research books that examine transition and development societies in a broad sense – including countries that have made a decisive break with central planning as well as those in which governments are introducing elements of a market approach to promote development. Books examining countries moving in the opposite direction will also be included. Titles in the series will encompass a range of social science disciplines. As a whole the series will add up to a truly global academic endeavour to grapple with the questions transition and development economies pose.

Also in the series:

Facilitating Transition by Internationalization
Edited by Marjan Svetlicic and Matija Rojec
ISBN 0 7546 3133 8

Modeling Russia's Economy in Transition
Peter Wehrheim
ISBN 0 7546 3299 7

Enhanced Transition Through Outward Internationalization
Andreja Jaklic and Marjan Svetlicic
ISBN 0 7546 3134 6

Forthcoming titles:

Economic Reforms and Capital Markets in Central Europe
Ken Morita
ISBN 0 7546 0884 0

Beyond Transition
Edited by Marek Dabrowski, Ben Slay and Jaroslaw Neneman
ISBN 0 7546 3970 3

Emerging Market Economies

Globalization and Development

Edited by
GRZEGORZ W. KOLODKO
*TIGER, Leon Kozminski Academy of
Entrepreneurship and Management*

ASHGATE

© Grzegorz W. Kolodko 2003

The editor has asserted his moral right under the Copyright, Designs and Patents Act, 1988, to be identified as the editor of this work.

Published by
Ashgate Publishing Limited
Gower House
Croft Road
Aldershot
Hants GU11 3HR
England

Ashgate Publishing Company
Suite 420
101 Cherry Street
Burlington, VT 05401-4405
USA

Ashgate website: http://www.ashgate.com

British Library Cataloguing in Publication Data
Emerging market economies : globalization and development.
- (Transition and development)
1. Economic development 2. Globalization 3. Capitalism
4. Developing countries - Economic policy
I. Kolodko, Grzegorz W.
338.9'001724

Library of Congress Cataloging-in-Publication Data
Emerging market economics : globalization and development / edited by Grzegorz W. Kolodko.
p. cm.
Includes bibliographical references and index.
ISBN 0-7546-3706-9
1. International economic integration. 2. Globalization--Economic aspects. 3. Economic development. 4. Globalization--Economic aspects--Developing countries. 5. Structural adjustment (Economic policy)--Developing countries. 6. Developing countries--Economic policy. 7. International economic relations. I. Kolodko, Grzegorz W.

HF1418.5.E54 2003
338.9--dc21

2003052112

ISBN 0 7546 3706 9

The articles in this volume comprise the proceedings of the Fourth International Conference on Globalization and Catching-up in Emerging Market Economies, Warsaw, 16–17 May 2002, organized by TIGER (Transformation, Integration and Globalization Economic Research), Leon Kozminski Academy of Entrepreneurship and Management (WSPiZ), Warsaw, Poland.

Printed and bound in Great Britain by Biddles Ltd, *www.biddles.co.uk*

Contents

List of Contributors

Keith Crane, The RAND Corporation, USA

László Csaba, Central European University, Budapest, Universitas Debrecen, Hungarian Academy of Science

Daniel Daianu, Academy of Economic Studies, Bucharest, Romania, and Visiting Professor, UCLA, Los Angeles, USA

Gang Fan, Director of the National Institute of Economic Research, China Reform Foundation, Beijing, China

Michael Keren, The Hebrew University of Jerusalem, Israel

Grzegorz W. Kolodko, Director of TIGER, Leon Kozminski Academy of Entrepreneurship and Management (WSPiZ), Warsaw, Poland, and John C. Evans Scholar in Polish and European Studies, University of Rochester, Rochester, NY, USA

Tadeusz Kowalik, Polish Academy of Sciences and WSPiZ, Warsaw, Poland

Nguyuru H. I. Lipumba, Senior Research Fellow, The Multi-Environmental Society (MESO), Dar es Salaam, Tanzania

D. Mario Nuti, University di Roma 'La Sapienza', Rome, Italy, and Visiting Professor, London Business School, UK

Gur Ofer, The Hebrew University of Jerusalem, Israel, The New Economic School, Moscow, Russia

Zbyszko Tabernacki, Global Insight Inc, Washington, DC, USA

Masahiro Taguchi, Okayama University, Japan

Rodrigo Vergara, Centro de Estudios Publicos (CEP) and Universidad Catolica de Chile, Santiago, Chile

George Vojta, President, Financial Services Forum, New York, USA

Introduction

Grzegorz W. Kolodko

Globalization is a multi-faceted process. Therefore, it gives rise to numerous interpretations, emotions, views and comments. This is natural, for aspects of globalization are not restricted to economic matters (which, nevertheless, are the main focus of this volume), but also include social, political and cultural issues. This historical, multithreaded process, unique though it is, can be viewed from as many different angles as there are ways to perceive one and the same reality. For some, globalization stands for the increasing uniformity of consumption patterns – the notorious MacDonaldization; others emphasize the subordination of weaker regions and nations to the interests of greater powers, especially, the transnational corporations whose income often exceeds by far the output of entire nations.

In this volume, globalization is discussed as a large and intricate economic phenomenon. It is understood as the historical liberalization process with the ensuing accelerated integration of the formerly quite isolated markets of goods, capital and (to a lesser degree) labor into a single world market. Thus emerging from the globalization process are the elements of a single world economy. This is a heavily interconnected system, although not all of its links are obvious at first sight. To discern them, penetrating economic analysis is not enough; one also needs to adopt various other perspectives: anthropological, sociological or even philosophical. Yet economics – both the macroeconomics of the modern world market and the political economy of the globalization process, which alters the appearance of this market – remains key.

Yet, what kind of market is it? This is the question addressed in this book – a joint work of more than a dozen scholars from several continents, most of whom sit on the Scientific Advisory Board of TIGER – Transformation, Integration and Globalization Economic Research – an independent economic think-tank affiliated with the Leon Kozminski Academy of Entrepreneurship and Management (WSPiZ) in Warsaw (www.tiger.edu.pl).

The authors ask many new questions and often provide innovative answers, while addressing the fundamental issues pertaining to the impact of the current globalization phase on output growth and the processes of socio-economic development. There is no question that globalization means not only progress – although progress does appear to be its dominant component – but also backwardness; it involves not only development and an ever increasing abundance of goods, but also the marginalization of entire social or occupational groups, or even regions; it not only promotes the transfer of technology and cultural goods, but also facilitates the spread of terrorism and social pathology. Thus the emergence of a new, global economic system, characterized by new types of technological, financial, commercial and investment interdependencies, as well as new forms of political and cultural relationships – formerly barely imaginable – evokes diverse responses. Obviously, various interpretations and behaviors follow: from euphoria on the part of some beneficiaries of the newly emerging economic arrangements, to anti-globalist sentiments and movements which have been gaining momentum in recent years.

The last-mentioned phenomena do not seem, as yet, to threaten globalization's further progress. But if the arrogance of the rich towards the poor, the strong towards the weak, the developed towards the backward continues, and if the real causes underlying the grievances of huge parts of society and considerable sectors of the world economy at a lower development level are ignored, such sentiments and movements may intensify, while the ensuing protests are likely to take a more organized form. Then some processes may get out of control – bearing in mind that many of them already unfold outside any *political* control – affecting the further progress of globalization. Such changes would hardly be welcome, because globalization *is* a good 'conception' for the future. The quotes are necessary here, because, in reality, no one ever conceived globalization: it came of its own accord – along with technological progress and economic liberalization, cultural change and new political agendas. And it came to stay, although the path of its further evolution, its trends and pace are far from settled.

All told, globalization brings more opportunities than threats. But is this statement true at all times and places? By no means. There exist individuals, groups, sectors, countries and regions that face more threats than opportunities. Under the circumstances, it is impossible to avoid situations that breed disagreement. Unless these are promptly defused using the right methods, they are likely to evolve into open conflicts, of which already there is no shortage. But who is to coordinate the policy to oppose such tendencies and situation in the absence of a world government in the world economy? Surely, it is becoming increasingly apparent that many problems can only be solved through better global coordination of activities.

Globalization opens additional, novel opportunities also for countries at a relatively lower development level, including those in the midst of the strenuous post-socialist transformation. But it also undoubtedly creates a new risk. And whereas the balance of these two tendencies appears to be favorable, the actual gains depend on the quality of the economic policy and the pursued strategy of socio-economic development. Therefore, the global economic game will never run short of winners or losers. But you don't become a winner or loser *because* of the ongoing globalization. Globalization means just new rules of the game, whose outcome will always predominantly depend on competent policies. And the latter must be based (this is a necessary but not sufficient condition) on sound economic theory. I hope this volume contributes to its development.

PART I
GLOBALIZATION, TRANSFORMATION AND GROWTH

Chapter 1

Globalization and Catching-up in Emerging Market Economies

Grzegorz W. Kolodko

1. Introduction

To believe is the privilege of politicians. Economists should *know*. The economic policy makers – who are typically economists put in charge of politics – usurp the prerogatives of both groups and mistake belief for knowledge. What they believe is that, the way the world is made, the poor should be able to catch up with the rich and reduce the enormous differences in the level of economic development. Yet, these differences somehow grow year by year. Today nearly half of the world's inhabitants live on less than two dollars a day, and a billion people – a sixth of mankind – subsist on less than a dollar.

Faith, of course, can help, but knowledge is of decisive importance. What then do we know about the capacity of the emerging, relatively backward market economies to catch up with the highly developed countries? What systemic arrangements and development strategies might lead to this objective? What historic lessons are there to be learned concerning the management of economic growth in the future? How to distinguish the inevitable legacy of the past, which can only evolve in time, from the economic policy options left open? These are the questions that should constantly be addressed, all the more so since the old answers become outdated as the development factors change.

A third of a century ago, in 1969, the United Nations set up an expert group, known as Pearson Panel, to suggest measures facilitating growth in less developed countries and to level out the differences in living standards. Guided by belief, rather than knowledge, the Panel proposed development strategies which supposedly promised the backward countries (many of which were then in the process of gaining independence after centuries of colonialism) to attain a 6-percent growth over the coming decades. Countries that managed thus to accelerate their economic growth were expected to become – mainly through the expansion of exports – self-reliant partners in the world economy by the year 2000.

The year 2000 has passed. And it turns out that the course of development outlined by the Pearson Panel is a rare exception rather than a rule. The United Nations established, therefore, a new expert group, this time headed by the former

President Ernesto Zedillo of Mexico, whose task is to advise on policies aiming to foster economic catching-up and, in particular, to implement the ambitious goals put on the agenda by the UN Millennium Summit – one of which was to reduce the number of people living in extreme poverty by at least half a billion until 2015. The Zedillo Panel believes that this could be achieved through rapid economic development, if only the rich countries would increase their annual assistance for poor countries to 0.44 per cent of their GDP. The trouble is, as we all know, that they would not (although they should) and so development aid lags at a paltry 0.22 per cent. Consequently, the numbers of the poor do not shrink, disparities in development level increase, and distances to catch up grow. The year 2015 will soon have passed, too, conceivably, without bringing any noticeable improvement. There will be few winners, many more losers, and all the remaining actors are also likely to be dissatisfied with the way the globalized economy operates and the living standards achieved. Can we do better than that?

This paper deals with the fundamental theoretical aspects of and practical prerequisites to the catching-up process in the emerging market economies. Following this introduction, Part 2 presents the hitherto efforts in this area and the actual socio-economic processes going on over the last decades. Part 3 describes the current phase of globalization and analyzes its influence on the trends in output change and its pace. Part 4 contains a characterization of the young, institutionally immature market economies which seek to boost their growth rate through integration with the global system. The disparities in development level between various countries and regions in the world economy are discussed in Part 5, along with their implications for the catching-up process. Finally, Part 6 is devoted to the policies of systemic reform and to conclusions concerning a desirable development strategy to foster fast, sustained growth in the emerging market economies.

2. Back to the Future

The past is gone. And so is the present, because in reality it does not exist, every passing moment turning instantly and irrevocably into the past. Thus all that is left is the future. Which is the most important thing. However, to be able to couch our expectations about the future in rational terms, we need a good understanding of the past. Otherwise, we will never manage to forecast future development processes with reasonable accuracy, or to actively shape these processes (which is even more important). For the socio-economic aspects of the future are not only the function of time and some chaotic development processes, but, first and foremost, depend on a conscious development strategy combined with a growth and distribution policy.

Throughout history, **only about 30 nations, with a total population of less than a billion – that is, about 15 per cent of mankind – has managed to attain a relatively high development level**, with GDP per head exceeding USD 15,000 in terms of purchasing power parity (PPP).[1] Outside North America and Western

Europe, this group comprises the member countries of the OECD from the Asia and Pacific region – Australia, Japan, South Korea and New Zealand – as well as Singapore. This level has also been achieved by some oil-exporting OPEC countries (Brunei, Kuwait and Qatar), certain economies with special structural characteristics (like the Bahamas, Martinique and Taiwan), and a few overseas territories of highly developed countries (like French Polynesia or New Caledonia). In 2001, the highest-income group was joint by the first and only post-socialist country thus far – the tiny (2 million inhabitants) Slovenia.[2] Next in line is the Czech Republic, where GDP per head is expected to exceed USD 15,000 in 2004.[3]

On the other extreme are countries unable to overcome the vicious circle of poverty. Some of them not only fail to close the staggering gap that separates them from highly developed countries, but keep plunging in stagnation and recession, lagging further and further behind not only economically, but also culturally. It happened in the past, and it happens, occasionally, today (Magarinos and Sercovich 2001). No doubt it will also happen in the future. Why? The answer is that only few countries in history managed to catch the train of progress. It was only possible if three favorable circumstances co-occurred.

First, economic development always requires technological progress. Without the spread of new manufacturing methods and the implementation of novel technologies that change the organization of production, no innovation is possible – and it is innovation that drives economic growth. Necessary – but not sufficient – conditions of technological progress also include, obviously, high-quality human capital, an adequate level of education and science, as well as efficient system arrangements in these areas (Kwiatkowski 2001).

Second, in order to sustain long-term development trends, it is essential to reform the institutional framework of an efficient market economy. Otherwise, even a relative technological superiority is no guarantee of rapid economic growth, as creative enterprise becomes stifled in such circumstances.[4] Obviously, creative enterprise is even less possible in technologically backward countries. Thus, without the capacity for economic reform, rapid output growth can hardly be relied on.

Third, **a creative feedback between technological progress and economic reform calls for political determination on the part of the political elites, who must be willing to upset the existing balance and to challenge the established position of conservative interest groups.** Only then can the 'new' gain the upper hand of the 'old', which is necessary for a sustained productivity growth. The fear of the temporary confusion that accompanies this kind of change often paralyzes the authorities, who then begin – through their reluctance to stimulate and institute the required reforms – to hamper rather than facilitate economic progress and socio-economic development.[5]

One needs to reminisce about the past – including more distant past, spanning several centuries – if for nothing else, then in order to realize, at the outset of a new millennium, that history is happening at all times. Now, too, because of the **three momentous processes coinciding today: the current phase of permanent**

globalization (Bordo, Eichengreen, Irwin 1999; Frankel 2001; Kolodko 2002a), **the post-socialist transformation** (Blanchard 1997; Lavigne 1999; Kolodko 2000a), and **the modern scientific and technological revolution** (Raymond 1999; OECD 2000; Payson 2000; Kolodko 2001d). It is in this context that we should perceive modern developments, so as to avoid missing the train of progress once again. Not everyone succeeded in this task in the past: actually, few did. The same thing is being repeated now: some will get on the train, some will be left waiting, and some might even get pushed off the platform.

Incidentally, this phenomenon has already been observed for two decades. This is shown, for instance, by a World Bank report (World Bank 2002a) which distinguishes – apart from the rich economies[6] – two main groups of states. Today the term 'developing countries' is less frequently used with reference to these, for the simple reason that some of them are hardly developing. Instead, one speaks about more globalized countries (MGC) and less globalized countries (LGC). This distinction is based on the participation in the international labor division, measured by the dynamics of foreign trade. A third part of the countries where the growth of the proportion of foreign trade volume to GDP in the 1980s and 1990s was steepest has been classified as MGCs, and the remaining two thirds as LGCs.[7]

The group of 24 countries which become more actively involved in the world economy (MGCs) has a total population of nearly 3 billion. The 49 countries less tightly integrated through foreign trade with the world system (LGCs) have about 1.1 billion inhabitants. The circumstances of the two groups differ widely, and changes in output level and dynamics, as well as the living standards, follow different trends in either group (Table 1.1).

Table 1.1: Characteristics of more and less globalized countries

Socioeconomic characteristics	More globalized countries (24 countries)	Less globalized countries (49 countries)
Population, 1997 (billions)	2.9	1.1
Per capita GDP, 1980 (USD)	1,488	1,947
Per capita GDP, 1997 (USD)	2,485	2,133
Inflation, 1980 (per cent)	16	17
Inflation, 1997 (per cent)	6	9
Rule of law index, 1997 (world average = 0)	-0.04	-0.48

Source: World Bank 2002a.

In 1980, GDP per head (in PPP terms) in the MGC group stood, on average, at less than USD 1,500; by 1997, it increased to nearly USD 2,500 – that is, by almost two thirds. In the LGC group, the increase amounted merely to about USD 200, or less than 10 per cent. Taking into account just the last five years, the respective proportions become even more striking. While the MGCs have kept developing at an average rate of about 5 per cent annually and managed to further increase GDP per head by almost USD 400, reaching about USD 3,100 in 2002, the LGCs have recorded an about 6-percent drop in GDP per head, to about USD 1,900 in 2002. Thus the difference in this respect changed from about USD 500 in favor of the LGCs in 1980 to about USD 1200 in favor of the MGCs in 2002. These are significant qualitative differences which alter the face of the modern world.

Such tendencies indicate that **within the time span of a single generation, the economies that take more active part in globalization managed to double their real income per head**. Unfortunately, the income of other societies, less involved in the development of international trade, did not increase, on average, at all. If a shorter time span is taken into account, and these processes are viewed solely from the perspective of the 1990s, we will see a 63-percent increase of GDP per head in the MGC group[8] and a drop by about 10 per cent in the LGC group[9] (Figure 1.1).

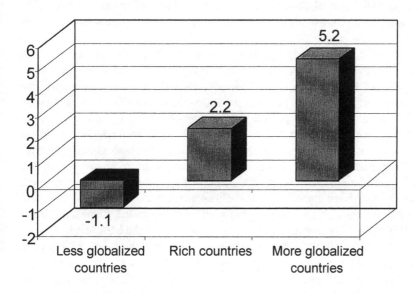

Figure 1.1: **Economic growth in the world economy, 1991–2000 (GDP per head in per cent)**

Source: Dollar and Kraay 2001.

However, one must not overlook in this context the fact that this general, fairly encouraging picture of change results mainly from the unprecedented progress attained by just two countries. But these were quite special countries, too: China and India, inhabited jointly by some 2.3 billion people. Therefore, their growth rate has an overwhelming impact on the indicators of the entire MGC group.

It is an important and noteworthy fact that both China and India – although they follow different routes and their progressive integration with the world economy and involvement in the worldwide competition likewise takes dissimilar paths – pursue development strategies by no means based on the neoliberal orthodoxy and the classical prescriptions that stem from the so-called Washington Consensus,[10] which has been invoked so often recently in mainstream economics and figured prominently in the recommendations given to many countries by the G-7 countries, the International Monetary Fund and the World Bank.

Both China and India are reforming their respective economies at their own, not too quick pace, but with a great deal of consistency and determination. They liberalize capital movements gradually and with moderation, while the exchange rates are effectively controlled by the state at all times. Moreover, their monetary policy is subordinated to the overall national policy, the top priority of which is rapid economic growth. To this end, state intervention is used in both countries more extensively than elsewhere, mainly in the form of industrial and trade policies. Such a combination of structural reform and development policy brings favorable results.[11]

Chinese GDP increased in the 1980s by as much as 162 per cent, which amounts to an average real year-to-year growth of 10.1 per cent. In the 1990s, growth was even faster, reaching 10.7 per cent annually, to produce a cumulative output increase of another 176 per cent. In 2000–2002, growth rate has somewhat declined, fluctuating around 7 per cent. Thus over the past 23 years – within the time span of a single generation – GDP in China has grown by a staggering 780 per cent! Given the population growth at the same time, the increase of GDP per head was, at 575 per cent, relatively lower, but this too is a giant leap – for which few historical precedents exist – in the field of economic catching-up and, consequently, the living standards. Yet the disparities remain enormous. It should be borne in mind that, despite this successful, great step forward, Chinese GDP per head (in PPP terms), still comes up to a mere 12 per cent of the USA level.

India, in turn, saw in the 1980s an average annual growth rate of 5.8 per cent, which increased to 6 per cent in the following decade. In the last three years (2000–2002), real GDP growth has been around 5 per cent. Thus the aggregate output growth within the time span of one generation (1980–2002) has totaled 264 per cent, or 130 per cent on a per head basis, because of the much higher population growth than in China.[12] Thus when it comes to closing the gap between rich economies and the MGC group, one should remember that if the world's two most populous countries were to be excluded from this group, the picture would be far less optimistic. The MGC population would then drop from three billion to 700 million, among which the income growth would be far less impressive.

On the other hand, there exist countries which have been thus far unable to cope. Not managing to reduce the gap, some of them have actually been losing distance. Unfortunately, from the point of view of the attained development level (or, to put it differently, relative backwardness), the latter group comprises nearly all the economies of Central and Eastern Europe and the former Soviet Union, in the midst of a lengthy and complex transition from central planning to free market. This transition is inseparable from the process of successive opening up to foreign contacts that will lead in time to full integration with the global economy (IMF 2000b; Kolodko 2000c and 2001a).

Characteristically, out of the total number of 28 post-socialist economies, only Hungary has found its way to the more globalized group. All the 15 post-Soviet republics, as well as the remaining 11 countries of Central and Eastern Europe and Mongolia, showed in the previous decade too low foreign trade dynamics[13] to qualify, using the World Bank methodology, to that group.

Of course, this fact by itself does not amount to much. Far more importantly, in the 1990s, the distance between these countries and more highly developed and affluent societies further increased. Whereas GDP in post-socialist countries plummeted in 11 years (1990–2000) in absolute terms by an alarming 28 per cent,[14] the seven most highly developed economies of the world – known as G-7 – recorded during the same years a 28-percent increase. Respectively, in the 15 European Union countries, growth amounted to 24 per cent and in OECD countries, to some 31 per cent.[15] Thus the already enormous gap between the post-socialist region and the most advanced economies was further dramatically broadened. Great as the distance was, now it is even greater.

This is highly significant. After all, **one of the fundamental economic arguments in favor of the post-socialist systemic transformation was – and remains – the conviction that market transition will contribute to greater economic efficiency and will soon lead to higher growth rates, compared not only with central planning, but also with the developed market economies.** Thus far, 13 years into the transition, this is hardly the case. In time, however, these predictions may materialize, although – as the experience of recent years shows – the economic transformation alone is not enough. What is needed is also an appropriate strategy of socio-economic development.

3. The Contemporary Phase of Globalization

Globalization is the historical process of liberalization and integration of goods, capital and labor markets, which have hitherto functioned largely in separation, into a single world marketplace. The qualification 'largely' is important, because even seemingly totally separate national or regional economic organisms are somehow interconnected, indirectly or directly, and some economic and financial flows do take place between them, albeit on a limited scale. As regards specific markets, their liberalization and consequent integration differs in scope and intensity.

There are differences between the markets of goods and services, many of the latter being unsuitable, in view of their specific form, to be traded globally, as they need to be consumed on the spot, the moment they are performed. Different still is the market of capital transfers, which follow different rules than the simple movements of goods. Yet another set of differences pertains to labor, whose international transfers have thus far been liberalized to the least extent – for economic, but also cultural and strictly political reasons, although the latter (expect for extremist political movements, like Haider's party in Austria or Le Pen's party in France) is rarely publicly admitted.[16]

To be sure, the scope of market integration has been changing across the historical phases of the globalization process (Frankel 2001). Globalization can be divided into periods in many different ways. Apparently, one can even speak about its permanent character, because globalization – that is, the extent to which particular product markets and regional markets have been liberalized and integrated – has been deepening all the time, although with varying intensity, long breaks or even occasional setbacks, as in 1914–45. In the history of permanent globalization thus construed, three particularly expansive phases can be distinguished:

- globalization of the Age of Exploration (16th to mid-17th centuries);
- globalization of the Industrial Revolution (mid-18th to 19th centuries);
- globalization of the Age of Virtual Discovery (last quarter of 20th century and beginning of 21st century) (Kolodko 2001b).

The World Bank distinguishes three phases of globalization, covering, respectively, the years 1870–1914, 1950–80 and recent times, past-1980 (World Bank 2002a). However, this periodization gives rise to serious reservations, for two reasons. First, it totally ignores earlier (pre-1870) peaks of international economic activity and links between numerous regional and national markets, as well as the ensuing qualitative changes. Second, the years 1950–80 cannot be considered a 'second phase of globalization', because, as the World Bank report itself confirms, that period involved only the integration of highly developed capitalist economies, that is, those of North America, Western Europe and Japan. This is quite a lot, but not enough to be considered a 'global economy'.[17] Remaining outside the scope of those integration processes were some huge areas: both the 'Second World' of socialist planned economies, and the 'Third World' of developing countries.

Six characteristics of modern globalization can be distinguished. First, thanks to the significant reduction of customs barriers,[18] the **volume of world trade increases very fast, nearly twice as fast as output**. While the global GDP increased in 1965–99, on the average, at 3.3 per cent a year, the volume of exports (and hence, in the global context, also imports) increased at 5.9 per cent per annum.[19] Foreign-trade growth was fastest in the MGC group: in the case of the East Asia and Pacific region, it stood at 10.1 per cent a year, on average. However, even in some LGCs foreign-trade dynamics exceeds that of GDP growth. As a result, the share of these countries in world trade increased from 19 per cent in 1971 to about 30 per cent in 2001.[20] Moreover, there have been favorable changes in the structure of these exports. In 1980, merely 20 per cent of exports from less developed countries consisted of processed manufactured goods; today this proportion exceeds 80 per cent (IMF 2000a).

Second, apart from some temporary disturbances caused by a series of financial crises at the turn of the previous decade, **capital flows have been steadily increasing**. Three decades ago, capital transfers from rich to less advanced countries stood at less than USD 28bn; in the record-breaking (thus far) year 1997, they were 11 times higher, reaching USD 306bn.[21] Growth of the transfer volume has been particularly explosive in the case of private portfolio investments: from a negligible USD 10m in 1970 to a record USD 103bn in 1996.

Third, there are **population migrations**. Although the modern-time movements are not as extensive as those in the years 1870–1910, when as much as about 10 per cent of the world population changed their permanent residence, their economic significance is considerable. Over nearly forty years (since 1965), the number of employees who have found work outside their country of birth has nearly doubled. Interestingly, the scope of migrations is greatest between less developed countries, rather than from those countries to rich ones.

Fourth, one should take note of the **dissemination of new technologies**, and in particular the spreading impact of the scientific and technological revolution connected with information and computer technologies (ICT). We witness the birth and development of a knowledge-based economy (Koźmiński 2002), with serious implications for countries seeking to catch up with more highly developed states. Progress pertains not only to the 'hard' manufacturing technologies, but also to new management and marketing methods, which greatly boost productivity and hence increase the output.

Fifth, an indispensable element of the current phase of globalization is the **post-socialist systemic transformation**. Indeed, one could hardly speak about globalization without including in this process the huge area of former socialist countries, inhabited by more than a quarter of mankind. On the one hand, this transformation acts as a catalyst facilitating market transition in the former centrally planned economies. On the other hand, it complements and completes the globalization process itself. Global economy means global capitalism (Hutton and Giddens 2000; Kolodko 2002c) and, therefore, it can only be based on the market. Thus the inclusion of Central and Eastern European countries, the Commonwealth of Independent States, China and Indochina in this process[22] will require the prior transformation of these areas into open and liberalized market economies.

Sixth, the radical transformation of the financial and economic structures and institutions is accompanied by far-reaching **cultural change**. Greater openness to the transfer of not only people, but, first and foremost, ideas – not least through the phenomenal growth of the Internet, which is a medium resistant to bureaucratic and political control – means that the world has shrunk considerably and increasingly acquires the characteristics of a 'global village'. But at the same time it has also enormously expanded by the creation of vast virtual spaces in which various cultural trends coalesce as if in a giant melting pot, while new forms of economic activity are being born (Kolodko 2001d; Zacher 2001).

Thus defined and characterized, **globalizations seems an irreversible process.** But is it really so? From the point of view of the incredibly accelerated information flow and decreased communication and transportation costs, it is. There is no way to undo technological progress and the explosive growth of the ICT sector – the two factors that have altered within the time span of one generation, right before our eyes, the face of the world.

What is it like then, the world's new face? First and foremost, it is heterogeneous, for not all the consequences of globalization are positive. The persistence or even, in some areas, increase of social inequalities (Dollar 2001), financial crises and their spread to other sectors of the world economy (including some economies based on relatively sound foundations and strong institutions), the dying off of some traditional branches of manufacturing in certain countries due to their low competitiveness, which creates rampant unemployment and poverty – these are but a few of the disadvantages of globalization. Further problems arise not only in the social and economic spheres, but also on the political or even military levels. As an extreme example, one could point at international terrorism, which, incidentally, can be viewed as a privatization of wars and military conflicts, or as an instance of the world trade in arms running out of control of powerful countries and the international organizations in which these countries play a dominant role, such as the UN or the WTO.

Therefore, the **possibility that the attained progress of globalization will be reversed cannot be ruled out.** It has happened so in the past, for instance, after 1914, when the then achieved level of globalization likewise seemed secure. Thus although technological progress cannot be checked, further liberalization of trade and capital movements – as well as, significantly, the increasingly liberalized transfer of labor – can be brought to a halt. The threat of renewed protectionism is real and cannot be ruled out a priori.[23] That would automatically entail the slowing down of globalization, which would deprive many nations of the chance to catch up with more advanced economies.

We keep looking at the world economy from the perspective of its component countries. This is not only due to the availability of appropriately aggregated statistical data (and hence the possibility to carry out various comparative analyses), but also – and mainly – because of the domination of the traditional way of thinking. Accordingly, although it would be more convenient to speak of the increasingly integrated world economy in terms of various regions, rather than countries and national economies, the traditional, 'nation-centered' thinking will continue to hold sway for many years to come. Superposed on it is the perception of the word economy as clearly divided into mature economic systems and 'emerging markets'.

4. The Emerging Markets

The notion of 'emerging markets' is blurred. It gets a different reading in the countries in which it was coined, that is, highly developed capitalist economies (Mobius 1996; Garten 1998; Gilpin 2001), and in the countries to which it directly applies. The latter is a large, if heterogeneous, group, with a well-defined center and hazy periphery.

It is easier to say with certainty what is *not* an emerging market than what is. One could say that **emerging markets do not include, by definition, either those highly developed market economies which have long evolved mature institutional systems, or those countries which have yet to set out on the path of market development.** Thus outside this group are all rich, institutionally mature countries. These comprise all the 'old' members of the OECD (except Turkey), and several countries which have attained a high development level in recent decades, acceding wholeheartedly to the world economic exchange and liberalizing their economic regulations.

It remains a moot point whether every relatively rich country can be excluded a priori from the 'emerging markets'. Should we include in this group – in view of their specific economic system and a certain immaturity of their market institutions, and in particular, barriers to competition and a lack of liberal deregulation – some oil-rich Arab countries which owe their relatively high development level solely to their natural resources? Could it really be that, say, Qatar or the United Arab Emirates, with a PPP-adjusted per capita GDP of, respectively, about USD 19,000 and USD 17,000, are more mature – already 'emerged' – market economies than Chile or Hungary? Or do they just happen to be richer than the latter? It would seem, therefore, that – at this end of the spectrum – inclusion in the category of developed markets should be based on the criterion of market-institution maturity rather than level of development alone.

At the opposite end of the list of countries that certainly cannot be included among the 'emerging markets' are four types of economies. The first one, rendered totally obsolete by the post-socialist transformation, comprises the orthodox socialist states, like North Korea and Cuba. The second is made up of countries which either by way of their own political preference, or through international sanctions imposed upon them, are largely isolated from broader contacts with the world economy, like Myanmar, Iraq or Libya. The third group consists of failed states with dysfunctional institutions, which are not only unable to take part in global economic exchange, but even internally appear ungovernable, such as Afghanistan and Bosnia-Herzegovina, or a fair number of African countries, like Somalia, Congo (former Zaire), Sierra Leone or Rwanda.

Finally, the fourth group – which is the most important source of candidates for an 'emerging market' status – comprises countries which are gradually approaching a stage in structural reforms, opening and liberalization where a qualitative change is about to take place that may soon enable them to take advantage of free global capital flows or international free trade. One can classify with this group some post-socialist countries which have belatedly embarked on the transformation, like Turkmenistan or Uzbekistan, as well as some of the former 'Third World' countries now facing profound economic and political reform, like Algeria or Iran, and, finally, countries about to overcome the turmoil of civil war and armed ethnic strife, like, formerly, Guatemala and Yemen and now, hopefully, Angola and East Timor.

Unfortunately, there are processes in the modern world going in the opposite direction, too. Economies whose markets were already 'emerging' may be set back in this process. This is particularly true of countries which become entangled – often quite unexpectedly – in destructive political and military conflicts, usually, though not always, of ethnic character. By way of exemplification, one could mention Kyrgyzstan and Nepal in Asia, Madagascar and Zimbabwe in Africa, or Haiti and Colombia in America.

Thus, generally speaking, **what is and what is not an 'emerging market' depends on the maturity of its institutions**, that is the rules of the economic market game – the law and culture – and the institutions enforcing the adherence to these rules. Thus a market which does not yet merit the name 'emerging' may have long been sufficiently developed from the institutional point of view.

Methodologically, it is also possible to treat as 'emerging markets' all economic systems which cannot be considered fully mature. Then one would also have to include in this category Iraq beside China, Belarus beside Poland, Libya beside South Africa, Cuba beside Mexico. Indeed, the classification here is a matter of convention, rather than sharp distinctions based on substantive criteria. This is not really the main point and there is no need to argue whether Singapore and Slovenia still count as 'emerging markets', as global investors would have it,[24] or whether Pakistan and Kazakhstan have already attained this status, although not as fast as some transnational corporations and the governments of the most highly developed economies would wish.

Of greater importance is the interpretation of the 'emerging market' category, as well as its theoretical and especially pragmatic implications. Does the fact that a country counts as an 'emerging market' has a bearing on its socio-economic development, and in particular, on its chances for accelerated growth, which are of special interest for us here? This is one of the issues that the two interpretations of the 'emerging markets' – from their own perspective and that of the advanced economies – are concerned with.

From the point of view of (institutionally) developed and (materially) rich countries, the 'emerging markets' are treated instrumentally. For these countries, they form yet another segment of the expanding field of economic activity. Thanks to its 'emergence', a new region of the world opens up for penetration by creating an opportunity to invest profitably surplus capitals, sell products and acquire resources, including relatively cheap labor. In this way an additional demand 'emerges' – and becomes globalized – which now can be satisfied, as the political, economic and financial barriers that used to block access to these regions of the world are being torn down. Such an approach emphasizes not so much a commitment to the socio-economic development of an 'emerging' market, as the opportunity to increase one's own capacity for expansion and to multiply the wealth of the already rich countries. The development of an 'emerging market' itself is only important inasmuch as it favors further expansion of the rich countries in a specific, new sales market. In other words, under the instrumental approach, rapid growth of an 'emerging market' is not a self-contained, supreme goal, but only an instrument to further the interests of other, more powerful actors in the global economic game – be it the highly developed countries or the great transnational corporations.

On the other hand, the 'emerging markets' themselves – which, incidentally, did not insist on being thus named – have a totally different outlook on this matter. What matters from their point of view is not the additional outlet created in their territory for the capital and goods from other, more advanced countries, but the **rapid maturation of their own economic systems, leading to the emergence of full-fledged market economies**. On this interpretation, the principal goal is not to create a new sales market for others, but to build a new, market system which is institutionally liberalized and progressively opens, much to its own benefit, to an expanding range of outside contacts.

Such a system should ensure a higher level of efficiency and faster output growth, hence also improving the living standards of the societies in countries described as 'emerging markets'. The object of the game is to have market *economies* emerge, rather than just markets. This distinction is significant, for it emphasizes the main objective, which is rapid growth, to be achieved by the creation of an open, market economy with strong institutions. But the fact that a given country can be classified as an 'emerging market' is in itself no guarantee that its economy is growing. If this is to be the case, many conditions must be met.

5. Development Gap and Catching-up

How, then, are we to understand catching-up? What is it supposed to be like and who is to close the distance to whom? Do we speak about Canada catching up with the United States,[25] Eastern Europe catching up with Western Europe, or perhaps Africa catching up with Southeast Asia? And with Europe, too? What are the prerequisites and implications of catching-up? To answer such questions, it is good to realize first what the starting point is, which the world economy has reached at the beginning of the 21st century. Different regions vastly differ in attained development levels.

So far some economies have been doing better than others. Over the past few decades, some have recorded considerable growth, while others are treading water or even falling behind with their development level. As a result, **huge differences in development levels exist between specific countries and regions of the global economy, and thus the less advanced economies face the task of closing an enormous distance**. In most cases it is plain to see that this distance cannot be made up for. But there should likewise be no doubt that for some emerging market economies, including several post-socialist countries, catching up with the highly developed countries is within reach (Kolodko 2001c and 2002b).

The potential reduction of distances in development levels should be seen in various perspectives. After all, we are not speaking about Sierra Leone catching up with the GDP of Luxembourg, the latter generating within a working week as much output (in terms of value) as the former does in two years. Nor are we speaking about Honduras overtaking the United States. But we do want to see Honduras, as well as other countries of Central America and the Caribbean, develop faster than their rich neighbor up north, overcoming in time their backwardness and poverty. The same can be said about Ukraine and Germany, Vietnam and Japan, Sudan and Egypt, or Papua New Guinea and Australia.

Closing the distances should be seen not only – or even not mainly – in the global context, but in a regional one. First one needs to catch up with one's close neighbors who have attained a relatively higher development level. **In the neighborhood of every country there are other, more highly developed economies, and reducing the distance to them should be one of the strategic political objectives.** Especially when these are adjacent countries, like Haiti and the far more prosperous Dominican Republic,[26] Costa Rica, which develops much faster than its neighbor, Nicaragua, Uganda, which does better than Tanzania, or Thailand, which has greatly outdistanced Myanmar. Such instances, as well as many others, demonstrate that the currently existing differences in development level are not only the function of geographical location and the available natural resources, but mostly result from the unequal efficiency of the respective economic systems and the varying quality of the development policy followed by specific countries.[27]

The same observation pertains to post-socialist countries, among which the pre-existing differences in development level changed in various ways over the first dozen or so years of the transformation, because of the varied duration and depth of the transitional recession (Kolodko 2000a; Blejer and Skreb 2001; EBRD 2002). Thus if Poland wants to improve its position, it should first close in on the Czech Republic and Hungary;[28] likewise, Uzbekistan should first attain the development level of Kazakhstan and Russia,[29] to be able to proceed further.

It seems, however, natural from the political and psychological points of view that, say, Turkmenistan looks up mostly to the nearby and culturally similar Turkey, Hungary wants to emulate the neighboring Austria, Estonia compares itself with Finland, Poland with Germany and Macedonia with Greece. The amount of catching-up differs in all these cases. The distance is least pronounced in the case of Turkmenistan, whose PPP-adjusted GDP per head is about 50 per cent of that of Turkey. The respective proportion stands at 45 per cent between Hungary and Austria, 37 per cent between Estonia and Finland, and 35 per cent between Poland and Germany. The most severe disparity occurs between Macedonia and Greece, where the ratio in question amounts to a mere 24 per cent.[30]

Let us add that we are not concerned in the present discussion with the catching up processes among highly developed economies (which, incidentally, is an interesting problem in its own right). In order to catch up with the US in terms of PPP-adjusted GDP per head, Canada would have to increase its output by 25 per cent. But the growth rates in both countries have been very similar in recent years, mainly because of their strongly correlated trade cycles. For South Korea to overtake Japan, its GDP per head would have to grow by 62 per cent. If New Zealand's per capita GDP were to equal that of Australia, it would have to be boosted by 35 per cent.[31] For Austria to be level with Switzerland, its per capita GDP would have to move 17 per cent up, whereas a similar outcome in the case of Portugal and Spain would require only a 12-percent growth.

Yet **even if GDP levels per head were fully equalized, this would by no means eliminate differences in living standards**, because the latter depend not only on the current income stream, but also on the resources accumulated – in some cases over many centuries.[32] This can be illustrated by the example of Finland and Sweden, which has been the more prosperous of the two for ages, partly due the exploitation of its eastern neighbor. Currently – since the turn of the previous decade – Finland enjoys a per capita GDP level (in PPP terms) amounting to 105 per cent of the OECD average, whereas the same indicator in Sweden stands at 103 per cent. In absolute numbers, this amounted in the year 2000 to about USD 24,900 and USD 24,400, respectively.

Catching-up has been even more efficient in the case of Ireland, which has managed to exceed the GDP of the United Kingdom (respectively, USD 25,060 and USD 24,390 at current exchange rates, or USD 28,500 and USD 23,900 in terms of PPP). However, the consumption level still clearly lags behind in Ireland. These differences remain conspicuous. A trip from London to Dublin is enough to see that it was Britain, and not Ireland, that was for centuries the center of an empire on which the sun never set. The legacy of that period can still be seen both in the regional proportions of income and wealth distribution, and in the functioning of the global economy.

Thus the average income level is greatly differentiated in modern world. The table below compares the ranking of 70 countries where the PPP-adjusted income per head exceeds USD 6,000 (or about a sixth of the current US level) with the 20 poorest countries of the world. Among the former group, there are just 12 out of the 32 post-socialist economies of Europe and Asia (including China and Indochina). In the latter group, there is just one post-socialist country: Tajikistan – the poorest of all the countries undergoing a systemic transformation.[33]

Reducing the existing differences in development level thus requires that the output growth rate should be high – markedly higher than in rich countries. This is obvious. But it is worthwhile to ask how big the difference in growth rates should be in order to reduce the distance in a perceptible way or, in some cases, eliminate in time the existing gaps.

**Table 1.2: Countries with highest and lowest GDP per head in PPP
(USA = 100)**

Highest purchasing power

1.	Luxembourg	129.2		36.	South Korea	48.7
2.	United States	100.0		37.	Bahamas	48.6
3.	Switzerland	90.1		38.	Martinique	46.3
4.	Norway	88.2		39.	Barbados	43.9
5.	Iceland	85.3		40.	Guadeloupe	40.6
6.	Brunei	85.1		**41.**	**Czech Republic**	**40.2**
7.	Belgium	80.6		42.	Bahrain	39.5
8.	Denmark	80.2		43.	Reunion	38.7
9.	Bermuda	79.7		44.	Argentina	37.4
10.	Canada	79.7		**45.**	**Hungary**	**34.6**
11.	Japan	78.9		46.	Saudi Arabia	34.6
12.	Austria	77.1		**47.**	**Slovakia**	**32.7**
13.	Netherlands	76.5		48.	Mauritius	28.0
14.	Australia	74.7		49.	Uruguay	27.4
15.	Germany	73.7		50.	South Africa	27.3
16.	France	72.1		51.	Chile	26.4
17.	Finland	70.8		**52.**	**Poland**	**26.3**
18.	Hong Kong	70.7		**53.**	**Estonia**	**25.7**
19.	Ireland	70.4		54.	Mexico	25.3
20.	Singapore	69.9		55.	Costa Rica	24.7
21.	French Polynesia	69.6		56.	Trinidad & Tobago	24.1
22.	United Kingdom	69.6		57.	Malaysia	23.9
23.	Euro area	69.5		**58.**	**Croatia**	**22.8**
24.	Sweden	69.4		**59.**	**Russia**	**21.9**
25.	Italy	68.9		**60.**	**Belarus**	**21.6**
26.	New Caledonia	66.2		61.	Brazil	21.4
27.	United Arab Emirates	64.5		62.	Botswana	20.5
28.	Cyprus	59.8		**63.**	**Lithuania**	**20.3**
29.	Israel	56.6		64.	Turkey	20.2
30.	Spain	55.9		**65.**	**Latvia**	**19.5**
31.	New Zealand	55.2		**66.**	**Romania**	**18.7**
32.	Macau	53.1		67.	Thailand	18.6
33.	**Slovenia**	**50.3**		68.	Tunisia	17.9
34.	Portugal	49.7		69.	Colombia	17.5
35.	Greece	49.5		70.	Namibia	17.5

Lowest purchasing power

1.	Sierra Leone	1.4	11.	Zambia	2.3
2.	Tanzania	1.6	12.	Nigeria	2.4
3.	Congo-Brazzaville	1.7	13.	Congo	2.5
4.	Burundi	1.8	14.	Madagascar	2.5
5.	Malawi	1.8	15.	Mozambique	2.5
6.	Ethiopia	1.9	16.	Chad	2.6
7.	Guinea-Bissau	2.0	17.	Rwanda	2.8
8.	Mali	2.3	18.	Benin	2.9
9.	Niger	2.3	19.	Burkina Faso	3.0
10.	Yemen	2.3	**20.**	**Tajikistan**	**3.1**

Post-socialist countries – in bold letters.

Source: Economist 2001.

Catching up is possible when the economic growth in a given country is at the same time:

- fast
- sustained
- endogenous.

So when can we say that growth is 'fast'? This is a relative matter, for the same absolute growth rate can be in same cases – in the context of one country or period – considered to be high, while elsewhere it is low. Undoubtedly, the average annual GDP growth of 3.3 per cent in the United States in the 1990s was very fast.[34] The neighboring Mexico recorded a similar rate during the same period, but this meant slow growth, because it not only failed to shorten the cumulative distance, but even, in view of the relatively weaker growth dynamics in per capita terms, resulted in an even greater income disparity.[35] In 1992–2001, overall GDP increased in Mexico, on average, by 3.2 per cent per annum. But calculated on a per capita basis, growth was merely 1.5 per cent annually. As a result, the distance between the two economies increased even further.

It should be noted that, from the point of view of growth rate dispersion and catching-up with the developed countries, this is the main difference between the market economies emerging from 'Third World' and 'Second World' (post-socialist) countries. Let us compare Latin America and the Caribbean with Central and Eastern Europe and the CIS. In the post-socialist economies, overall output grows at the same rate as output per head, as the population, generally, does not change. On the other hand, in the emerging market economies of America, population is increasing steeply. In extreme cases, the spread between GDP growth rate in overall and per capita terms exceeds two percentage points. During the previous decade, it reached 2.6 percentage points in Paraguay (respectively, +1.7

and –0.9 per cent), and 2.1 points in Ecuador and Venezuela (respectively, +2.0 and –0.1, and +2.4 and +0.3 per cent). In the entire Latin America and Caribbean region, GDP grew on average at 2.9 per cent a year, but on a per capita basis, the increase dwindled to a lame 1.2 per cent annually, that is, below the social perception threshold. Worse still, in as many as five countries of the region (Ecuador, Jamaica, Haiti, Cuba and Paraguay), output per head was lower in 2001 than 11 years before, although it was only in two of these countries (Cuba and Haiti) that overall output shrank (ECLAC 2002).

Thus if growth is to qualify as fast, it should be qualitatively higher in per capita terms than in highly developed countries. The term 'qualitatively' is used here to imply that, in time, the differences in development level will perceptibly diminish. Bearing in mind the disparities existing at the very outset, it might be assumed that **rapid growth presupposes at least double the growth rate of developed economies**. In the last-mentioned group, the average annual growth over the last 35 years has stood at 3.2 per cent in overall terms, or 2.4 per cent on a per capita basis. Accordingly, rapid growth should amount to at least 5 per cent annually in per head terms. At this rate, GDP doubles approximately every 14 years, so within the time span of a single generation it quadruples. If so, even if the starting point was low, qualitative changes for the better take place and the distance to more developed economies is substantially shortened.

What makes this point important is that less advanced economies – both from the MGC and LGC groups – are characterized by faster population growth than rich countries. One exception from this rule is post-socialist countries, where, in general, population does not increase. In the years 1995–2000, as many as 17 out of the 20 countries with the lowest natural increase (which indeed took negative values) were post-socialist countries. According to UN demographic forecasts, this tendency will continue to prevail until 2005. Among the top 20 countries with the largest absolute population decrease during this period – from –0.1 per cent annually in the Czech Republic, Poland and Slovenia, to –1.0 and –1.1 per cent, respectively, in Bulgaria and Estonia – there are 16 countries of Central and Eastern Europe and the CIS. In all these cases overall growth rate can be equated with per capita growth rate.

Unfortunately, situated at the opposite end of the spectrum are many of the world's most backward and poorest countries, including two post-socialist economies which have lost much of their national income to local conflicts: Bosnia-Herzegovina and Cambodia. The average natural increase rate in this group varies these days from 2.8 per cent in Cambodia to 3.2 per cent in Mauritania and Chad, to as much as 8.5 per cent in Rwanda (Table 1.3).

Table 1.3: Fastest and slowest growing population, 2000–2005 (annual average growth in %)

Fastest growth

1.	Rwanda	8.5	11.	Mauritania	3.2
2.	Liberia	7.1	12.	Gambia, The	3.1
3.	Yemen	4.2	**13.**	**Bosnia-Herzegovina**	**3.0**
4.	West Bank and Gaza	3.8	14.	Congo-Brazzaville	3.0
5.	Somalia	3.6	15.	Uganda	3.0
6.	Niger	3.5	16.	Angola	2.9
7.	Saudi Arabia	3.5	17.	Jordan	2.9
8.	Oman	3.3	18.	Madagascar	2.9
9.	Togo	3.3	19.	Singapore	2.9
10.	Chad	3.2	**20.**	**Cambodia**	**2.8**

Slowest growth

1.	**Lithuania**	**–1.2**	**11.**	**Moldova**	**–0.3**
2.	**Estonia**	**–1.1**	**12.**	**Romania**	**–0.3**
3.	**Bulgaria**	**–1.0**	**13.**	**Serbia, Montenegro**	**–0.2**
4.	**Ukraine**	**–0.9**	14.	Austria	–0.1
5.	**Latvia**	**–0.6**	**15.**	**Czech Republic**	**–0.1**
6.	**Russia**	**–0.6**	16.	Italy	–0.1
7.	**Georgia**	**–0.5**	**17.**	**Poland**	**–0.1**
8.	**Hungary**	**–0.5**	**18.**	**Slovenia**	**–0.1**
9.	**Belarus**	**–0.4**	19.	Sweden	–0.1
10.	**Kazakhstan**	**–0.4**	20.	Switzerland	–0.1

Post-socialist countries – in bold letters.

Source: Economist 2001.

If, then, 'fast growth' could be conventionally defined as a real per capita GDP growth of 5 per cent plus annually, another question arises: what is 'sustained growth'? It could be assumed, also by convention, that **sustained growth pertains to a macroeconomic reproduction process which spans a period of at least ten to twenty years, allowing per capita national income to double at roughly half-generation intervals.** Such criteria of sustained growth are undoubtedly met by China's economic expansion over the last 25 years or the doubling of the GDP by Ireland during the 1990s and its continued growth at about 5 per cent annually in the first years of the current decade.[36]

Likewise, the average growth of per capita GDP by 6.4 per cent annually in South Korea in 1965–2002 can be labeled both rapid and sustained. Unfortunately, the same cannot be said about growth in Poland over the last decade.[37] Even though GDP increased in 1994–7 – in the course of the implementation of the plan known as 'Strategy for Poland' (Kolodko and Nuti 1997) – by as much as 28 per cent, likewise increasing on a per capita basis by 6.4 per cent annually on average, this prosperity was too short-lived, being prematurely interrupted by erroneous economic- and especially financial-policy decisions, implemented since 1998. As a result, the economy was brought down to near stagnation in 2001–2, with a mediocre growth of 1 per cent annually. Thus the distance to developed countries began to increase again, instead of being progressively shortened – which, by the way, is still possible (Kolodko 2002a).

The trouble is that few economies indeed are capable of keeping to the rapid-growth path for an extended period. Out of the 20 fastest growing countries in the 1980s, which recorded an average GDP increase of 4.5 to 10 plus per cent a year, only eight made it again to the top twenty in the 1990s.[38] These eight countries with fastest-growing output are: China, Vietnam, Singapore, Malaysia, India, Taiwan, Oman and South Korea. It should be noted that the first five countries on this list developed in the 1990s even faster than in the 1980s. It is intriguing or, indeed, fascinating to observe that virtually all of them followed policies which were a long way off the Washington Consensus and monetary orthodoxy, which usually inform the IMF-proposed structural adjustment programs.

What is more, the situation on the opposite pole was going from bad to worse during the period in question. Whereas in the 1980s, there were 11 national economies with a negative average yearly growth – from –6.8 per cent in Iraq to – 0.1 per cent in Mozambique and Niger – the number of such countries doubled in the 1990s, reaching 22. One of the reasons was the post-socialist transformation, intended to boost economic growth. But it turned out that this effect could not be expected at this phase: as many as 16 post-socialist economies saw a negative average annual growth in the 1990s, while by 2002, only seven[39] out of the 28 post-socialist countries have exceeded their GDP levels of 1989.

Finally, there is the third prerequisite of the catching-up process – the endogenous character of growth. It is indispensable in that **only by building, during one phase of rapid growth, the foundations of continued expansion in the following phase, can the self-sustaining character of growth be assured**. The endogenous growth mechanism is thus intimately connected with the market's institutional infrastructure and a high propensity to save and invest. Taken together, these factors should ensure an adequate level of internal accumulation of capital and high efficiency of its allocation.

The average per capita GDP (in PPP terms) in OECD countries will approach USD 25,000 in 2003. Bearing in mind what has been said earlier about catching-up with highly developed neighbors, this amount should be seen as a long-term goal for countries at a medium development level, including the relatively less developed OECD countries, like Turkey, Poland, Mexico, Slovakia, Hungary, Czech Republic, Greece, South Korea and Portugal. And, it should be borne in mind at all times, per capita income throughout the OECD, which is composed of 30 countries with a total of some 1.16bn people, runs up to a mere two thirds of the US level. The emerging markets, including all post-socialist economies, will keep lagging far behind that last-mentioned country for generations to come. But countries at a lower development level should strive to successively reduce the distance to the next richer group.

From the point of view of the attained development level, the World Bank – as well as some other international organizations – distinguishes in its reports three groups of economies: low income, middle income – further subdivided into lower middle income and upper middle income – and high income. Superposed on these statistics in the two lower-income groups is a geographical division into six regions. Post-socialist economies are included in the Europe and Central Asia group (Table 1.4).

Table 1.4: Populations and income level in the world economy (2000)

	Population (millions)	Gross national income per head (in USD)	PPP gross national income per head
World	**6,057**	**5,140**	**7,410**
Low income	2,460	410	1,980
Middle income	2,695	1,970	5,680
Lower middle income	2,048	1,130	4,600
Upper middle income	647	4,640	9,210
High Income	903	27,680	27,770
East Asia & Pacific	1,855	1,060	4,130
Europe & Central Asia	474	2,010	6,670
Latin America & Caribbean	516	3,670	7,080
Middle East & North Africa	295	2,090	5,270
South Asia	1,355	440	2,240
Sub-Saharan Africa	659	470	1,600
Euro area	304	21,730	23,600

Source: World Bank 2002b.

Evidently, the distance to the rich countries that the economies at medium and lower advancement levels should make up for, is truly astounding. In many, or, indeed, in most cases, closing the existing gap is practically impossible – at least in the foreseeable future. Certainly not in this century. And what happens afterwards – we will see. For the time being, let us reiterate, **the point is to have poorer economies develop faster than richer ones**. The focus, therefore, should not be on coming abreast of the richest, but rather on efficiently closing the distance, and gaining on them rather than lagging ever further behind. All the more so since the rich do not intend by any means to stay put. Assuming that their per capita GDP increases at a similar rate as it has in the last 35 years, after two more generations it will have reached (on a PPP basis) some USD 90,000. Even if the less advanced countries manage to maintain a high growth rate – 5 per cent annually, on average – most of them will still bring up the rear. In some cases, indeed very far behind the leaders (Table 1.5).

Table 1.5: Catching-up in the first half of the 21st century

GDP per capita in PPP (in USD)[a]

Year	2000	% of high income group in 2000	2012	2025	2050	% of high income group in 2050
Low income	1,980	**7.1**	3,225	6,705	22,705	**25.0**
Middle income	5,680	**20.5**	9,250	19,230	61,135	**67.3**
Lower middle income	4,600	**16.6**	7,490	15,580	52,750	**58.0**
Upper middle income	9,210	**33.1**	15,000	31,190	105,615	**116.2**
Post-socialist economies[b]	6,670	**24.1**	10,865	22,590	76,490	**84.1**
High Income	27,770	**100.0**	35,200	50,240	90,900	**100.0**
Euro area	23,600	**85.0**	29,920	42,700	77,250	**85.0**

[a]   GDP per capita in a given year under the assumption that the average rate of growth since 2001 will be 2.4 per cent in the case of high income economies and 5.0 per cent in the case of all emerging market economies.
[b]   Central and Eastern Europe and the CIS.

Source: Author's own calculation.

But it is a well-known fact that many countries – both among the MGC group and, especially, the LGC economies, undergoing marginalization – are unable to attain such growth dynamics. This is also true of some post-socialist economies, in the case of which less favorable geographical location combines with a misguided economic policy and an institutional weakness of the emerging market. Some countries not only failed to achieve high growth dynamics in the past, but will likewise be unable to do so in the future. In recent history, only a few countries managed to overcome their age-old backwardness. Among these, one should mention especially South Korea, whose per capita GDP has attained about 50 per cent of the USA level, Singapore (70 per cent), Hong Kong (71 per cent), Ireland (72 per cent) or Finland (71 per cent), where sweet herring with potatoes is a national dish not because everybody loves it, but for the simple reason that as late as the 1950s many Finns could afford little more.

There is compelling evidence that many other nations have begun to catch up with more advanced economies. This is true of the already mentioned Costa Rica in Central America and the Dominican Republic in the Caribbean, as well as Chile (an 86-percent GDP increase during the 1990s) in South America. Countries doing fine in Africa include Uganda and Côte d'Ivoire (44-percent growth in the 1990s), Egypt (54 per cent) and Ghana, where the proportion of population living in poverty had dropped during the 1990s from 53 to 43 per cent.[40] In Asia, apart from China, Vietnam and India, mention is also due to Malaysia, which, thanks to its unorthodox strategy, doubled its income in the previous decade, and Bangladesh, which saw a 58-percent increase of its national income in the 1990s.

As regards post-socialist countries, there are grounds to believe that rapid growth will continue, among others, in Azerbaijan, Estonia, Latvia and Kazakhstan, and in Europe – in Albania, Hungary and Slovenia. Some other economies, too, especially the countries in the process of integration with the European Union may – although this is by no means automatic – enter the path of rapid and sustained growth, kept up by the endogenous mechanism of extended macroeconomic reproduction. It would be unreasonable to expect that all the countries from this group will manage, in the space of a generation or two, to increase their output at a rate conventionally described as rapid, but there are many reasons to believe that their growth dynamics will be better than in the richer countries, including the European Union (Kolodko 2001c and 2002b). Alternative growth paths for this group, differing in output dynamics, and their consequences in terms of per capita GDP changes in the current half-century are presented in Table 1.6.

Table 1.6: GDP per head (PPP) in a given year assuming 3, 4, and 5% average annual rate of growth

	GDP in 2002 (in PPP)*	3 per cent			4 per cent			5 per cent		
		2012	2025	2050	2012	2025	2050	2012	2025	2050
Slovenia	15,850	22,598	33,186	65,496	25,376	42,254	104,143	28,464	53,674	164,480
Czech Republic	13,380	19,077	28,015	55,290	21,422	35,669	87,914	24,029	45,309	139,169
Hungary	11,790	16,810	24,686	48,719	18,876	31,430	77,467	21,173	39,925	122,631
Croatia	11,500	16,396	24,078	47,521	18,412	30,657	75,561	20,652	38,943	119,615
Estonia	10,900	15,541	22,822	45,042	17,451	29,058	71,619	19,575	36,911	113,374
Slovakia	10,730	15,298	22,466	44,339	17,179	28,604	70,502	19,270	36,336	111,606
Poland	8,290	11,820	17,357	34,256	13,273	22,100	54,470	14,888	28,073	86,227
Latvia	8,040	11,463	16,834	33,223	12,872	21,433	52,827	14,439	27,226	83,626
Belarus	6,980	9,952	14,615	28,843	11,175	18,608	45,862	12,535	23,637	72,601
Romania	6,200	8,840	12,981	25,620	9,926	16,528	40,737	11,134	20,995	64,488
Russia	5,625	8,020	11,778	23,244	9,006	14,995	36,959	10,102	19,048	58,507
Bulgaria	5,570	7,941	11,662	23,017	8,918	14,849	36,598	10,003	18,862	57,935
Lithuania	4,190	5,974	8,773	17,314	6,708	11,170	27,531	7,525	14,189	43,581
FYR Macedonia	3,970	5,660	8,312	16,405	6,356	10,583	26,085	7,130	13,444	41,293
Turkmenistan	3,960	5,646	8,291	16,364	6,340	10,557	26,019	7,112	13,410	41,189
Kazakhstan	3,550	5,061	7,433	14,669	5,684	9,464	23,325	6,375	12,022	36,975
Yugoslavia	3,390	4,833	7,098	14,008	5,427	9,037	22,274	6,088	11,480	35,260
Armenia	3,330	4,748	6,972	13,760	5,331	8,877	21,880	5,980	11,277	34,636

Ukraine	2,950	4,206	6,177	12,190	4,723	7,864	19,383	5,298	9,990	30,684
Bosnia-Herzegovina	2,700	3,850	5,653	11,157	4,323	7,198	17,740	4,869	9,143	28,083
Uzbekistan	2,700	3,850	5,653	11,157	4,323	7,198	17,740	4,869	9,143	28,083
Kyrgyzstan	2,560	3,650	5,360	10,579	4,099	6,825	16,821	4,597	8,669	26,627
Azerbaijan	2,540	3,621	5,318	10,496	4,067	6,771	16,689	4,561	8,601	26,419
Albania	2,290	3,265	4,795	9,463	3,666	6,105	15,047	4,113	7,755	23,819
Georgia	2,290	3,265	4,795	9,463	3,666	6,105	15,047	4,113	7,755	23,819
Moldova	2,090	2,809	4,125	8,636	3,094	5,151	13,732	3,404	6,419	21,739
Tajikistan	1,028	1,466	2,152	4,284	1,646	2,740	6,755	1,846	3,841	10,693

* GDP for 2002 - in 2000 dollars.

Source: GDP in 2002 - PlanEcon 2001a and 2002b. Growth scenarios – author's own calculation.

The distance to the rich countries that post-socialist economies have to make up is in many cases enormous. For Kazakhstan to reach today's income level of the United States, its GDP would have to grow, until 2050, at the average annual rate of 5 per cent. This seems hardly probable, although this country does have too the potential for rapid growth for ten or twenty years. In the case of poor countries, like Albania or Georgia, whose GDP per head (in PPP terms) stood at about USD 2,300 in 2002, even if such a growth rate were maintained in the time span of two generations, they would still be below today's income of rich countries. It follows that one should try to catch up with one's neighbors. Albania will need as much as 48 years of an average growth of 4 per cent annually to reach today's per capita income level of Slovenia; Georgia in 2025, after 23 years of growth at 5 per cent a year on average, will not yet have reached the level then attained by Croatia, even if the latter country were to develop at an average rate of merely 3 per cent annually.

In post-socialist economies, the attainment of the current level of rich countries – that is, a per capita GDP of USD 27,000 – would require its current level to increase by a factor ranging from 1.7 in the case of Slovenia, to more than 26 in the case of Tajikistan (Figure 1.2). Even if this does happen one day, the rich countries will then be still richer and the pursuit of the moving target will go on (Kolodko 2000b).

Now, in the 21st century, chances to catch up with more developed countries, although unevenly distributed, are opening up before quite a few emerging market economies. This is a result of the contemporary phase of globalization, which, as we know, also poses numerous threats. While trying to avoid the latter, many emerging market economies can make good use of the new opportunities: Argentina and Ukraine, Brazil and Russia, Chile and Poland, Nigeria and Pakistan, Iran and Thailand, Costa Rica and Malaysia, Mexico and Croatia, Tunisia and Sri Lanka. Half a century from now, some of them will count among high-income countries, while others may even be demoted to the low-income group. It is time to address the question of what this will depend on.

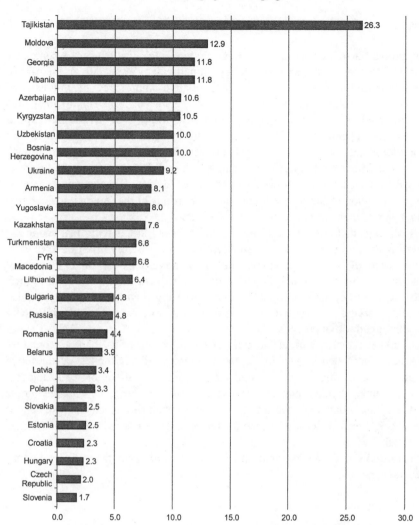

The coefficients show how many times the country's GDP must multiply to catch up with the income level of a rich country, e.g., 27,000 dollars.

Figure 1.2: Catching-up with high-income countries in emerging post-socialist markets

Source: Author's own calculation.

6. Determinants of Fast Growth

Many growth factors exist, but the current phase of globalization brings some new elements into economic theory and policy. In particular – especially in the case of more globalized countries (MGC) – the relative importance of the external environment, in relation to the domestic market, is increasing. **Demand for goods manufactured in a given country and the supply of available capital increasingly depend on tendencies prevailing in other parts of the world and in the global economy as such.** A national economy may enjoy long-term growth only on condition that both effective supply and real demand are on the increase. The dynamics of these two flows thus determines the general economic dynamics, with globalization changing the traditional proportions of the internal and external components of their structure, in favor of the latter.

This means that **only those countries can succeed in ensuring fast economic growth which, on the one hand, can stimulate, in a possibly inflation-free way, the increase of internal demand, and take advantage of their increasing openness and international competitiveness to tap the external demand, and, on the other hand, are capable of not only creating their own capital, but also attracting foreign savings and turning them into long-term capital, enhancing their own productive powers.**

On taking a closer look at the mere dozen or so emerging market economies which have succeeded in overcoming the development lag in the last decades, one can notice that this success stems from a combination of two sources: macroeconomic stability and human capital. Without these, no catching up is possible, either today, or in the future. Only those countries which can take care of these two factors will have a chance for rapid, sustained growth. But even this is not enough.

Sustained social development and rapid economic growth crucially depend on six factors:

- human capital
- financial and real capital
- mature institutions
- magnitude of the markets
- policy quality
- geopolitical location.

The combination of these factors will decide in the coming years about the success or failure in catching up with the rich countries.

The role of **human capital** is increasing in the current phase of liberalization and integration, which unfolds in the course of yet another stormy scientific and technological revolution connected with the ICT expansion and growth of the knowledge-based segments of the economy. For this reason, the high quality of education at all levels and relatively high spending on research and development will increasingly act as growth stimulants.

The trouble is that globalization entails, by definition, migrations, which also involve the educated. As a result, instead of education, or brain training, we often witness **brain draining**. It is felt in many emerging market economies, also the post-socialist ones, from which there is an outflow of mostly highly skilled workforce to more developed countries. In this way, the relative competitiveness and development potential of the countries where these people were educated and trained is adversely affected. This is an aspect of globalization which limits the catching-up potential.

These migrations are paralleled by large-scale movements of poorly educated people. Unskilled labor looks for a new and better place in the global village, thus not only improving their own material situation, but also contributing in a specific way to a reduction of development disparities. By changing the balance of regional and local labor markets, such flows contribute to the relative increase of wages in the countries that people leave (supply of unskilled labor is dwindling so average wages go up) and their relative decrease in the countries in which they arrive (supply of unskilled labor increases so average wages go down).[41] Currently, such dependencies can be observed, for instance, between Mexico and the United States, Algeria and France, Ukraine and Poland, Vietnam and Thailand, Indonesia and Australia, Mozambique and South Africa, or Bolivia and Chile.

Thus if the outflow of workforce – and especially skilled labor – does not favor high growth rates, measures should be taken to avoid it. This is no simple task in a liberalizing world, and is best accomplished by overcoming the vicious circle of low growth rates and population outflow. **The reason why people leave their native land is not the low income levels in that country, but, rather, the lack of realistic prospects for perceptible and speedy improvement in this field.** People do return to their homeland, too – bringing with them their experience, acquired knowledge and savings[42] – if they can view their country's development perspectives with optimism. Feedback thus arises which can be either favorable, or detrimental to development.

Poland, for example, recorded in 1994–7 net (positive) immigration, because of its unprecedented economic dynamics and a significant improvement not only in the current living standards, but also in the level of social satisfaction and optimism about the future. More people were coming back to Poland – quite often equipped with new knowledge and experience gained abroad – than were leaving the country. This tendency was reversed a couple of years later because of the unnecessarily dampened growth rate. In 1999–2001, at least a quarter of a million people, mostly young and educated, left their country for faster developing regions of the world economy. Some of them, regrettably, for good.

Development must be based on **real and financial capital**. For many countries at a medium or low development level, its shortage is the principal barrier to economic growth. Achieving and maintaining such growth requires, in the first place, the formation of domestic capital, while foreign investment and aid can only play a supplementary role. Systematic capital formation requires financial equilibrium and a high propensity to save. Both are difficult to attain in backward countries, especially in the absence of well developed institutions of financial intermediation – the banking sector and the capital market.

If the low propensity to save is aggravated by capital flight – which is quite often the case in emerging market economies – the problem is hopeless.[43] However, when the banks and other organizations manage to accumulate an increasing flow of savings and turn it into active capital, a great deal depends on systemic regulations which should facilitate efficient capital allocation. Otherwise, the apparent abundance of assets might not be productively employed as capital (de Soto 2000).

Foreign capital, which should increasingly be referred to as 'originating from other parts of the global economy', can only supplement domestic capital in the financing of development. A strategy for catching-up with the richer countries cannot be based on the assumption that this process will be financed by capital from these countries. It can only play an auxiliary role. This applies both to foreign investment, especially direct (FDI), and to the aid of the richer for the poorer.

The influx of FDI itself, and, consequently, the increased presence of foreign companies on the market of a given country, is not in itself a guarantee of progress and accelerated growth. Sometimes it just demonstrates that domestic companies are weak and their products are unable to satisfy the demand not only in other parts of the world economy, but even at home. However, foreign capital may contribute to the growth of output and an improved efficiency of the emerging market economies in which it is invested, if four processes take place.

First, the incessant **process of 'creative destruction'** of the old firms by new ones must indeed be creative in the sense that the penetration of foreign capital and the influx of FDI result in the disappearance of obsolete (mostly domestic) companies which are uncompetitive and unable to expand on the world market, but this is more than compensated for by the emergence of new companies, offering more competitive jobs and better products. Such replacement processes occur everywhere – also in the most highly developed countries[44] – and constitute the main vehicle of technological progress and microeconomic efficiency improvement, which, in the long run, should translate into faster growth.

Second, **changes in the market and price structure should facilitate competition and foster the economies of scale.** Foreign companies have their obvious interest in driving out domestic firms. Given the unequal power of companies to resist such pressures, this affects especially small and medium-size enterprises. The ultimate impact of this kind of competition on output dynamics depends, on the one hand, on the openness of the market, the extent of protectionism and support for domestic entrepreneurs, and, on the other hand, on the general reduction of manufacturing costs (and relative prices) resulting from the extended scope of production and the accompanying reduction of trade markups.

Third, **foreign direct investment functions today as the principal transmission belt for new technologies** – including ICT – being transferred to the emerging markets. The most important thing here is an appropriate proliferation mechanism that will spill-over the technologies to related spheres of economic activity and other enterprises. This is not as obvious as it might seem at first glance, for this type of impact would be in the interest of the recipient countries, but not necessarily of the multinational investors. In fact, these interests are often at cross-purposes here. This is due to the fact that over 80 per cent of all FDI originates in just six rich countries – in order of magnitude, the United States, Great Britain, Japan, Germany, Switzerland and the Netherlands – and it is these countries that derive profits from licenses and patent fees, absorbing a total of 90–98 per cent of revenues from this source.[45]

Therefore, foreign (global) investors may occasionally hinder, rather than facilitate, the spread of technological progress. But an appropriate development policy response to this threat should not restrict the influx of FDI, but just the opposite, encourage its increase. The greater the number of modern companies (including foreign ones) which apply modern technologies operating on a given emerging market, the faster is its overall long-term growth.

Fourth, the inflow of direct investment involves a constant know-how transfer, resulting in the **improved skills of local employees in the areas of management and marketing**. Quite often it is the lack of basic skills in these areas that hampers output expansion and economic growth. Foreign investment is usually directed to export-oriented sectors – particularly in those countries where the size of the local market is limited – and the penetration of foreign markets requires greater skills. In time, this knowledge accumulates and finds use on the domestic market as well, with all the beneficial effects on productivity, efficient goods trade and growth rate.

While most emerging markets, regardless of internal capital accumulation, may and should count on private foreign investment to give their rapid growth strategy an additional boost, some countries may also rely on **foreign aid**. These need not be the poorest countries, for transfers of this kind are also a function of geopolitics, regional policy and regional integration processes. Thus, for instance, foreign aid on an extremely large scale has been directed in recent decades to Ireland, whose success in catching-up with the most highly developed countries would not have been possible without the aid received from the European Union.

Unfortunately, the stream of foreign aid flowing from the rich to the poor countries largely dried up in the 1990s. Despite the UN recommendation, undoubtedly appropriate, as it is, that highly developed countries should bring up the relative amount of development aid to 0.7 per cent of their GDP, the actual proportion dropped over the previous decade to 0.22 per cent. This resulted from the combination of naïve belief that private direct investment would be more than adequate to compensate for this loss, and reasonable doubts about the ability of some of the poorest countries to absorb the received aid in a sensible way (Easterly 2001).

Rather than to places where capital seems to be particularly needed, FDI is far more prone to flow to areas where growth dynamics is already high and a vibrant emerging market exists. At the same time many instances can be quoted of misallocation of funds directed, in the form of non-repayable aid, to countries in particularly strained circumstances, mainly in sub-Saharan Africa. Undoubtedly, without a substantial **increase of the scale of assistance to the poorest economies** – both in the form of the cancellation of debt of those highly indebted poor countries[46] (which cannot be expected to be repaid anyway) and new funds for the financing of human capital and infrastructure development – these economies will not only be unable to enter the category of emerging markets, but will not even manage to make sufficient progress to join the MGC group, where growth rate considerably exceeds the average.

Mature institutions are of fundamental importance for sustaining a high growth rate. The trouble is that the emerging economies are characterized – by definition – by still underdeveloped institutions and too liquid, as well as frequently opaque, rules of the market game. This affects allocative efficiency and impedes growth. Importantly, weak institutions create relatively greater inefficiencies and waste. Everything – with the possible exception of corruption, money laundering and organized crime – functions in such circumstances less efficiently than in institutionally mature economies.

This is why structural reform and successive institution building are so important for the emerging markets (Porter 1990; North 1997; Kolodko 1999b). Today this truth is generally acknowledged and, thankfully, its importance is emphasized by influential international organizations (World Bank 2001), although this was not always the case. The involvement of such organizations in the institution building in the emerging market economies appears to go beyond the direct participation in the financing of various projects. The campaign to overcome the development lag is largely fought on the institutional front, where the framework for the functioning of the young market economies is being strengthened.

The **size of the markets** also has a bearing on growth rate. Under globalization, markets undergo integration, and so they expand in size. At the same time every national economy relinquishes part of its sovereignty over the part of the world market it represents. Thus its capacity to interfere with the market is reduced, which may be a good thing or a bad thing, depending on the effectiveness of the intervention policy. At any rate, a larger market provides a better scope for the proliferation of technological progress and the reduction of manufacturing costs due to the economies of scale. A larger market also stimulates enterprise, as it exposes companies to greater competition from other manufacturers. All this has an impact on the production pace and thus may be able to enhance the capacity for catching up.

In a closed economy, the only way for a market to expand was through the increase of internal demand (and supply). Now markets expand because liberalization and globalization are in progress. Some of the emerging post-socialist market economies face in this context the integration with one of the largest and best-developed markets – the European Union.[47] This is often expected to lead to a rapid convergence and reduction of development disparities between the Union's old members and the candidate states. It should be clearly pointed out, however, that **integration with the European Union by no means automatically entails accelerated economic growth.**

Unquestionably, the integration does create opportunities for such growth, but if these opportunities are to be utilized, many requirements, discussed above, must be met. Some countries achieved this feat in the past, other failed to do so (Daianu 2002). When Ireland joined the European Union in 1973, its GDP stood at a mere 59 per cent of the Union's average. Now it takes pride not only in having caught up with, but also having overtaken others, as this indicator currently exceeds 120 per cent. Greece, on the other hand, joined the Union in 1981 with an income equivalent to 77 per cent of the EU average, and now its relative position has eroded, as the indicator in question has dropped to just 66 per cent. Similar mechanisms will continue to operate in the future – some actors may succeed, and some may not.

This will depend on the **quality of economic policy**, since membership in the European Union – or in any other integration organization elsewhere, be it NAFTA[48] in America, ASEAN[49] in Asia, or SADC[50] in Africa – does not preclude conducting one's own, national development policy. It does restrict, even more so than globalization does, the members' political – and especially economic – sovereignty, depriving the governments and central banks of the use of certain economic policy instruments previously at their disposal, but this does not render this policy totally impossible. Such a policy should, generally, consist in maximizing the advantages offered to the emerging markets by globalization and in mitigating the inevitable risks brought by globalization.

Besides, of course, one can always celebrate or bemoan one's **geopolitical situation**. Its geographical component is unalterable, but it is possible to endeavor to change the political circumstances for the better. In the long run, some actors even succeed in this task. This is particularly likely when they manage to utilize fast growth to catch up with the economies which made the forward leap a long time ago.

Notes

1 'Purchasing Power Parities (PPPs) are the rates of currency conversion which eliminate the differences in the price levels between countries. PPPs are obtained by evaluating the costs of a basket of goods and services between countries for all components of GDP; PPPs are given in national currency units per US dollar.' (OECD 2001, p. 13). Because of the relatively higher (in dollar terms) cost of living in the US than in the remaining OECD countries, GDP calculated in PPP terms is, in most of the cases, higher than GDP calculated at the current market exchange rate of a given currency. For

instance, with respect to Poland, the OECD estimates the purchasing power parity of the zloty at 1.98 to a dollar. This means that, at the average market rate of 4.35 zlotys to a dollar in 2000, the zloty equivalent of one dollar bought in Poland 2.19 times more goods and services from the representative basket than one dollar did in the United States. In 2001, this proportion decreased to 2.07 because of the appreciation of the zloty by 5.9 per cent (the average exchange rate amounted to 4.1 zlotys to a dollar). Only in six countries (Denmark, Iceland, Japan, Norway, Sweden and Switzerland) is GDP per head calculated in PPP terms is lower than GDP in current exchange rate terms. Characteristically, all the European countries from this group remain outside the euro area. These are the 'more expensive' countries in the sense that a dollar exchanged for their domestic currencies buys less than it does in the US, because of the price differentials. For the inhabitants of these countries, the US is 'cheap'. In the remaining countries this relationship is reversed, and there is an inverse correlation between this price differential on the one hand, and the relative development level of a given country and the degree of adjustment of its internal prices to world prices, on the other. For example, within the OECD, the spread between PPP-adjusted and current-rate GDP is largest in Slovakia and smallest in the United Kingdom. In the age of globalization – in view of the progressive market liberalization and integration – differences in this field can be expected to shrink gradually. In the United States, GDP calculated at current rates and at PPP is, by definition, the same and amounts in 2002 to about USD 37,000 per inhabitant.

2   According to the estimates of the Washington-based PlanEcon (since 2002 DRI-WEFA, Inc.), per capita GDP in Slovenia (in PPP terms) amounted in 2001 to USD 15,372 (PlanEcon 2001b). By way of comparison, the same source puts Poland's GDP at USD 8,137. The OECD estimates the latter at 15 per cent more, that is, about USD 9,400. These discrepancies stem from the different methodologies on which the calculations are based.

3   According to OECD estimates, GDP per capita in the Czech Republic – taking into account the 3.5 per cent growth rate in 2001 and another 4 per cent or so expected in 2002 – approaches (in PPP terms) USD 14,900 in 2002, while the PlanEcon forecast for the same year mentions USD 13,376 (PlanEcon 2001b).

4   In fairly remote times – at the beginning of the 16th century – that was the case with China, which then surpassed Europe in technological advancement. However, the lack of necessary reform and the conservatism of the power structures stood in the way of an economic acceleration – particularly at a later stage, when 18th- and 19th-century Europe took excellent advantage of the subsequent phases of the scientific and technological revolution.

5   A positive example is provided by the changes in Japan in the second half of the 19th century under the Meiji reform; a negative one can be furnished by Ukraine, which failed to utilize its relatively better position as regards the state of the production facilities and the technology at its disposal in the 1990s. It is important to note that such losses cannot be made up for at a later time. Thus neither contemporary China is making good the losses, despite its impressive growth, nor is Ukraine, even if it manages to hold on to the rapid development path it entered at the beginning of the present decade. This

is so because the time that was once wasted is irrevocably lost, and no contemporary (or future) economic growth will offer compensation for this loss, as this growth begins at a lower level than it would, had the past opportunities been appropriately utilized. Today these opportunities can only be seen as a more or less distant past, whose promise – if not totally squandered – was at best inadequately exploited.

6   Interestingly, included among the 'rich economies', apart from the initial 24 member states of the OECD, are not only Hong Kong, Taiwan, South Korea and Singapore, but also Chile, whose GDP per head (in PPP terms) is the same as Poland's. In both cases it amounts to about 26 per cent of the American income.

7   'The "more globalized" – the top third of developing countries in terms of increased trade to GDP between 1970s and 1990s – are Argentina, Bangladesh, Brazil, China, Colombia, Costa Rica, Côte d'Ivoire, the Dominican Republic, Haiti, Hungary, India, Jamaica, Jordan, Malaysia, Mali, Mexico, Nepal, Nicaragua, Paraguay, the Philippines, Rwanda, Thailand, Uruguay, and Zimbabwe. The "less globalized" are all other developing countries for which we have data. The less globalized group is a very diverse set of countries. It includes failed states whose economic performance has been extremely poor. It also includes some countries of the former Soviet Union that went through a difficult transition in the 1990s. Some of the less globalized countries have had stable but not increasing trade, and positive but slow growth.' (World Bank 2002a, p. 51).

8   Per capita GDP in these countries kept growing at increasingly faster rates in the last decades of the previous century: from 1 per cent in the 1960s, to 3 per cent in the 1970s, 4 per cent in the 1980s and 5 per cent annually, on average, in the 1990s.

9   In highly developed countries, GDP per head grew at the average rate of 2.1 per cent a year. Thus it increased during the 1990s, in real terms, by another 23 per cent, yet in the richest among the major economies – the United States – the aggregate growth was over 38 per cent (3.3 per cent average overall growth, or 2.8 per cent in per capita terms).

10 The essence of this concept of economic policy is presented by Williamson (1990 and 1997). For a criticism of the 'Washington Consensus', see North (1997), Stiglitz (1998) and Kolodko (1999b).

11 It should be added that a similar observation pertains to some other countries which boast success in attaining relatively higher growth rates and overcoming the development lag. In Asia, for instance, this is true of Vietnam, and in Africa – of Uganda.

12 Whereas the population of China increased in those years by ca. 30 per cent, India recorded a nearly 50-per cent population growth. If the current demographic forecasts prove accurate, the population of these countries should increase by the year 2015, respectively, by 8.5 and 18 per cent, reaching 1.41bn in China and 1.23bn in India. Thus every third inhabitant of the Earth will live in one of these two populous countries, whose development level will have an even greater impact than today on global averages.

13 This pertains especially to exports, whose slow growth creates problems which are fairly typical of the entire region, connected with a high trade deficit and a deficit of the balance of payments.

14 This indicator differs from region to region and from state to state. In nine economies of Central and Eastern Europe (Croatia, the Czech Republic, Estonia, Hungary, Latvia, Lithuania, Poland, Slovakia and Slovenia), economic growth began after just three years of transitional recession, in 1993. As a result, in the year 2000 their GDP reached 107 per cent of the 1989 level. In six other states of Southern and Eastern Europe (Albania, Bosnia-Herzegovina, Bulgaria, Macedonia, Romania and Yugoslavia), the recession lasted four years, having begun already in 1989). In that region, as the slump was much deeper, the GDP of the year 2000 reached only 73 per cent of the level of 1989. In the CIS area, that is, the 12 economies of the Commonwealth of Independent States (Armenia, Azerbaijan, Belarus, Georgia, Kazakhstan, Kyrgyzstan, Moldova, Russia, Tajikistan, Turkmenistan, Ukraine and Uzbekistan), this indicator came up to 61 per cent, partly because these countries, on average, returned to the growth path only in 1996, after five years of recession in 1991–5 (EBRD 2001).

15 This group also comprises the new member states which joined this organization in the 1990s, including four post-socialist countries (the Czech Republic, Hungary, Poland and Slovakia). However, their relative contribution to the GDP of the entire organization (respectively, 0.5, 0.5, 1.3 and 0.2 per cent) is so small that the development tendencies within this group have very little impact on the overall growth in OECD countries. Even if these countries were excluded from the calculation, the GDP growth in the remaining OECD countries in the 1990s – rounded off to the tenth of a percentage point – would amount, on average, to ca. 2.5 per cent annually.

16 This can be illustrated by examples from various corners of the world economy – from the openly hostile treatment of the Asian immigrants in Australia and their deportation to South Pacific islands, to the expulsion of illegal Chinese immigrants from Hong Kong back to China, to the introduction of stringent visa requirements for CIS citizens traveling to the formerly 'fraternal' countries of Central and Eastern Europe, to tough immigration quotas for the inhabitants of Central America trying to settle in North America. Of course, such restrictions are far less strict – or, indeed, sometimes replaced with material incentives – in the case of highly skilled employees who are in short supply in the developed economies. The boom of the so-called new economy in the US is a case in point, where a number of measures were introduced to facilitate the arrival of specialists in the areas of computer hardware and software, as well as Internet technologies, educated elsewhere – mostly in India and China, but also in some post-socialist transforming economies.

17 This group of highly developed countries, although inhabited by merely 15 per cent of the world population, generates 57 per cent of the global income, and its share in the world exports of goods and services amounts to 76 per cent. However, in spite of its decisive influence of the global economy, it must not be equated with the world at large.

18 In the last decade and a half – since the mid-1980s – customs tariffs have been reduced by about 10 per cent in the LGC group and by about 33 per cent in the MGC group.

19 This long-term tendency is not undermined by the stagnation of the world trade volume in 2001–2002, which is a temporary occurrence, as was the slowing down of growth in 2000–2001. The World Trade Organization estimates that the global trade volume

dropped in 2001 by about 1 per cent and is likely to increase by about the same amount in 2002, returning to the level attained in the year 2000.

20 It should be noted that out of the 20 countries with the relatively highest proportion of foreign trade volume to GDP, exceeding 50 per cent, only four are highly developed countries, namely, Belgium, Ireland, Luxembourg and Singapore. This group also includes three post-socialist economies: the Czech Republic, Estonia and Slovakia.

21 In terms of capital flows, and especially direct investment, post-socialist economies occupy a specific position. In 1990–2001, they officially absorbed more than USD 150bn, of which the greatest part – almost USD 60bn – was channeled to Poland. During the same period Poland invested abroad – mainly in the neighboring post-Soviet republics – less than USD 600m, that is, a hundred times less. Similar proportions are observed in other countries of the region, except Russia. Another type of emerging markets comprises countries which invest more capital abroad than they absorb from foreign sources, like Hong Kong or South Korea. In post-socialist emerging markets, the scarcity of capital makes direct investment a one-way process: funds flow into these countries. Obviously, there are exceptions, connected especially with the export and flight of capital, as was the case in Russia in the 1990s or after the fall of the fraudulent pyramid schemes in Albania in 1996–8.

22 Of course, among post-socialist countries, one should also include Mongolia, to which the above remarks and generalizations also apply, although it is usually left out in the published statistics, because of its marginal contribution to the world economy.

23 In a sense, this threat remains a fact all the time. Even the World Bank (2002a) says that, by cautious estimates, the protectionist practices of rich countries alone cost the poorer countries as much as about USD 100bn a year, that is, double the amount of foreign aid they receive.

24 In some international analyses, certain countries are occasionally included in two groups simultaneously. For instance, Hong Kong, South Korea, Singapore and Taiwan have been treated by the IMF and the World Bank for a couple of years now as advanced economies, whereas investment banks still classify them as emerging markets.

25 Per capita GDP (in PPP terms) in Canada is just 80 per cent of the US level.

26 Although the Dominican Republic and Haiti coexist on the same island, the GDP of the former increased in the 1990s by 82 per cent and that of the latter dropped by 11 per cent (ECLAC 2001).

27 In the long run, the economic system is also shaped by the policy being implemented, although in a short-term perspective it may have a serious impact on the effectiveness of this policy. Incidentally, this is one of the significant differences between emerging and mature markets.

28 PlanEcon (2001b) estimates per capita GDP (in PPP terms, year 2000 prices) in Poland, Hungary, and the Czech Republic in 2002, respectively, at about USD 8,300; USD 11,800 and USD 13,400. According to the World Bank, the Hungarian and Czech income exceeds that of Poland, respectively, by 32 and 53 per cent.

29 PlanEcon (2001a) puts per capita GDP (in PPP, year 1995 prices) in those three countries, respectively, at USD 2,700; USD 3,550 and USD 5,625.

30 The indicators quoted above for the Turkmenistan-Turkey and Macedonia-Greece pairs (pertaining to the year 2000) should be taken with due caution, as the respective per capita GDP figures (in PPP terms) have been calculated using slightly different methods: the OECD methodology in the case of Greece (USD 16,000) and Turkey (USD 6,800) (OECD 2001) and the PlanEcon methodology in the case of Macedonia (USD 3,900) (PlanEcon 2001b) and Turkmenistan (USD 3,400) (PlanEcon 2001a).

31 As it happens, the Australian economy has been developing faster than New Zealand's over the past dozen or so years, thus increasing the distance between the two: the average GDP growth in Australia in 1990–2002 has reached as much as 4.2 per cent, as compared with 3 per cent in New Zealand.

32 Real consumption depends on both current income and the degree of depreciation of the accumulated consumption assets. It should be added that the notion of living standards is far broader than consumption – even if the latter is construed in so-called true terms (Pohorille 1982). It depends on many factors, including the general level of education and culture, health, public security and the state of the environment. Attempts are being made to measure these standards by means of the Human Development Index (HDI), calculated under the United Nations Development Program (UNDP 2001). It should be noted that from the point of view of HDI disparities, the distance between the emerging post-socialist market economies and the rich countries is noticeably smaller than in the case of per capita GDP (Kolodko 2000a). Whereas there are just four post-socialist countries (Slovenia, the Czech Republic, Hungary and Slovakia) among the 50 countries with highest per capita GDP levels (in PPP terms), four other post-socialist countries (Poland, Estonia, Croatia and Lithuania), in addition to the above-mentioned four, are listed among the top 50 in terms of HDI.

33 According to a PlanEcon forecast, per capita GDP (in PPP terms) in Tajikistan was expected to reach USD 1,028 in 2002, whereas at current exchange rates it stands at a mere USD 204 (PlanEcon 2001a). The ratio of per capita GDP between the richest EU member – Luxembourg – and the poorest CIS economy – Tajikistan – amounts to 42-to-1 in PPP terms, but calculated at current exchange rates, it increases to 243-to-1.

34 In the euro area, the annual GDP growth in the same period was just 1.8 per cent, thus increasing (rather than reducing) the distance between these 12 advanced economies and the USA to more than 50 per cent.

35 Per capita GDP in Mexico (in PPP terms) amounts to about 25 per cent of the US level, but it should be borne in mind that income disparities in Mexico are much greater than in the United States, with the Gini coefficient for these two countries of, respectively, 53.1 and 40.8. If the extreme deciles and quintiles of the Mexican population derive, respectively, 1.3/41.7 and 3.5/57.4 per cent of the total income, the respective indicators for the US stand at 1.8/30.5 and 5.2/46.4 per cent (World Bank 2002b).

36 The IMF forecasts that, in 2003, Ireland will remain the fastest growing economy among the rich countries and its GDP will increase by a further 6.2 per cent (IMF 2002).

37 In Poland, thanks to the reforms of the pre-transformation period, the transitional recession was the shortest in the region, lasting merely three years: from mid-1989 to mid-1992. Growth has thus continued for 10 years, although during the two quarters at

the turn of 2001/2002, it was brought down to a negligible rate of 0.3 per cent (on a year-to-year basis).

38 There are also cases like Burundi, which maintained in the 1980s an average annual growth of 4.4 per cent, placing it among the twenty fastest growing economies, only to end up in the following decade, in the aftermath of a devastating ethnic and military conflict, with a negative growth of 2.9 per cent annually, among the twenty slowest growing (or, to be precise, fastest shrinking) countries.

39 This threshold was crossed, in chronological order, by Poland, Slovenia, Albania, Hungary, Slovakia, the Czech Republic and Uzbekistan (EBRD 2002). The next post-socialist economies to achieve this will be, in all probability, Estonia and Croatia, around 2005.

40 Oddly enough, this feat was attained despite the relatively low growth rate of 2.0 per cent (in per capita terms) in 1983–2001.

41 During the 'second phase of globalization', in accordance with the World Bank periodization, that is, in the years 1870–1914, migrations had an even stronger impact on the changing economic dynamics than did goods trade or capital transfers (World Bank 2002a). In those years, 'Emigration is estimated to have raised Irish wages by 32 per cent, Italian by 28 per cent and Norwegian by 10 per cent. Immigration is estimated to have lowered Argentine wages by 22 per cent, Australian by 15 per cent, Canadian by 16 per cent and American by 8 per cent.' (Lindert and Williamson 2001, p. 19).

42 Of course, one does not have to return home in order to transfer the savings made abroad to one's native country. It is estimated, for instance, that the transfers to India made by Indians working worldwide are six times higher than the entire official aid received by that populous country.

43 According to World Bank estimates, about 40 per cent of African countries' private capital was kept outside the continent in the 1990s. If the poorest continent thus finances, de facto, the development of other parts of the global economy, it is small wonder it remains the poorest.

44 In the United States, in every five-year period as much as some 35 per cent of all companies go into liquidation, particularly in the small and medium-size enterprise sector (Dunne, Roberts and Summelson 1989). But even among large companies, with 250 or more employees, this indicator amounts to 16 per cent (Bernard and Jensen 2001).

45 It should be added that most of these funds are cross-invested in the richest countries, while the poorest continent – Africa – receives only about 1 per cent of the global direct investment flow. There were years when a small country like Ireland attracted more investment than this vast continent in its entirety.

46 In particular, this refers to the 41 economies that make up the so-called HIPC group (Highly Indebted Poor Countries), out of which as many as 35 are located in Africa. In some cases – like Mozambique – they spend more on the servicing of their foreign debt owed to rich countries than on education and health together. Under such circumstances, there is no chance for development.

47 The share of the European Union in the global output is estimated at about 20 per cent in PPP terms and 27.8 per cent at current exchange rates. By way of comparison, the same indicator for the United States stands at 29.9 per cent.

48 The core of NAFTA, or the North American Free Trade Agreement, is United States. The other members of the grouping are Canada and Mexico. NAFTA has almost 400 millions inhabitants and its GDP exceeds 8 billion dollars, that is about 17,000 per head. Of course, Mexico brings this average significantly down.

49 ASEAN (the Association of Southeast Asian Nations) was established in 1967 and initially included only five members: Indonesia, Malaysia, the Philippines, Singapore and Thailand. Brunei joined in 1984, Vietnam in 1995, Laos and Myanmar in 1997 and Cambodia in 1999. The population of the ASEAN region counts about half billion people, yet the total GDP of it is less than a tenth of the GDP of the USA or European Union. However, ASEAN is strongly committed to openness and active external economic links (not only due to the export-oriented Singaporean economy), hence it is well advanced into integration with the global economy, more than the other regions. The foreign trade turnover of this grouping matches its GDP and hovers at around 800 billion dollars.

50 SADC (the Southern African Development Community) includes 14 members from the southern part of continent: Angola, Botswana, Democratic Republic of Congo, Lesotho, Malawi, Mauritius, Mozambique, Namibia, Republic of South Africa, Seychelles, Swaziland, Tanzania, Zambia, and Zimbabwe. The entire grouping contributes half of Africa's GDP, yet a major part of it is coming from just one country, i.e., the Republic of South Africa.

References

Bernard, Andrew B. and Bradford Jensen, J. (2001), 'Who Dies? International Trade, Market Structure, and Industrial Restructuring', *National Bureau of Economic Research Working Paper*, No. W8327 (June), National Bureau of Economic Research, Cambridge, MA.
http://papers.nber.org/papers/w8327.pdf

Blanchard, Olivier (1997), *The Economics of Post-Communist Transition*, Oxford University Press, New York.

Blejer, Mario I. and Skreb, Marko (eds) (2001), *Transition. The First Decade*, The MIT Press, Cambridge, MA, London, England.

Bordo, Michael D., Eichengreen, Barry and Irwin, Douglas A. (1999), 'Is Globalization Today Really Different than Globalization a Hundred Years Ago?', *NBER Working Paper*, No. W7195 (June), National Bureau of Economic Research, Cambridge, MA.
http://papers.nber.org/papers/w7195.pdf

Daianu, Daniel (2002), 'Is Catching-up Possible in Europe?', *TIGER Working Paper Series*, No. 19 (May), Transformation, Integration and Globalization Economic Research (TIGER) at the Leon Kozminski Academy of Entrepreneurship and Management (WSPiZ), Warsaw.
http://www.tiger.edu.pl/publikacje/TWPNo19.pdf

De Soto, Hernando (2000), *The Mystery of Capital. Why Capitalism Triumphs in the West and Fails Everywhere Else*, Basic Books, New York.

Dollar, David (2001), *Globalization, Inequality, and Poverty since 1980*, World Bank (November), Washington, DC.
http://econ.worldbank.org/files/2944_globalization-inequality-and-poverty.pdf

Dollar, David and Kraay, Aart (2001), 'Trade, Growth, and Poverty', *Policy Research Working Paper*, No. 2199 (June), World Bank, Washington, DC.
http://econ.worldbank.org/files/2207_wps2615.pdf

Dunne, Timothy, Roberts, Mark and Samuelson, Larry (1989), 'The Growth and Failure of U.S. Manufacturing Plants', *Quarterly Journal of Economics*, Vol. 112, No. 4, pp. 1203–50.

Easterly, William (2001), *The Elusive Quest for Growth: Economists' Adventures and Misadventures in the Tropics*, MIT Press, Cambridge, MA.

EBRD (2001), *Transition report 2001. Energy in Transition*, European Bank for Reconstruction and Development, London.

EBRD (2002), *Transition report update*, European Bank for Reconstruction and Development (May), London.

ECLAC (2001), *Preliminary Overview of the Economies of Latin America and the Caribbean*, United Nations Economic Commission for Latin America and the Caribbean (December), Santiago de Chile.
http://www.eclac.org/publicaciones/DesarrolloEconomico/3/LCG2153P/lcg2153i.pdf

ECLAC (2002), 'Preliminary Overview of the Economies of Latin American and the Caribbean 2001', *ECLAC Notes* (Special Issue), No. 20 (January).

Economist (2001), *World in Figures. 2002 Edition, The Economist* in association with Profile Books, London.

Frankel, Jeffrey (2001), 'Globalisation of the Economy', in Joseph Nye and John Donahue, *Governance in a Globalizing World*, Brookings Institutions Press, Washington, DC.

Garten, Jeffrey E. (1998), *The Big Ten: The Big Emerging Markets and How They Will Change Our Lives*, Basic Books, New York.

Gilpin, Robert (2001), *Global Political Economy. Understanding the International Economic Order*, Princeton University Press, Princeton-Oxford.

Hutton, Will and Giddens, Anthony (eds) (2000), *Global Capitalism*, The New Press, New York.

IMF (2000a), *Globalization: Threat or Opportunity?*, International Monetary Fund (April), Washington, DC.
http://www.imf.org/external/np/exr/ib/2000/041200.htm

IMF (2000b), *World Economic Outlook. Focus on Transition Economies*, International Monetary Fund, Washington, DC (October).
http://www.imf.org/external/pubs/ft/weo/2000/02/pdf

IMF (2002), *World Economic Outlook. Recessions and Recoveries*, International Monetary Fund, Washington, DC (April).
http://www.imf.org/external/pubs/ft/weo/2002/01/index.htm

Kolodko, Grzegorz W. (1999a), 'Ten Years of Postsocialist Transition: the Lessons for Policy Reforms', *Policy Research Working Paper*, No. 2095 (April), World Bank, Washington, DC.
http://econ.worldbank.org/docs/424.pdf or
http://papers.ssrn.com/sol3/papers.cfm?abstract_id=170888

Kolodko, Grzegorz W. (1999b), 'Transition to a market economy and sustained growth. Implications for the post-Washington consensus', *Communist and Post-Communist Studies*, Vol. 32, No. 3 (September), pp. 233–61.

Kolodko, Grzegorz W. (2000a), 'From Shock to Therapy. The Political Economy of Postsocialist Transformation', Oxford University Press, Oxford-New York.

Kolodko, Grzegorz W. (2000b), 'Globalization and Catching-up: From Recession to Growth of Transition Economies', *IMF Working Paper*, WP/00/100 (June), International Monetary Fund, Washington, DC.
http://www.imf.org/external/pubs/ft/wp/2000/wp00100.pdf
or http://papers.ssrn.com/sol3/papers.cfm?abstract_id=248423

Kolodko, Grzegorz W. (2000c), 'Post-Communist Transition. The Thorny Road', Rochester, NY, and Woodbridge, University of Rochester Press, Suffolk, UK.

Kolodko, Grzegorz W. (2000d), 'The "New Economy" and the Old Problems. Prospects for Fast Growth in Post-socialist Countries', *EMERGO. Journal of Transforming Economies and Societies*, Vol. 7, No. 4 (Autumn), pp. 21–37.

Kolodko, Grzegorz W. (2001a), *Moja globalizacja, czyli dookoła świata i z powrotem* [My Globalization, or Around the World and Back Again], TNOiK, Toruń.

Kolodko, Grzegorz W. (2001b) 'Globalisation and Transformation: Illusions and Reality', *Technical Papers*, No. 176 (May), OECD Development Centre, Paris.
http://www1.oecd.org/dev/publication/tp/Tp176.pdf
or http://papers.ssrn.com/sol3/papers.cfm?abstract_id=258435

Kolodko, Grzegorz W. (2001c) 'Globalization and Catching-up: From Recession to Growth in Transition Economies', *Communist and Post-Communist Studies*, Vol. 34, No. 3 (September), pp. 279–322.

Kolodko, Grzegorz W. (2002a), '2025: Two Histories of Economic Growth', *TIGER Working Paper Series*, No. 12 (September), Transformation, Integration and Globalization Economic Research (TIGER) at the Leon Kozminski Academy of Entrepreneurship and Management (WSPiZ), Warsaw.

Kolodko, Grzegorz W. (2002b), 'Globalization and Catching-up in Transition Economies', Rochester, University of Rochester Press, NY, and Woodbridge, Suffolk, UK.

Kolodko, Grzegorz W. (2002c), 'Tygrys z ludzką twarzą' [Tiger with a Human Face], TNOiK, Toruń.

Kolodko, Grzegorz W. and Nuti, D. Mario (1997), 'The Polish Alternative. Old Myths, Hard Facts and New Strategies in the Successful Transformation of the Polish Economy', *Research for Action*, 33, The United Nations University World Institute for Development Economics Research (UNU/WIDER), Helsinki.
http://papers.ssrn.com/sol3/papers.cfm?abstract_id=170889
or http://www.tiger.edu.pl/kolodko/working/wider/WIDER_1997.pdf

Koźmiński, Andrzej K. (2002), 'Jak zbudować gospodarkę opartą na wiedzy?' [How to Build a Knowledge-based Economy?], in Grzegorz W. Kolodko (ed.), 'Rozwój polskiej gospodarki. Perspektywy i uwarunkowania' [Development of Polish Economy. Perspectives and Determinants], Wydawnictwo WSPiZ, pp. 155–66.

Kwiatkowski, Stefan (2001), 'Intellectual Entrepreneurship and Sustainable Economic Development in Europeans Post-Communist Countries', *EMERGO. Journal of Transforming Economies and Societies*, Vol. 8, No. 1 (Winter), pp. 2–12.

Lavigne, Marie (1999), *The Economics of Transition: From Socialist Economy to Market Economy*, Macmillan, Chatham, Kent.

Lindert, Peter H. and Williamson, Jeffrey G. (2001), *Globalization and Inequality: A Long History*, World Bank (April), Washington, DC.
http://econ.worldbank.org/files/2872_lindert_williamson.pdf

Magarinos, Carlos A. and Sercovich, Francisco C. (2001), *Gearing Up for a New Development Agenda. Marginalization vs Prosperity: How to Improve and Spread the Gains of Globalization*, United Nations Industrial Development Organization (UNIDO), Vienna.

Mobius, J. Mark (1996), *On Emerging Markets*, Pitman Publishing, London.

North, Douglass C. (1997), 'The Contribution of the New Institutional Economics to an Understanding of the Transition Problem', *WIDER Annual Lectures*, No. 1 (March), The United Nations University World Institute for Development Economics Research (UNU/WIDER), Helsinki.

OECD (2000), 'A New Economy? The Changing Role of Innovation and Information Technology in Growth', Organisation for Economic Co-operation and Development, Paris.
http://www.oecd.org/dsti/sti/stat-ana/prod/growth.htm

OECD (2001), *OECD in Figures. Statistics on the Member Countries*, Organisation for Economic Co-operation and Development, Paris.

Payson, Steven (2000), *Economics, Science and Technology*, Edward Elgar Publishing, Cheltenham, UK-Northampton, MA, USA.

PlanEcon (2001a), *Review and Outlook for the Former Soviet Republics*, PlanEcon, Inc. (October), Washington, DC.

PlanEcon (2001b), *Review and Outlook for Eastern Europe*, PlanEcon, Inc. (December), Washington, DC.

Pohorille, Maksymilian (ed.) (1982), *Tendencje rozwoju konsumpcji. Postulaty i uwarunkowania* ['Trends in Consumption Development. Postulates and Determinants'], Państwowe Wydawnictwo Ekonomiczne, Warszawa.

Porter, Michael E. (1990), *The Competitive Advantage of Nations*, The Free Press, New York.

Raymond, Susan U. (ed.) (1999), *Science, Technology, and the Economic Future*, Johns Hopkins University Press, Baltimore, MD.

Stiglitz, Joseph E. (1998), 'More Instruments and Broader Goals: Moving toward the Post-Washington Consensus', *WIDER Annual Lectures*, No. 2 (January), The United Nations University World Institute for Development Economics Research (UNU/WIDER), Helsinki.

UNDP (2001), *Human Development Report 2001*, Oxford University Press, New York.

Williamson, John (1990), 'What Washington Means by Policy Reform', in John Williamson (ed.), *Latin American Adjustment: How Much Has Happened?*, Institute for International Economics, Washington, DC.

Williamson, John (1997), 'The Washington Consensus Revisited', in Louis Emmerij (ed.), *Economic and Social Development into the XXI Century*, Inter-American Development Bank, Washington, DC.

World Bank (2001), *World Development Report. Building Institutions for Markets*, The World Bank, Washington, DC.

World Bank (2002a), *Globalization, Growth and Poverty: Building an Inclusive World Economy*, A copublication of the World Bank and Oxford University Press, Washington, DC.
http://econ.worldbank.org/prr/structured_doc.php?sp=2477&st=&sd=2857

World Bank (2002b), *World Development Indicators 2002*, The World Bank, Washington, DC.

Zacher, Lech W. (2000), 'The "New Economy" as an Interaction of Technology, Economy and Society', *EMERGO. Journal of Transforming Economies and Societies*, Vol. 7, No. 4, (Autumn), pp. 38–53.

Chapter 2

Transition as Development[1]

László Csaba

Thirteen years have elapsed since the conclusion of the round table talks in Poland in April 1989, which marked the onset of systemic transformations in Central and Eastern Europe. The peoples of the region have been given a chance to overcome the blind alley of the Soviet model and return to the mainstream of human development. This span of time is long enough to allow for some theoretical generalizations. In the present study we analyze the present state of 'transitology', at a time when the frontrunners of change are likely to join the European Union by 2004, thus establishing their position as fully-fledged market economies of the European brand. This is a decisive factor in the formation of their economic and political order, allowing them to avoid that particular variant of 'east European capitalism' which has evolved in the countries that do not stand a chance of EU accession in the near future and thus miss an anchor for their strategic decisions in the spheres of policy and economy.

In answering the question of 'what has been left' or alternatively, 'what we have learned' we adopt the following approach. First we survey some salient findings of transitology proper. Then we attempt to put these in the context of new development economics (Todaro, 2000; Meier and Stiglitz, eds, 2001), interpreting the ups and downs of poor countries within the context of general economics. Then we compare the remaining institutional reforms in the region with the ongoing structural reforms of the welfare states in Western Europe. Finally, we search for a basis of collective choices that would enable the EU to enlarge eastward in a way that amounts to more than a minimalist alibi exercise. Our focus is thus on the overall landscape and theoretical novelties, while detailed substantiation of some of the points is left to the references.

From Ideology to Sustainable Development

According to conventional wisdom in economics, and also in the predominant view in historiography, the collapse of the Soviet empire was built into the system and inevitable. Still its speed and timing, as well as its very occurrence remained a surprise to the overwhelming majority of analysts. The situation is best reflected in the fact that the G7 meeting of Houston, convening in December 1990, entrusted the tasks of analyzing and assisting the Soviet economy to institutions whose only common denominator was that the Red superpower was no member to any of them. The joint effort of these (IMF, OECD, IBRD, 1991) – and the parallel endeavors of the European Communities (EU, 1990) – produced weighty volumes; however, by the time of their publication, the object of research – the Soviet Union – had ceased to exist.

Even in more academic analyses the confusion was considerable. Sovietologists, on the one hand, tended to be versed in the languages and customs of the region, not so much, however, in standard economics and its applications. Likewise, academic – and especially macroeconomic – departments had little idea, if any, about command economy in general and the societal context of Central and Eastern Europe in particular.

This applied, basically, also to the international agencies, as their – limited – experience with Hungary and Romania was of little assistance in managing the problems of a disintegrating Soviet empire or a collapsing communist economy in Poland. As a contemporary survey (Murrel, 1995) neatly proves, the lack of knowledge of the specific post-communist context tended to be 'remedied' by reliance on shallow analogies to the experience of international financial institutions (IFIs) in developing countries, or a direct application of textbook solutions, without much care about the institutional or historic context into which these insights were to be transposed.

At the level of policy advice, reliance on simplistic adaptations of otherwise elaborate policy conceptions proved even more widespread. Ideological leanings, experimenting spirit and mechanistic application of what the current wisdom on poor countries suggested were combined to produce quick fixes.

Uncritical reliance on standard, pre-cooked solutions, coupled with ideological postulates stressing speed over quality, and instrumentalizing the concept of spontaneous institution emergence for trivial political ends, often swept away any attempt at analyzing local conditions on their own right. This led – as Stiglitz (2000, pp. 552–7) retrospectively illustrates – to a neglect of those *contextual circumstances* which decide about the success or failure of the application of a proven theoretical insight to policy-making. Thus the quest for speed and the resultant policy improvisation (lacking a systemic coherence) has often brought about partial reforms yielding paradoxical outcomes, with unintended side-effects dominating over desired and planned objectives.

Correct theories translated into haphazard policy implementation thus produced perverse outcomes in a number of cases. Suffice it to mention some of the better known cases: in Hungary, public utilities were privatized with a stroke of a pen in late 1995, without, however, their prior regulation. Thus public monopolies were simply transformed into private (or, in some cases, foreign public) monopolies. With 'real owners' established, the chances of further liberalization and deregulation (called for by the EU process) are slim, and low efficiency has been built into the system for many years. The introduction of voucher privatization in Russia in 1992–4, at the height of hyperinflation, could not stand a chance of testing the Coase theorem, nor could it build a reform constituency. Similarly, introducing a fully funded private pension system in Kazakhstan in 1999 – while the capital market was lacking – can hardly bring about those benefits on which the general arguments for pension privatization are based.

On the other hand, it would be wrong to ignore the fact that local economists – of a great variety of persuasions – have been, as a rule, poorly equipped to deal with the theoretical and policy challenges of transformation. The contemporary vogue – reform economics – functioned within a self-constraining framework of market socialism, which never addressed questions related to a real market order (like capital market regulation, banking crises, credit crunches or the conflicting demands of exchange rate policy). Its positive message – over and above the critical account of the *status quo ante* – has evaporated in the face of the in-between solutions and ersatz-solutions left behind by the political drive toward real markets and real democracy.

Even in Hungary, where by the mid-1980s economics had long overcome any form of socialism and focused on such issues as capital market, private property and opening up the economy (cf. Kornai, 1990; Kornai, 2000; Csaba, 2002b), these insights had only inadequate influence on policy decisions and institutional options. Until late 1989, the state administration held more radical transformation projects to be politically infeasible. Later, the daily struggle for retaining the solvency of the country dominated any broader considerations, at least until 1992. The former opposition (post-transition ruling parties), stepping in the footprint of the 1956 revolution, called for a third road, based on self-management solutions, with private property and competition playing a subordinate role at best (Laki, 1991; Lányi, 1996). As the two analyses quoted above show in detail, the program of democratic parties was populist rather than pro-market, on occasion going back on the radicalism of the projects adopted by the outgoing socialist administration.

These critical and self-critical remarks do not imply that the entire economic profession were unable to interpret and solve real-world puzzles. Already the earliest analyses (Blommestein, Marrese and Zecchini, 1990) highlighted the focal role of *stabilization* and large-scale *privatization*.[2] In calling for trade reform and *outward* looking policies, including currency convertibility, local analysts joined forces with the leading authorities of the time and elaborated common propositions in line with the mainstream of the day (Köves and Marer, eds, 1991). Consulting has been involved, with a fair degree of overzealousness, making these activities a favorite topic of local humor. But jokes apart, international agencies, private actors, governments, and – predominantly – *the EC/EU played a formative role in the transformation process*, through PHARE, the Europe Agreements and the resultant harmonization of legal systems to the acquis communautaire. The EC has never shied away from an independent role; its policy advice represented a special line in providing guidance for new democracies (Portes, ed., 1991). The latter – despite the latter-day legend of colonialism – had been, from the very outset, a *co-operative endeavor*: local experts were involved, their output was published – although policy advice was furnished by the incumbent apparatus.

In hindsight, the early transitological literature can be divided into two major categories. The *policy oriented* category tended to be dominated by issues that later proved irrelevant or misleading. These included the debate over shock therapy versus gradualism, the theories of how to escape stagnation, how to increase the numbers of domestic owners, how to create capitalism without large capitalists, restitution and reprivatization, and, finally, the search for the optimal technology of privatization. In the more *theoretical category*, an attempt was made to apply the western economic theories currently in vogue. These included an early version of the political economy approach, portraying the building of *reform coalitions* and providing compensation for losers as the major feasibility conditions of successful change (Roland, 1991). Others highlighted the relevance of *fiscal federalism* for finding new equilibria in Russia (Schneider, 1993), and also highlighted the role of *corporate governance* as the link between ownership change and efficiency gains (Dallago, 1994).

Analysts from transition countries tended to see privatization as an exclusively or predominantly political issue of power redistribution. Their major aim was to break the backbone of the old guard an create stakeholders in the new arrangements (Chubais and Vishnevskaia, 1995). From this angle, classical economic and business considerations and the related success indicators, such as the number of successful corporate *turnarounds*, or the share of companies with improved performance in total output, are by definition *secondary* at best. If the considerations inherent in economic analysis – such as wealth creation, welfare improvement, growing efficiency, better combination of factors – are openly de-emphasized, the resultant absence of these is hardly a surprise (and even less of a proof of the inefficiency of economic theories).

Anybody familiar with the dismal performance of economic reforms of the socialist period, doomed by recurrent recentralization waves, would subscribe, even in hindsight, to the need for radical solutions in order to attain the point of no return. The more we conceive the Soviet empire as a rent-seeking society, with large numbers of conceived or real beneficiaries having no clue about the real cost of their welfare (and not interested in securing its sustainability with their own effort), the more we may condone revolutionary options. However, already early analysts, sympathetic to this point of view (Malle, 1994/2001) have underscored the fact that both the economic efficiency and social acceptance of privatizations are crucially dependent upon the quality of those *institutional and regulatory changes that accompany* (or not, as the case may be) the transfer of property rights. These will decide whether the transfer of property to private owners is tantamount to the introduction of a *competitive order* and an open society, or public monopolies and the profits accruing to them are merely passed over to private persons. The prosperity of the latter is conditional upon their success in preserving *entry barriers* that preclude any new effort to combine factors in a more efficient manner. If monopolist rent-seeking works, there is no reason to expect privatizations to be efficiency enhancing and welfare improving, not even in the long run.[3]

Seen from this angle, the dismal performance of the Newly Independent States is anything but surprising, and can by no means be attributed to an overdose of 'monetarism' or 'neoliberalism'. Likewise, a privatization based on favors and aimed at nominating a new clientele, while state activism and regulation remain all-pervasive – as is the case under the Putin presidency – will not improve performance; the oil-boom fed upswing can only be short-lived. This does not prove, contrary to what is usually asserted, the uniqueness of Russia, but the *universal relevance* of the economic laws formulated above. A state-led monopolistic economy can *not* be expected, on the basis of available theories, to be *more efficient*, if changes are restricted to property structure, while all other incentives, allocational mechanisms and the overall economic environment remain hostile to any major innovation.

Since the mid-1990s, two new features have dominated transitological literature. One of them is the *transformational recession* (Kornai, 1994), which proved to be a protracted process in all cases except for East Germany and Poland. The second is the *return of successor parties* and the related perception of a threat of societal regression – a point studied mostly in the political science literature (Körössényi, 1995).

With the benefit of hindsight, it is hard to overlook the fact that the fears pertaining to both developments proved exaggerated. Growth did resume, in East Germany already in 1991, in Poland in 1992, and in the rest of the region in 1993–4, but only from 1999 in the NIS. True, growth proved to be sustainable only in those countries which not only preached, but also implemented the agenda of stabilization, liberalization and privatization (SLIP), and, moreover, complemented these steps with *institution building* and solid *macropolicies*. This point has been most forcefully proven by the World Bank (1996) but also by analysts from within the region (Kolodko, 2000b, pp. 57–86).

What institutional/*structural reforms* were needed to get on the path of sustained growth? These included changes in the banking system (i.e. the establishment of financial intermediation proper), and the creation and efficient regulation of capital markets (these are needed to improve allocative efficiency). But further reforms were needed in the inherited welfare systems, immediately related to the focal issue of long-run *fiscal sustainability* (through the problem of intergenerational accounting and the implicit debt of the pension system).

In other words, handling a prime economic problem – the sustainability of the general government position[4] – required interdisciplinary analyses, as is richly documented by one of the pioneering volumes on the subject (Nelson, Tilly and Walker, eds, 1999). The underlying issues here are all related to value judgments and, ultimately, to matters of worldview: the scale and ways of ideal redistribution, the role of state versus civil society in providing public goods and services, the share of centralized versus municipal self-financing in covering the costs of public activities, the new mix of solidarity versus self-care, or the economic value of health.

In a pluralistic society, based on the coexistence of competing values and life strategies, it is by definition impossible to expect a professional consensus to emerge: *public choices* are needed, and these have to be anchored in constitutional arrangements, i.e. laws that cannot be changed by a new legislation adopted by a simple 50 per cent plus one vote majority. Until a consensus is reached, it might be in vain to expect successor governments to sustain commitments assumed by their predecessors without taking into account their objections. Unless it is *sustained over several election cycles*, no change in the health and pension systems is likely to be successful, and the same goes for the municipalities' role in the economy ('Europe of Regions'). Those reforms are likely to continue long after the EU accession of the frontrunner transition countries (an issue to which we shall come back below). Thus no decision is helpful that is based exclusively on financial or narrow professional considerations, but does not enjoy wide public endorsement.

As far as the return of *successor (post-communist) parties* is concerned, the related fears proved to be unfounded. Global comparisons of the experience of the 1980s and early 1990s (Williamson, 1994) had already proven by that time that leftist parties turned out to be quite efficient promoters of market-oriented reforms (years before New Labor was conceived). This had to do with their high level of organization as well as their social embeddedness. To the examples provided by the volume quoted above, one could add those of France since the mid-1980s or Italy and Greece in the mid-1990s. From among the transition countries, we may list the governments of Hungary in 1994–8, Poland in 1993–7 and the Czech Republic in 1998–2002 (under a minority government). It seems that these have been setting the trend, rather that constituting deviations in need of special (culture- and history-based) explanation.

This outcome is hardly surprising if we take into account the fact that left wing parties in central Europe (not in the NIS) represent mostly the *winners of the transformation*, such as entrepreneurs, civil servants, individuals benefiting from their cultural and social heritage and the like. The more we accept the relevance of inherited skills and starting positions as determinants of privatization outcomes, the less surprised we are to see this. Those in small and micro-business, unsuccessful entrepreneurs (oriented towards local markets only), losers in the transition process, and strata permanently *dependent on transfers* (e.g. pensioners or farmers) tend to group around right-wing parties in protest of the outcomes of the changes. This has lead to the revival of splits according to the interwar lines, with unreconstructed, statist conservative parties becoming a lasting feature of the scene. This may solidify a division of economic platforms which runs contrary to what is observed in most core countries: in Central and Eastern Europe, the left calls for deregulation and privatization, while the right demands more redistribution and state protectionism. In empirical terms, such a division clashes with the models prevailing in political science, still quite widely represented in continental Europe.[5]

At the turn of the millennium, transitology took yet another twist. Primarily in the context of EU accession, external performance measurements have become formal and continuous, while competition for foreign investment has also intensified. In this dimension, the increasing *differentiation* among transition countries has come to the focus of attention among analysts. This growing divergence has been regularly documented using a wide array of indicators by all institutions dealing with the region, from the Transition Reports of EBRD, to the Economic Survey of Europe of the UN Economic Commission for Europe in Geneva, to publications of various regional research institutes, banks and rating agencies. This analytical material, which has been widely presented (most recently e.g. Hare, 2001; Csaba, 2002a), divides transition countries into three different categories, confronted with *three different research programs*.

First is the *frontrunner group*, where the SLIP agenda has been concluded, the system of financial intermediation and the rule of law are in place, not contingent upon particular political forces remaining in power. These economies are on a *secular growth path*, even though the rate of growth is naturally volatile by the country and period. EU membership has been within reach since the middle of the decade. Here the question is how to *accelerate welfare reforms*, how to build up a social consensus around the major trends of change and how to secure better professional foundations for these processes. The issue is to meet the deadlines and parameters that are vital for a successful integration into the EU. The subject of the debates is thus no longer what needs to be done, but *how and at what speed*. What needs to be done is an issue by and large settled by the prospect and nature of EU accession. This holds for a wide range of issues, from monetary policy to environmental regulations.

In the *second group*, EU membership remains a long-term objective. Still, for the same reason, day-to-day decisions are hard to reach. In this group there is a demand for an answer why transition has remained only a partial success. Social and political forces call for normative approaches that should lead to more successful policymaking and institution-building solutions. A typical case is Romania, where in the elections of 2000, over 70 (!) per cent of the electorate turned their back on various westernizing forces. The returning post-communist party does not enjoy an absolute majority in the legislative, thus is unable to institute any step to change the status quo. There is a serious *gap* here between *economic rationality and social acceptability*, which is also the case with other members of this group. It is a situation for which the greater part of the literature on policy reform offers little or no remedies, since no society can be lead to prosperity against its revealed preferences. On the other hand, a weak government is usually unable to institute major reforms, since such steps involve by their very nature imminent and certain costs, whilst benefits are uncertain and can be reaped only in the future. Thus democratic processes may or may not lead to the selection of a more viable, more efficient institutional setting; the 'law' of natural selection may or may not apply in socio-economic processes (Hoff and Stiglitz, 2001, pp. 394–7). In societies which lag behind, there is a tendency to reinterpret the path dependency insight of North (1990) in terms of the inevitability of governance failures in less developed countries and to put the entire blame on those informal institutions which replace the defunct or mismanaged formal ones. While anyone familiar with the original argument would clearly see this as perverting a valid scientific claim, it is hard to overlook the fact that references to path dependency are often used instrumentally to justify interventionism in policy-making and the quest for national models of economic development (which is, in the end, no less than a relapse to the historicism of von Schmoller).

A *third group* of countries consists of the NIS and Southeast European states, where the level of per capita GDP, according to official and internationally comparable data,[6] by and large, still lags at about 70 per cent of the Soviet-era level, and in some cases – like Georgia, Bosnia and Moldova – it is even lower, closer to 40 per cent of the pre-crisis value (UN ECE, 2001/1, p. 254). In these societies, daily *crisis management* is the name of the game and all the *rest*, including wider-ranging structural reform projects, tends to belong to the realm of poetry. Here the major task of research is to find the reasons – over and above incidental factors, like civil wars or corrupted régimes – for the failures and the *inability to correct*. Unilaterally culturalist explanations are obviously unsatisfactory for an analytical economist. Good analytical answers are badly needed in such cases as Ukraine, which is a country of France's size, Belarus – comparable in size to Greece or Austria – not to speak of the Caucasian and Balkan countries. These constitute the real puzzles for the western community in general and for the *Ostpolitik* of the EU in particular.

To wrap up what has been said, transitology is becoming an ever *narrower field on its own right*. One part of the countries under discussion 'qualifies' for European studies; another one shows a striking affinity to the traditional topics of development economics. While the latter branch of study – as will be shown – has made important advances in understanding the dynamics of less developed and less successful economies, the learning process (of transition countries looking south) is still in its infancy, partly in consequence of the early improvisation. Still, it is hard to overlook the fact that such *traditional topics* in development economics as vicious circle phenomena, or the ways to create an outward-oriented economy or to fight corruption, might have a *direct bearing on countries in transition*.

The New Political Economy of Development

Development economics was born right after World War II as an antidote to the neoliberal mainstream, reflecting revolutionary ideas and showing little appreciation for the type of formal approaches that has come to dominate major departments and journals ever since[7] (for an excellent summary, cf. Meier, 2001). This has made it a bestseller among many policy-makers in the Third World, and likewise in the leading departments of major world universities. *Desarrolismo* is a shorthand for anti-American, import-substituting nationalist and populist policies in South America, though literally it means only 'supportive of development'.

The *original paradigm* of development economics was based on the negation of western market-oriented concepts and policies, and of the laissez-faire of the colonial period. It emerged as a rejection of the materialist West, equated with moral decay, political oppression, racism, and a free market culminating in the Great Depression of 1929–33 and its dire consequences for the periphery. In order to overcome dependency, it advocated state planning (even if no Soviet advisors were around, the current official statistics of the Soviet Union tended to be taken at face value, which resulted in a sincere admiration for the non-capitalist alternative). It also took for granted the idea of import substitution as a means of nation building and state building – an idea that has acquired global appeal ever since the Friedrich List, under the banner of economic nationalism. Furthermore, it took for granted that the state must play a leading role in accelerating economic development (based on various theories of the big push, originating with Rosenstein-Rodan). The central state administration (in the hands of the vanguard) – rather than civil society, municipalities, private capital of domestic or foreign origin – was to become the sole *owner*, *regulator* and *organizer*, constrained only by its own ideological beliefs. The central state was to become the driving force and guarantor of accelerated change.

The more heavily the strategy relied on priorities which deliberately limited the scope of the market – or ones which were just incongruous with, say, the long-time priorities of the market agents, or made recoupment uncertain – the more inevitable it became to *repress the financial sector* by means of highly inventive regulatory measures and justifications (Lal, 1993). It seemed obvious that monetary processes must be (or are by their very nature) instrumental, subordinate to 'real processes', which were to be co-ordinated basically by the bureaucracy.

It is common knowledge that the more sophisticated an economy and society is, and the higher is its development level, *the greater is the role of prices as the major instrument of co-ordinating* millions and tens of millions of individual decisions, if welfare is to be increased. Therefore, it was inevitable and predictable that the more the financial system is repressed and the longer this repression lasts, the higher are the costs in terms of lost (sacrificed) welfare at any point of time. The longer such an arrangement persists, the greater the lag it leaves behind.

The dominance of bureaucratic co-ordination caused, as it did in the Soviet-type economy, first efficiency losses and later on stagnation. Alternatively, countries tried to borrow in order to bridge the revenue shortfall. But the more money was lent, in the absence of domestic corrective and absorption mechanisms, the less growth could materialize, and adjustment was merely postponed (Easterly, 2001, pp. 101–20). Recurring *payments crises* – and the high visibility of interrupted and never finished grand prestige projects – had a sobering effect. Experience opened up the way to the 'monetarist counterrevolution' of the 1970s and 1980s, leading to the gradual change of paradigm in most developing countries.

The *new paradigm* is built upon the appreciation of market-led growth and overcomes the ideological elements derived from the principle of negating everything resembling the western experience. It is generally acknowledged that the same *principles*[8] of solid macro- and micromanagement that work in OECD countries should be valid for less developed countries, and cultural differences can no longer be invoked to justify profligate or simply unprofessional policies. Development is conditioned by public policies ensuring price stability, export-led growth and providing investments for such public goods and externalities that private agents tend to undersupply (more on that in Behrman and Srinivasan, 1995, pp. 2467–96).

What has been said implies a *Copernican turn* in development economics. On the other hand, the story just means that the discipline of *standard economics has returned into the discourse about poor countries*, and nothing more. Underdevelopment and ways of overcoming it can now be discussed in standard economic terms, following the logic and procedures of standard economic analysis. This return of economics took place in a slow, evolutionary manner, through a substantial amount of trial and error as well as open scientific exchanges – as documented in rich detail by the four volumes of the *Handbook* quoted above. In most of the cases and throughout this process, there was no sign of the oft-alleged dictates of the IMF,[9] wrongdoings of the Chicago boys, tricky stockbrokers and fund-misusers from Harvard, corrupted media multipliers and other folkloristic elements still dominating much of the social science discourse in large parts of the globe. But even if in some individual cases such discourse is substantiated (which is very rarely the case), anecdotal evidence and the related incidental factors can hardly explain the turn of the tide in an entire strand of international intellectual endeavors. As we have seen – and our references prove this *in extenso* – this turn can by no means be attributed to the western triumphalism that followed the collapse of the 'evil empire', as it had taken place a *decade earlier*, in the 1980s. The largely pragmatic and policy-level agreement among the various trends of thought came to be known as the Washington Consensus, and later on – with reference to lessons from transition failures, and with a new emphasis on institutions – as the post-Washington Consensus (Williamson, J. 2000; Kolodko, 2000a, pp. 119–40).

Development economics has long been studying phenomena that cropped up as queer novelties for transitology or Sovietology. This applies *a fortiori* to cases when the transformation failure is rooted in the disintegration of formal institutions, regulatory arrangements or even the core state itself. Fuzzy property rights, the lack of independent judiciary and the inability to enforce private contracts by an impartial third agent, rampant corruption, malfunctioning of formal institutions and the resultant informalism, the dominance of traditional networks over imported arrangements, or the impacts of a sizable irregular economy are all among the evergreens of development studies.

The encounter of the 'neoliberal' mainstream with 'exotic' themes proved to be quite productive. One of the fortresses of formalized approaches, growth theory, and the wide and sophisticated econometric arsenal could now become *applied to real-world issues*; moreover, these instruments facilitated the settlement of debates.

In comparative analyses, quantitative methods helped clarify the contribution of various factors to economic success. Applications often allowed the relevance of specific theoretical or methodological propositions to be verified. All in all a variety of contradictory observations, successes and failures could be interpreted within a *single theoretical framework*. Moreover, by reliance on analytical concepts and quantitative methods several long-debated issues could be settled. One of these was the ancient dispute over *import substitution versus export orientation*. Especially following the second oil price hike of 1979, the superiority of export-led policies became evident: the countries adopting this line were disadvantaged in terms of natural endowments, and yet their growth proved *sustainable*, whereas the windfall tended to create 'Dutch disease' symptoms and temporary booms in the resource-rich economies in the Middle East. The sustainability of outward orientation went hand in hand with the broad concept of *market orientation* and supportive *institutions*, over and above the narrow prioritizing of external sectors (Balassa, 1993). Long-term analyses have shown that export-led growth is not based on the financial support for sectors selling abroad, but implies a broad liberalization strategy extending beyond the trade sectors. Its intensity, sequencing, timing and overall professionalism explain the cases when this option proved successful and sustainable (Greenaway, Morgan and Wright, 1998).

In order to test the above finding, several analyses have been carried out, probing into the causes of the inefficiency of import substitution policies. These indicated *governance failures* as a major reason, inherent in the original state-centered paradigm (relying heavily on the right choices by the vanguard as opposed to the use of decentrally available social knowledge). This problem has been exacerbated by the frequency of *state capture*.

Third, it proved unjustified to assume that the core *state* would by definition stand for the *public purpose*. State administrations, especially in weak states and under non-democratic arrangements, still predominant in the majority of developing countries, tend to *fall victim to the redistributory tendencies of traditional societies*. State jobs are used to boost employment and serve as rewards for political loyalty rather than to function on meritocratic principles. Cases which do not fit into a typical public choice model, where public policy players maximize their own personal welfare and power rather than any abstract public good, are hard to find, especially in Africa and Central America. This tendency can be reversed if the state becomes *decreasingly involved* in protecting palpable interests (the protective state should only guard unambiguous public goods, such as price stability, competition, rule of law, public security – but not individual producer interests or pre-set redistributory outcomes). On the other hand, the smaller the size of the productive state, i.e. the scope of goods and services provided by the central state, the lower is the propensity (or: the weaker is the motivation) to abuse it.

It can be clearly seen from this angle how *insufficient* is the reliance on such traditional models of growth where development is based primarily on *physical capital accumulation*. These models – which were invoked to justify import substitution – tended to downplay or neglect a key element of endogenous growth, which is the *accumulation and spread of knowledge* in societies (Bruton, 1998). While the accumulation of physical capital may be managed by governmental action – at least in the short and medium run – the accumulation and spread of knowledge can only be *lubricated, but not created* by the authorities.

These insights have lent additional weight to an approach that has always emphasized, albeit sometimes from a minority position, the *social conditioning* of the market as a system. In contrast to the simplistic reading of the Harrod-Domar model, it considers the market as the fundamental coordination mechanism through which the vicious circle of poverty can be overcome (Hayek, 1989; Bauer, 2000). Adherents to this approach interpret as a revolution in development economics the movement from state-led approaches, emphasizing physical capital accumulation, towards a broader, more realistic and socially conceived version of *growth promoting mechanisms*. In this framework, the market rules and institutions – which occasionally emerge spontaneously, but are largely man-made – lead the countries *out* of the low-level steady-state equilibria, relying on the related incentives, allocation and accumulation mechanisms (Dorn et al., eds, 1998).

It is worth emphasizing that a market-based approach to development is by no means equivalent to the revival of the 'night watchman state' ideal. Instead of preaching the minimal state, a *strong state* is required: one constrained by constitutional, legal, procedural and other democratic checks and balances (Buchanan, 1977). A civilized market is one constitutionally constrained and protected, where the state is a *regulator* and an arbitrator, but *by no means a day-to-day manager of affairs*, producer or protector of individual concerns. Reliance on self- interest of market actors alone will hardly guarantee the respect for those cultural and civilizational norms that have evolved over centuries, whereas the constitutional rules that secure the latter are setting the rules of the game, but not its pre-determined outcomes (Vanberg, 2001, pp. 2–36).[10]

It is interesting to recall that these 'new' insights *were already available by the time systemic changes had started* in Central and Eastern Europe. In a volume published on the occasion of the 25th anniversary of the Harvard Institute of International Development (Perkins and Roemer, eds, 1991), the contributors came out against a unilateral emphasis on trade liberalization as a panacea and called on public authorities to supplement these steps with institution-building measures. True, this call implied something different from what is actually seen in the region, namely, the state replacing (in a Gerschenkronian way) the market. Instead, it advocated a market-supportive state, where interventions build market institutions and overcome co-ordination and information failures, much the same way as it was put forward more recently by Hoff and Stiglitz (2001, pp. 397–412). This requires, in the HIID view, a slim, but well-paid (rather than underpaid) state administration, based on meritocracy and transparency, which refrains from interventionism and day-to-day crisis management. Such an administration may become the *anchor for those reforms* that may lead stagnant societies out of their vicious circles. The timing of sectoral reforms and their pace in this normative view are conditioned by the ability for and speed of social learning, collective choices and interactions in the democratic process of deliberations.

Thus we have come to what a contemporary classic, Robert Bates and Anne Krueger (1993, p. 463) called the *orthodox paradox*. This means that extending the scope of the market requires strengthening the core state, while the policy of grievances and individual rationality (of buying clients) must be *subordinated to collective rationality* (geared towards, e.g., transparency and accountability). In concrete terms this requires financial discipline (such as the balanced budget proviso for the constituent states of the USA), limiting the scope of redistribution (especially if carried out on discretionary basis or in a non-transparent fashion), strengthening the rule of law in the economy, and, last but not least, enhancing the role of *technocratic agencies* (which are not subject to daily political pressures).

As we can see, this broad approach abandons the previous narrow interpretation of reforms embraced by IFIs and most of the literature, restricted to changes in some sectors or policy areas. In the 1990s, reform came to imply deep changes pertaining to the macroeconomic *allocation* mechanism, *decision-making* structures at the macrolevel, and the way *legislation* works (a classical area of political science).

It is in this context that representatives of standard macroeconomics also call for reinterpreting the role of the state as a precondition for stabilization to sustain. In order to attain this, Dornbusch (1993) advocates improving the *administrative capacity* by way of decentralization, by empowering local municipalities with financial competences, with improved transparency and accountability at all levels and in all areas.[11] Reform policies should ensure that support goes indeed to the most needy. They can create mobilizing visions, build a consensus around focal issues, ensure consistency among reforms running in parallel, and thereby contribute to the social acceptance of economic change. In this way, thorough *reform policies may sustain a single electoral cycle and thus deliver.* This is, trivially, a side condition of such undertakings as a successful pension reform, and also brings considerable benefits in terms of improving administrative capacities, strengthening the rule of law, or *changing informal institutions* such as social norms (e.g. the (un)acceptability of taking bribes or applying kinship criteria in making appointments).

Importantly, the institutional focus of the new political economy of development is *by no means a rehash of the state-centrism* of the old paradigm. This is, to a large degree, a generalization of the experiences of three decades of statist developmental strategies. Such an insight follows directly from the experience of non-capitalist development initiatives in sub-Saharan Africa (Paulson, ed., 1999), where the state turned out to be more of a problem than an agent of solution. The volumes quoted above provide ample empirical evidence of how and why governments trapped within various vested interests proved *unable to perform the elementary functions of public policy*, thus *aggravating* the situation that had already been critical anyway. State failure in these cases *lies at the heart of market failure*, which is only aggravated by non-neutral redistributory practices.

If foreign investors with a large bargaining power come in, they may further distort the outcomes.

The deeper is the distrust in the abilities of the state as a provider, the stronger is the case for large-scale privatizations; this does not depend on the level of development. The best empirical overview of comparative country experiences to date (Meggison and Netter, 2001, esp. pp. 380–81) proves that private corporations tend to outperform their publicly-owned competitors and mixed-ownership firms alike. This experience is global and the tendency is overwhelming.

It is true, however, that the *change of ownership,* as seen above, *does not lead on its own,* and in the absence of other conditions, *to improved efficiency*: privatization works in a context. According to the survey quoted above, mass privatization proved to be the least efficient form of ownership change. Its popularity is derived from exigency situations, at least in political terms. A preferential treatment of employees was observed in 91 per cent of cases. Privatization technologies and terms often emerged as an outcome of competing regional, employment, financial, organizational and prime political strategies. As a rule, a privatization proves lastingly efficient if it also contributes to the *broadening of the local capital markets,* by the public quotation of shares. This is the best indicator of whether or not corporate governance has improved, that is, whether a new combination of factors will lead to greater efficiency or just to a changed distribution of rents. Further requirements are the introduction of international accounting standards, the enforcement of disclosure rules and the improvement of the *quality of macroeconomic governance.*

These findings corroborate the conclusions of Stiglitz (2000, p. 577). He blames the reformers in transition countries not only for the neglect of the contextual factors listed above, but also for their tendency to downplay the *feasibility constraints* of any major reform under *democratic conditions.* The further we get beyond the elementary SLIP phase, the more involved we become in administrative and welfare reforms, i.e. in the *modus operandi of the power structures and of millions of people.* Changes in these areas shape the nature of societies. Thus the *public may choose something different from an option derived from comparative institutional or economic studies.* The more willing we are to acknowledge that backtracking is often a result of half-hearted or incoherent reforms, the less likely we become to be taken by surprise. In this context, the literature typically mentions the liberalization of east Asian financial markets: carried out without sound institutions and regulation, but with a fixed rate of exchange. Such conditions invited and triggered the crisis. In turn, liberalizing strategies may well have lost their popular appeal irrespective of their substantive features.

Welfare Reforms and EU-maturity – a Special Feature of Central European Development

As we have seen above, the success of the frontrunner countries in transition has rested, to a large degree, on the *anchor function of the EU*. As long as EU membership could provide a rallying point for otherwise conflicting forces, it helped to build consensus around major institutional features of the market economy. Likewise, with the implementation of the third stage of the economic and monetary union, and especially with the introduction of the euro as the sole currency in 12 EU states, accession sets qualitative and quantitative tasks for the candidate countries. Given the disparity of economic power (the accession countries account for just about six per cent of the GDP of EU-15) and the expected timing of the enlargement in the middle of the decade, the major features of institution building and policy reforms are pre-set by the Europeanization context. This is true, even though the overlap between the endogenously derived institutional features and the ready-made solutions of EU-15 may not be complete. For instance, the adoption of Pillar Three items (justice and home affairs), or involvement in Pillar Two (common foreign and security policy) may be in conflict with e.g. good neighborly policies, or the need to fight terrorism on a global (rather than regional) scale.

The quality of institutions was shown to be vital for the long-run growth potential of any country. This insight has gathered momentum through the studies of the east Asian crises. In the latter case, conventional macroeconomic indicators, debt exposure measures and other types of quantitative information failed to perform their early warning function (Lamfalussy, 2000). This may also explain why the early search for quantitative indicators of EU maturity was discontinued and gave way to assessments of a more qualitative nature. The share of the 100,000 pages of the acquis already translated, the number of negotiation chapters closed, or the share of private firms in GDP creation no longer count as factor deciding about the EU-fitness of any candidate. Already by introducing the phase of acquis screening, the EU has indicated its legitimate interest in delivery (as opposed to formal compliance with its criteria).

It would be hard to overlook the fact that a consistent implementation of the acquis is likely to entail yet another systemic change for the transforming countries. The need to qualify for the EMU, the implementation of environmental standards, or the community-level control of state aids, to mention but a few, will surely pose a challenge even to the frontrunners. Likewise, it is hard to deny that the EU is also facing a similar reform of its internal arrangements, owing to the large number and diversity of applicants, but also under the pressure of globalization (Cassel, ed., 1998). Knowing the substance of the Nice Treaty and the schedule of the Convention, it is unlikely that this rearrangement will be concluded by the time of first accessions. Thus a decade-long gradual reform is the most likely outcome. All the more so since democracy does allow for representing sectoral and other vested interests that will lose out in the course of what is a win-win game at the macrolevel.

On the following pages, we adopt a deliberately one-sided view and list only those tasks that are to be mastered by the transition countries. These are viewed from the angle of the new political economy of development, i.e. the extent to which they contribute to a sustainable growth within the EU. High growth in modern economic theory does not eliminate the need to fight inflation, thus the 'high growth-moderate inflation' model, which used to perform quite well in several catching-up countries, does not seem to be relevant for our country group.

1. First and foremost, a further disinflation has become an urgent task. This follows not only, and not even primarily, from the relatively close date of EMU membership, but also from the observation that transition countries managed to bring down inflation below the 8–10 per cent level only at times of economic recession. This means that organic disinflation that would not require major sacrifices in terms of growth is yet to come about. As we are confronted with the propensity of representative democracies to overspend, we will realize that this is hardly a trivial a task to accomplish.

Moderate inflation figured prominently in several catching-up stories among the emerging market economies. Broader enquiries into its causes have highlighted the importance of social and psychological factors in bringing about this outcome. Particularly, a lack of credibility and the widespread use of backward-looking indexation formulae are made responsible for sustaining moderate inflation even at times when 'fundamentals' would allow for a non-inflationary growth (Cottarelli and Szapáry, eds, 1998). Analysts tend to disagree over how best to overcome this problem. In the volume quoted above, some advocate tripartite agreements, while others call for more monetary and fiscal orthodoxy, applied in a co-ordinated fashion. In both cases the objective is to diminish the share of state expenditures in GDP and to restructure their inherited priorities. Since at the bottom line we talk about rolling back universal entitlements, this is a prime political issue that relates to the basics of the welfare model of each reforming country.

Thus lasting and organic disinflation is hardly possible without transparency in public finances, which allows policy agents to find out who pays what for whom, thus making public choices at all feasible. Otherwise, a typical Olsonian case of a well-organized minority misleading and dominating the disorganized majority is the likely outcome of spontaneous interplay of policy processes. In order to ensure sustained improvements, countries with a less than convincing history of fiscal solidity, and those of low credibility, may usefully employ medium-term fiscal targeting. If the major priorities and numbers of such a plan are made public, both the EU Commission and market players can verify its fulfillment; similarly governments can claim their precommitments as binding constraints when faced with improvised and politicized pressures for more spending. This practice has already been efficiently implemented by the EMU countries, while accession countries may well have to conform to additional requirements in terms of code of conduct that would limit discretionary interventions, but help continuous improvements in the field of fiscal solidity (Braga de Macedo, 2001). Such arrangements – as EU countries have recently experienced – may not go hand in hand with political expectations at times of downturns.

2. On the other hand, a continuous decrease of public dues may prove infeasible and even undesirable. At certain times, as in 1998–2002 in the Czech Republic, or in Romania, the government may not enjoy a solid legislative majority, which obviously limits the room for major expenditure rollbacks. A similar outcome may result from the specific social background of center-right parties in central Europe, discussed above. Several structural disproportions have been diagnosed but not solved in the frontrunner reforming countries, such as the redefinition of the role of farming, environment, and health care. Whatever way these structural problems are solved, it is unlikely to be less costly, since many implicit cost and debt items are becoming explicit in the course of reforms. In order to attain this, a strong state as described above – i.e. one that is capable of liberating itself from the dominance of economic vested interests and of regulating in the interest of preserving diversity (Bruszt, 2002) – would be of vital importance. This normative view, however, is not to be mistaken for a forecast, thus the pressure for redistribution is unlikely to diminish.

3. Maybe the most controversial item is our third point, the redefinition of the role of the state in the provision of welfare. As a recent major volume (Kornai, Haggard and Kaufmann, eds, 2001) illustrates, this requires a truly interdisciplinary approach and policy dialogue as a side condition for any measure to become implementable. By studying the experiences of the 1990s, the editors highlight the importance of blocking powers, the role of formative personalities capable of building up reform coalitions, the need to redistribute inherited checks and balances among various branches of power, and the dangers of state capture. While the authors call for introducing conservative financial principles in the welfare-related areas, they also highlight the need for a non-conservative, heterodox analytical approach to these issues and the necessity to integrate sociological, political-science and psychological insights into the reform projects. Only this makes the way for right sequencing and consensual deliberation that allow for sustainable reforms.

Analyzing the failure of reforms in Latin America and the NIS, Rüdiger Dornbusch (2000, p. 85) underscores the fact that governmental activity should not be restrained to correcting market failures and building market infrastructure, plus providing law and order. For a major welfare reform to succeed and market oriented reforms to survive, a certain degree of redistribution needs to be preserved, or else disintegration or regression to authoritarianism may be the unintended, but inevitable, outcome. This leads us back to the need to redefine explicitly new expenditure priorities that allow for a socially acceptable operation of the market mechanism, while not replacing the fundamental co-ordination mechanism with a prearranged selection of outcomes.

4. Fourth, a solid and stable system of financial intermediation remains a key component of any viable market economy. This task should not be declared either trivial or resolved, even though those transition countries which are also members to the OECD have actually liberalized all, including short-term capital-account transactions, in 1999–2001. In the long run, joining the eurozone will provide an answer to the question. In the medium run, however, it is not clear how crisis-resistant the financial sector of the best transition performers actually is. As a recent analysis of Poland, Czech Republic, Hungary, Slovakia and Slovenia indicates (Schardax and Reininger, 2001), the banking sector in each of these countries has already undergone a major change. The share of foreign ownership has proven predominant, reaching a maximum of 76 per cent in Slovakia. Banking supervision and regulation has substantially improved, disclosure requirements are no longer just promulgated, but also enforced. Thus problems of corporate governance in the banking sector seem to have found a solution. True, as a corollary, corporate restructuring is no longer financed by domestic banks, with parent companies and the international capital market providing most of the funding for big-company restructuring. Local capital markets continue to play an auxiliary role at best, serving to channel some portfolio investment into the corporate sector, but not mediating the bulk of financial flows. The sunny side of this phenomenon is the diminished vulnerability and exposure of Central European financial systems to international speculation.

The major correction in the international capital markets in 2001, together with the marginalization of regional stock exchanges, highlighted the importance of the economies of scale and scope in financial intermediation. Therefore, Central European capital markets also joined their West European counterparts in the search for strategic alliances. In this process, the logic of industrial organization, i.e. searching for a leading center, dominated over politically oriented intra-regional alliances. With the unfolding of this global tendency, it is beyond doubt that local economic activity will require local funding and services, thus ensuring a lasting role for Central European stock exchanges. Meanwhile, the biggest and brightest companies, i.e. the blue chips, will be increasingly oriented towards global capital markets so as to reduce costs and also the leverage that host governments may exert over them.

5. The more we realize the fact that, in structural terms, it is the future role of farming and the environment that will pose the major challenge for the eastward enlargement of the EU, the more it calls for an interdisciplinary endeavor. In the traditional approach based on microeconomic consideration, incumbents and candidates are irreconcilable adversaries. In a nutshell, candidates tend to form their expectations in terms of the common agricultural policies of the EEC in the 1960s and 1970s. The crux of these was income redistribution in favor of farming

by way of market protection, guaranteed prices and the resultant increases in land prices that further limited new entry. Meanwhile, the gradual reform started in 1992 and, supplemented with the 1999 Berlin compromise (Schrader, 2000), has put European farming on a different track. The role of market coordination is gradually increasing, while net contributors have set a series of ceilings on agriculture-related outlays. Instead of supporting production, various non-production-related rural development projects have been coming to the fore. Rural living is no longer tantamount to generating income from agriculture at a time tourism is the third largest global industry, and when the Internet allows for the new economy to overcome distances more easily than ever. These changes, in line with the US and developing country claims represented in the Doha Round of the WTO, allow little leeway for the producer interests in accession countries to dominate the talks the way domestic policy considerations would indicate. In short, the EU is unlikely to invest what has not been invested into CEE farming over the last 50 years or so.

It is hard to overlook the fact that the macroeconomic role of farming is typically a case for collective choice, since it will determine the ensuing type of nation and society. Candidate countries have not yet gone through the phases which the incumbent EU members completed in the 1960s to 1980s. Thus territorial, employment, social, transport, human, infrastructural, educational and environmental omissions all add up to what looks like a sectoral problem.

In theory, the best answer to this challenge is what the European Commission proposed in January 2002 by making a trade-off between diminishing direct supports but compensating for this with greater access to and entitlements from structural funds. The only 'minor' flaw in this respect is the very limited ability of candidate countries to draw on these, as is indicated by the very low utilization of funds earmarked for them in the PHARE, SAPARD and ISPA programs. Moreover, as intra-EU experience has shown, drawing on these sources and making best use of transfers are two different things.

Seen from this angle, the issue of EU accession and the related controversy over direct income supports (DIS) to farmers appears in a different perspective. These call for a major rethinking of such crucial points as regional development strategy, administrative reform, education, social stratification and the related longer-term visions, not least concerning the rational expectations based thereon. These are mostly unrelated to the most vocally discussed items, such as the distribution of DIS between farmers from the candidate and incumbent countries. Still, these are poorly researched and formulated issues, which goes, among others, for those of public versus private forms of transport (and the related infrastructural developments), industrial or bio-agriculture, Internet-based or industry-based society, a serving or a servicing state (to rephrase Buchanan's productive and protective state), together with the related levels of public dues that millions of taxpayers are willing to accept, and similar strategic options.

Answers to these comprehensive challenges are unlikely to be simple; still, it is the median voter who will finally decide which of the high-flying ideas will be legislated, especially at the constitutional level. Moreover, this will decide the final cost-benefit balance of the actual EU accession, including the type and sustainability of growth in the acceding economies. If societies resist the fundamentals of an EU-compatible policy, as the growth of Euroscepticism may indicate, the real issue is transformed from the traditional questions of convergence and its time span, into a different one: what kind of global economy do we want to integrate with and in what capacity, once the EU option has been practically rejected.

Integration, Globalization and Questions

We have attempted to survey *three interrelated programs of research*: transitology, EU enlargement studies and the new political economy of development. It sounds like a trivial observation that transition countries wish to join the EU not primarily for the transfers, but to enhance their global competitiveness. For the time being, precious little is known for sure about how to reach the point of competitiveness. The conditions are *easy to axiomatize but hard to deliver* – be that credibility, solid finances, good governance or transparent regulations. Our survey has shown that transformation studies and the new political economy of development overlap in highlighting the need for institutions, in the reliance on the major approaches and methods derived from the mainstream, and in acknowledging the need to rely more extensively on the findings and insights of other social science disciplines. The nature of what is called *second generation* reforms is *largely identical* in the two approaches, and so is their aim: sustainable development.

There are at least three groups of reasons why second generation reforms are more difficult to master than first generation (SLIP) reforms were (Krueger, 2000, p. 591).

1. Already in order to launch these, reliance on the political decision mechanism is needed.
2. Given the diversity of issues involved, and in view of the heavy dependence of rationality criteria on culture and on value systems, there is no standard cookbook to go by, of the kind available for trade liberalization or inflation stabilization.
3. In the areas and sectors to reform, the present arrangements have persisted for several decades, and are thus often seen as the only possible/natural way. Likewise, the financial and equity constraints of reform are less than universally understood. Thus even those who would profit from the changes may well be mobilized against them (e.g. in health care systems).

Let us recall that second generation reforms include clashes among value systems (judgments), thus a professional consensus is hard to achieve even within a single country, not to mention the EU or global dimensions. Thus the travails of continuous social dialogue as well as the dominance of trial-and-error methods cannot be eschewed or bypassed. The more counter-arguments and counter-examples are known, the more analyses are called for. Oftentimes we are simply unaware of those factors that, ultimately, put a severe constraint on the applicability of otherwise elegant theoretical constructs.

Any of the major issues of these reforms involves a series of trade-offs. When we consider the relationship between education and growth, the need to protect investors without suppressing entrepreneurship and innovation,[12] or the interface of trust and control (especially in high-responsibility posts, like those of surgeons or investment bankers, where other people's health or wealth is at risk) it is next to impossible to follow the 'if you cannot quantify it, do not talk about it' dictum of the technical economist. The broader approaches found in recent contributions to the literature did manage to endogenize some of the quality factors, but only at the expense of rigor, which used to be the economists' prizest possession in their armory (Saint-Paul, 2000). On the other hand, the general applicability of abstract (formal) methods allowed for the incorporation of some qualitative aspects, including the social conditions of innovation, into analytical models. This has lead to the politicization of the entire growth theory (Hibbs, 2001).

In trying to apply general growth theory to EU accession, we have surveyed five major problem areas. We hope to have demonstrated that any economic theory aspiring to political applicability/feasibility (or simply to social relevance) needs to be open to the interface with other social sciences and their insights. Economists are unable to determine, on their own, the salient features of efficient and workable legal systems, or the complexities of environmental options that may be contingent upon advances in various natural sciences. Some of the more controversial experiences of the last decades, such as the privatization of British railways, or the exorbitant costs of US private health care, caution against making direct policy inferences even from well-established theoretical insights.

There is no single best option outside of the framework of democratically legitimated public choices. This can be easily demonstrated by simply listing the major areas of current intra-EU reform debates: the future of farming, the costs of environmental protection, the need to overcome the democratic deficit while working efficiently in a community of 25 or more countries, the ways of finding efficient forms of regional development, the conditions of transferability of social security claims within the EU, or the modalities of setting up an independent rapid-reaction European force, all require interdisciplinarity and democratic deliberation alike. Therefore, our starting question about the possibility of a purely economic theory of reforms can be answered in the negative, for reasons inherent to the subject matter, although without having to give up the fundamentals of the discipline.[13]

Allowing for interdisciplinarity also paves the way for the insight that taking on board post-communist countries, whose number may be close to the current incumbent membership, will inevitably redraw the EU itself. The enlargement will be 'not just another accession' (Eatwell et al., 1995) but will trigger the revision of integration theory paradigms, from intergovernmentalism to the system of entitlements and setup of common institutions. Success of the related theories in all the three areas will be directly measured by the ensuing development of European states – in a global perspective.

Notes

1   Previous versions of the present article have been presented at the international conference of Europa Universität Viadrina, 'Transformation as Large-Scale Institutional Rearrangement' (Frankfurt/O, October 11–12, 2001) and to the workshop of Financial Research Inc. (Budapest, April 3, 2002). Comments of the participants, as well as of Huricihan Islamoglou are acknowledged, with the usual caveats.

2   Quite a heated debate went on in several transition countries (especially in Russia and in Southeast Europe), centered on the claim that stabilization was nothing more than an IMF straightjacket or a product of ideological overzealousness. Thus many people (publishing e.g. in *Acta Oeconomica* and other Sovietological journals) called for policies that downplayed stabilization, i.e. advocated a 'growth first financial discipline later' approach.

3   This insight had been explicitly formulated by the ordoliberals (Böhm, 1933/1982; Eucken, 1948) in Germany and by the theory of collective action (Olson, 1982) in the US, well ahead of the east Asian crisis or the debacle of the NIS in the 1991–9 period.

4   'General government' becomes little more than a buzzword, if we take it to cover not only the central budget, but also pension funds and other items not figuring in the state's central budget, approved by parliament (but constituting public spending).

5   The statist economic platform of the CSU in Germany, of Partido Polpular in Portugal, of the Danish Republicans, of Alleanza Nazionale or of the Greek Nea Dimokratia is comparable to the stance of the Hungarian or most Polish parties on the right.

6   This version is hotly debated in the literature, with Anders Aslund (2001) going as far as to question any real welfare (as opposed to environmental, military or power) loss and call transformational recession a statistical artefact.

7   For this reason some of the pioneers in the area, such as Holis Chenery, Evsey Domar or Simon Kuznets qualified as growth theorists (owing to their quantitative orientation that ensured canonic acceptability). The similarly oriented *Journal of Development Economics* is thus more of a forum of the mainstream than of developmental discourse.

8   Harberger (2001, pp. 549–557) highlights the need to avoid rigidity, especially doctrinaire approaches to policy issues where *discretion* and *common sense* (e.g. in assessing administrative capacities) cannot be substituted with general references to textbook solutions or to abstract theoretical models. Thus this insight by no means implies the mechanistic copying of even 'best practices' or an indiscriminate use of

benchmarking. The emerging Basle Two agreement is a nice example of how and why decentral assessments – differently tailored within the same logic – may be the only practicable solution.

9   Even authors sympathetic to the international financial institutions (e.g. Krueger, 1998; Williamson, J., 2000) consider as by and large *unsuccessful* most of the attempts by the IFIs to be involved in institution building in developing and transforming countries. Currently also the IFIs themselves stress the need for domestic 'authorship' of reform packages. Moreover the quoted authors consider the mere emergence of a common language, a common intellectual framework for discussing issues, and personal contacts among wide segments of policy-makers – also on the second and third levels – as lasting accomplishments of the IFI-sponsored structural reform projects of various sorts.

10 A *strong* state thus should not be confused, as is often the case, with an *activist* one, with interventionism and aggressive wielding of power, as the Putin administration seems to interpret this call. It is worth noting that the ordoliberals of the 1930s developed their theory as a reaction to limitless and arbitrary state interventionism in Germany that ended up in totalitarianism. In opposition to it, they call for *cutting back discretion to the minimum* and for a rule-based government (Böhm, 1933/82, Eucken, 1948). In the United States a similar debate over rules versus discretion took place in the 1970s in the context of monetary policy (Kydland and Prescott, 1977). Later on, the victorious position of rule-based management was modified somewhat, with reference to drawbacks of too rigid interpretation of any of the golden rules for policy-making and theories alike (DeLong, 2000).

11 Discussing this point, a leading authority of institutional economics, Oliver Williamson (2000, p. 611), notes that the functioning and embeddedness of bureaucracy largely remained a mystery for the social sciences. Neither formalized approaches, nor political science, could come up with an interpretation that could be accepted as a new paradigm. By the same token his own institutional approach remains also open-ended.

12 On Basle Two, everybody is in agreement – except for the banks concerned; similarly, everybody seems to favor IAS, except the US profession of accountants and consultancies after the Enron case.

13 In descriptive terms, public choice approaches would flatly exclude the feasibility of reforms. Still, these have occurred and will occur, thus in a descriptive and normative sense we have to leave the door open for a concurring theory, even if it is a heterodox one.

References

Aslund, Anders (2001), 'The Myth of Output Collapse after Communism', Carnegie Endowment for International Peace, Russian and Eurasian Programme, Working Papers, No. 18 (March), Washington.

Balassa, Béla (1993), 'Outward Orientation', in Balassa, Béla, *Policy Choices for the 1990s*, Macmillan, Basingstoke, pp. 3–53.

Bates, Robert and Krueger, Anne (1993), 'Generalizations Arising from the Country Studies', in Bates, R. and Krueger, A. (eds), *Political and Economic Interactions in Economic Policy Reform*, Basil Blackwell, Oxford, pp. 444–72.

Bauer, Peter (2000), 'From Subsistence to Exchange', in Bauer, P., *From Subsistence to Exchange and Other Essays*, Princeton University Press, Princeton, pp. 3–15.

Behrman, Jere and Srinivasan, T.S. (eds) (1995), 'Introduction to Policy Reform, Stabilization, Structural Adjustment and Growth', in Behrman, J. and Srinivasan, T.S. (eds), *Handbook of Development Economics*, Vol. 3B, Elsevier, Amsterdam, pp. 2467–96.

Blommestein, Hans, Marrese, Michael and Zecchini, Salvatore (1990), *Centrally Planned Economies in Transition*, OECD, Paris.

Böhm, Fritz (1982), 'The Non-state ("Natural") Laws Inherent in a Competitive Economy', in Stozel, W., Watrin, C., Willgerodt, H. and Hohmann, K. (eds), *Standard Texts on the Social Market Economy*, G. Fischer Verlag, pp. 107–13 (originally published in German in 1933), Stuttgart.

Braga de Macedo, Jorge (2001), 'The Euro in the International Financial Architecture', *Acta Oeconomica*, Vol. 51(3), pp. 287–314.

Bruszt, László (2002), 'Market-making as State-making: Constitutions and Economic Development in Post-communist Eastern Europe', *Constitutional Political Economy*, Vol. 13(1), pp. 53–72.

Bruton, Henry (1998), 'A Reconsideration of Import Substitution', *The Journal of Economic Literature*, Vol. 36(2), pp. 903–36.

Buchanan, James (1977), 'Law and the Invisible Hand', in Buchanan, James, *Freedom in Constitutional Contract*, Texas A&M University Press, College Station, pp. 2–39.

Cassel, Dieter (ed.) (1998), *Europäische Integration als Ordnungspolitische Gestaltungsaufgabe*, Duncker und Humblot, Schriften des Vereins für Socialpolitik, Band 260, Berlin.

Cottarelli, Carlo and Szapáry, György (eds) (1998), *Moderate Inflation*, joint publication of the IMF and the National Bank of Hungary, Washington, Budapest.

Csaba, László (2002a), 'Transition and Integration in Central and Eastern Europe', in Mänicke, K. (ed.), *Zehn Jahre Wende in Osteuropa*, Verlag Peter Lang (in print), Frankfurt am Main.

Csaba, László (2002b), 'Economics: Hungary', in Kaase, Max and Sparschuh, Vera (eds), *Handbook of Three Social Sciences in Central and Eastern Europe*, Wissenschaftzentrum Berlin & Informationszentrum Berlin, Paris: Maison des Sciences de l'Homme, Collegium Budapest, Brussels / Fifth Framework Programme, (in print), Berlin.

Chubais, Anatoly and Vishnievskaia, Marina (1995), 'Russian Privatization in mid-1994', in Aslund, Anders (ed.), *Russian Economic Reform at Risk*, Frances Pinter, London, and St. Martin's Press, New York, pp. 89–99.

Dallago, Bruno (1994), 'Some Reflections on Privatization as a Means to Transform the Economic System: the Western Experience', in Wagener, Hans-Jürgen (ed.), *The Political Economy of Transformation*, Physica Verlag, Heidelberg and New York, pp. 113–44.

DeLong, Bradford (2000), 'The Triumph of Monetarism?' *The Journal of Economic Perspectives*, Vol. 14(1), pp. 83–94.

Dorn, James, Hanke, Steve and Walters, Alan (eds) (1998), *The Revolution in Development Economics*, The Cato Institute, Washington.

Dornbusch, Rüdiger (1993), *Stabilization, Debt and Reform: Policy Choices for Developing Countries*, Harvester Wheatsheaf, New York.

Dornbusch, Rüdiger (2000), *Keys to Prosperity: Free Markets, Sound Money and a Bit of Luck*, The MIT Press, Cambridge (Mass.).

Easterly, William (2001), *The Elusive Quest for Growth*, The MIT Press, Cambridge (Mass.) and London.

Eatwell, J., Ellman, M., Karlsson, M., Nuti, M.D. and Shapiro, J. (1997), *Not 'Just Another Accession'. The Political Economy of EU Enlargement to the East*, Institute for Public Policy Research, London.

European Commission (1990), 'Stabilization, Liberalization and Devolution. Assessment of the Economic Situation and Reform Process in the Soviet Union', *European Economy*, No. 45. (special issue).

Eucken, Walter (1948), 'On the Theory of the Centrally Administered Economy. An Analysis of the German Experiment', parts I and II, *Economica*, new Vol. 15(1), pp. 79–100 and No. 2, pp. 173–93.

Greenaway, David, Morgan, William and Wright, Paul (1998), 'Trade Reform Adjustment and Growth: What does the Evidence Tell Us?' *The Economic Journal*, Vol, 108, No. 450, pp. 1547–61.

Harberger, Arnold (2001), 'The View from the Trenches: Development Processes and Policies as Seen by a Working Professional', in Meier, Gerald and Stiglitz, Joseph (eds), *Frontiers of Development Economics*, Oxford University Press for the World Bank, pp. 541–61.

Hare, Paul G. (2001), 'Institutional Change and Economic Performance in the Transition Economies', in UN Economic Commission for Europe, *Economic Survey of Europe*, No. 2, Geneva and New York, pp. 77–94.

Hayek, Friedrich August (1989), *The Fatal Conceit*, The University of Chicago Press (second edition), Chicago.

Hibbs, David (2001), 'The Politicization of Growth Theory', *Kyklos*, Vol. 54, nos. (2–3), pp. 293–316.

Hoff, Karla and Stiglitz, Joseph (2001), 'Modern Economic Theory and Development', in Meier, G. and Stiglitz, J. (eds), *Frontiers of Development Economics*, Oxford University Press for the World Bank, pp. 389–459.

IMF/OECD/IBRD (1991), *A Study of the Soviet Economy*, Vols. I–III, Government Printing Office, Washington, D.C.

Kolodko, Grzegorz W. (2000a), 'Ten Years of Post-socialist Transition: The Lessons for Policy Reforms', in Kolodko, G.W., *Post Communist Transition: The Thorny Road*, University of Rochester Press and Boydell&Brewer Ltd., Woodbridge, Suffolk (UK), Rochester, N.Y, pp. 57–86.

Kolodko, Grzegorz W. (2000b), 'The Washington Consensus Revisited', in Kolodko, G.W., *From Shock to Therapy*, Oxford University Press for the UN University, pp. 119–42. Oxford etc.

Kornai, János (1990), *The Road to a Free Economy*, W.W. Norton, New York.

Kornai, János (1994), 'Transformational Recession', *The Journal of Comparative Economics*, Vol. 19(1), pp. 39–63.

Kornai, János (2000), 'Ten Years After. The Road to a Free Economy: The Author's Self-evaluation', in Stiglitz, J. (ed.), *The Annual World Bank Conference on Development Economics*, IBRD, Washington, pp. 1–30.

Kornai, János, Haggard, Stephan and Kaufmann, Robert (eds), (2001), *Reforming the State: Fiscal and Welfare Reforms in Post-Socialist Countries*, Cambridge University Press, Cambridge etc.

Körössényi, András (1995), 'Reasons for the Defeat of the Right', *East European Politics and Societies*, Vol, 9, No, 3.

Köves, András and Marer, Paul (eds), (1991), *Foreign Economic Liberalization: Experiences of Socialist and Market Economies*, The Westview Press, Boulder (Col.).

Krueger, Anne (1998), 'Wither the IMF and the World Bank?' *The Journal of Economic Literature*, Vol., 36, No, 4, pp. 1983–2002.

Krueger, Anne (2000), 'Agenda for Future Research', in Krueger, Anne (ed.), *Economic Policy Reform: the Second Stage*, The University of Chicago Press, Chicago and London, pp. 585–94.

Kydland, F. and Prescott, E. (1977), 'Rules Rather than Discretion: The Inconsistency of Optimal Plans', *The Journal of Political Economy*, Vol. 87(3), pp. 473–92.

Laki, Mihály (1991), 'Economic Programmes of the Ex-opposition Parties in Hungary', *East European Politics and Societies*, Vol. 5(1), pp. 73–92.

Lal, Deepak (1993), *The Repressed Economy*, Edward Elgar, Aldershot (UK) and Brookfield (USA).

Lámfalussy, Alexandre (2000), *Financial Crises in Emerging Markets*, Yale University Press, New Haven.

Lányi, Kamilla (1996), 'Szociális piacgazdaság – nálunk, most?' [A social market economy for Hungary, now?], in *2000*, Vol. 8(4), pp. 8–17.

Malle, Silvana (1994), 'Privatization in Russia: A Comparative Study in Institutional Change', in Csaba, László (ed.), *Privatization, Liberalization and Destruction*, Dartmouth Publishing Co, Aldershot (UK) and Brookfield (USA), pp. 71–101 – reprinted also in Pejovich, Svetozar (ed.) (2001), *The Economics of Property Rights*, Vol. I, Edward Elgar, Cheltenham (UK) and Northampton (Mass., USA), pp. 403–33.

Megisson, William and Netter, John (2001), 'From State to Market: A Survey of Empirical Studies on Privatization', *The Journal of Economic Literature*, Vol. 39(2), pp. 321–89.

Meier, Gerald (2001), 'The Old Generation of Development Economists and the New', in Meier, G. and Stiglitz, J. (eds), *Frontiers of Development Economics*, Oxford University Press for the World Bank, pp. 13–50.

Murrel, Peter (1995), 'The Transition According to Cambridge, Mass.' *The Journal of Economic Literature*, Vol. 33(1), pp. 164–78.

Nelson, Joan, Tilly, Charles and Walker, Lee (eds) (1999), *Transforming Post-Communist Political Economies*, The National Academy Press, Washington.

North, Douglass (1990), *Institutions, Institutional Change and Economic Performance*, Cambridge University Press, Cambridge etc.

Olson, Mancur (1982), *The Rise and Decline of Nations: Economic Growth, Stagflation and Social Rigidities*, Yale University Press, New Haven.

Paulson, Jo Ann (ed.) (1999), *African Economies in Transition*, Vols. I and II, St. Martin's Press, New York.

Perkins, Dwight and Roemer, Paul (eds) (1991), *Reforming Economic Systems in Developing Countries*, The Harvard University Press, Cambridge (Mass.).

Portes, Richard (ed.) (1999), 'The Path of Reform in Central and Eastern Europe', *European Economy*, special issue No. 2.

Roland, Gérard (1991), 'Political Economy of Sequencing Tactics in the Transition Period', in Csaba, László (ed.), *Systemic Change and Stabilization in Eastern Europe*, Dartmouth Publishing Co, Aldershot (UK) and Brookfield (USA), pp. 45–64.

Saint-Paul, Giles (2000), 'The New Political Economy', *The Journal of Economic Literature*, Vol. 38(4), pp. 915–25.

Schardax, Franz and Reininger, Thomas (2001), 'The Financial Sector in Five Central and Eastern European Countries': an overview, Oesterreichische Nationalbank, Vienna, *Focus on Transition*, Vol. 7(1). pp. 30–64.

Schneider, Friedrich (1993), 'The Federal and Fiscal Structures of Western Democracies as a Model a Federal Union in Former Communist Countries?' in Wagener, Hans-Jürgen (ed.), *On the Theory and Policy of Systemic Change*, Physica Verlag, Heidelberg and New York, pp. 135–54.

Schrader, Jörg-Volker (2000), 'CAP Reform, the Berlin Summit and EU Enlargement', *Intereconomics*, Vol. 35(5), pp. 231–42.

Stiglitz, Joseph (2000), 'Reflections on the Theory and Practice of Reform', in Krueger, Anne (ed.), *Economic Policy Reform: the Second Stage*, The University of Chicago Press, Chicago and London, pp. 551–81.

Todaro, Michael (2000), *The Economics of Development*, 7th edition, Oxford University Press, Oxford.

UN Economic Commission for Europe (2001), *Economic Survey of Europe*, No. 1, Geneva and New York.

Vanberg, Viktor (2001), *The Constitution of Markets: Essays in Political Economy*, Routledge, London and N.Y.

Williamson, John (1994), 'In Search for a Manual for Technopols', in Williamson, John (ed.), *The Political Economy of Policy Reform*, Institute of International Economics, Washington, D.C., pp. 9–47.

Williamson, John (2000), 'What Should the World Bank Think about the Washington Consensus?' *The World Bank Research Observer*, Vol. 15(2), pp. 251–64.

Williamson, Oliver E. (2000), 'The New Institutional Economics: Taking Stock, Looking Ahead', *The Journal of Economic Literature*, Vol. 38(3), pp. 595–613.

World Bank (1996), *From Plan to Market*, Oxford UP for the IBRD, Oxford and Washington.

Chapter 3

Governing Incomplete Globalization[1]

D. Mario Nuti

1. Introduction

It is a commonplace that the last thirty years have seen a process of fast *globalization*, understood as increasing world economic integration[2] through international trade and investment. In the period 1970–2000 the share of exports in world GDP has risen threefold from about 8 per cent to 24 per cent.[3] Capital flows grew tenfold over the period. Foreign direct investment by advanced to less-developed countries boomed from USD 28bn in 1970 to a peak of USD 306bn in 1997, and has only declined slightly since then. Portfolio investment grew from USD 10bn in 1970 to a peak of USD 103bn in 1996 (World Bank, 2000). Global transactions in foreign exchange are an increasingly large multiple of central banks' reserves (see Frankel, 2000; Feldstein, 2000; DfID 2000).

Two major factors underlie this globalization process:

1. The fall of transport, communications and transaction costs in the private sector, due to the diffusion and cheapening of air freight and of containerization, the increasing importance of weightless tradable, the development of information technology (Frankel, 2000) – all leading to what has been called 'The Death of Distance' (Cairncross, 1997). The average incidence of transport costs (measured by the difference between *cif* and *fob* prices) is now of the order of only 4 per cent (Frankel, 2000).
2. The fall in policy barriers to foreign trade (tariff and non-tariff) and to investment on the part of the public sector, due to trade liberalization rounds (within GATT/WTO), to the internationalization of financial markets, the increasing importance of international financial institutions (especially the IMF and the World Bank), and the opening of former centrally planned economies in their transition to markets – which raised not so much the level but the market orientation of their economic integration in the world economy.

Both factors and their various manifestations have the equivalent, indeed identical, effect of reducing *trade costs*, therefore, from the viewpoint of their impact on globalization measured by the share of world trade in GDP, there is no reason to distinguish between them.

In this paper, after considering briefly the evolution of globalization since the late 19th century and the specific features of the current round (Section 2), it is argued that such a process is just as notable for its incompleteness as it is for its progress. Section 3 sets a benchmark for *complete* globalization, as a world in which resources are allocated as in a single, competitive, closed economy, governed by global governance institutions. Today's global world is a far cry from such a notion of complete globalization, as witnessed by the missing or inadequate institutions of global governance (Section 4); the persistence of barriers to trade and factor movements, and especially the recent proliferation of trade blocs (Section 5); or the presence of a number of phenomena which remain 'puzzles' difficult to explain in a globalized world (Section 6). This state of affairs reduces the net benefits actually obtained from globalization and fails to distribute fairly its gross costs and benefits across countries and groups, thus, at least to some extent, explaining current widespread opposition to globalization (Section 7). Section 8 concludes that the growth of global governance institutions may or may not be feasible and desirable, but ultimately constrains the continued growth of globalization.

2. The Evolution of Globalization

We could debate *ad nauseam* whether globalization is a new phenomenon or follow the 'back to the future' view that it is a mere continuation of a secular trend, begun in the 19th century (or 1498 or 1492 or even earlier) and interrupted in the 20th century during the two World Wars and the interwar period. As the current round of globalization is decisively different from its earlier incarnations (see World Bank, 2001) this issue is completely immaterial.

Nineteenth-century globalization consisted primarily in the integration of raw materials markets, so much so that historians measure its intensity by the dispersion of international prices for such materials. From 1870 to 1914, transport progress (from sail to steam) and the negotiated reduction of trade barriers allowed a better utilization of land and natural resources, with a dramatic growth of international flows of commodities, capital and labor; the share of world exports and GDP doubled to 8 per cent over the period. In less-developed countries foreign capital more than trebled, rising from 9 per cent to 32 per cent of their income. Migrations (mostly from Europe towards America and Australia, but also within the South) involved over 10 per cent of world population. The average world income growth rose yearly from 0.5 per cent in the previous half century to 1.3 per cent, increasing inequality.

In 1914–44, globalization went into reverse, with a post-World War I world characterized by isolationism, nationalisms, monetary instability and depression, protectionism, the growth of fascism and communism. Poverty and inequality increased and at the end of the 1940s the share of world exports in income had fallen back almost to the level of 1870; in the more advanced countries former trade shares recovered only around 1970.

In the second wave of globalization (1950–80 using the periodization adopted by World Bank, 2001) the cost of maritime transport fell by about a third, there was an increase in intermediate products trade and an agglomeration of production. Economic integration increased primarily among developed countries, with a series of multilateral agreements within GATT; their economies grew rapidly, accelerating their convergence within the group. Less-developed countries continued their specialization in primary products, broadly insulated from capital flows, and developed more slowly thus diverging further from advanced economies.

In the current wave, promoted by the factors mentioned above in the Introduction, less-developed countries benefit from globalization by raising the share of manufacturing products in their exports from 25 per cent to 80 per cent. The foreign trade share of a number of countries, such as Brazil, China, India, Mexico, Hungary, increases enormously. Twenty-four less-developed countries (with a population of 3 billion people) have doubled their share of foreign trade in GDP, significantly accelerating their per capita income growth (1 per cent in the 1960s, 3 per cent in the 1970s, 4 per cent in the 1980s, to 5 per cent in the 1990s). If we define 'extreme poverty' as a per capita income below USD 1 per day (World Bank, 2001), the number of poor in these countries fell by 120 million between 1993 and 1998. These countries narrow their gap with respect to developed countries, where income growth is only 2 per cent, but the other less-developed countries (2 billion inhabitants) remain excluded from these processes and become marginalized; their income per capita actually falls.

Other distinguishing features of the current wave of globalization are:

1. A much greater integration of financial markets, accompanied by large-scale capital flows, while migratory flows are constrained and discouraged (see below);
2. A fall in the share of tradable in GDP, within which traded output grows faster than its share in GDP, thus understating the measurement of globalization by trade/GDP ratios;
3. A greater share of services in foreign trade;
4. A greater geographical dispersion of individual stages (or processes) in the production of given items, as well as other forms of intra-industry trade;[4]
5. A drastic increase in the weight of Multi-National Enterprises (MNEs), now representing about a third of world trade;
6. The emergence of small states with an exceptionally high ratio of foreign trade to GDP;
7. The monetary and economic disintegration of post-communist economies, with the break-up of old trade blocs – Comecon, USSR and the ruble area, the Yugoslav and Czecho-Slovak federations – whose members' integration was centrally planned and is now market oriented. This has involved a very deep

qualitative change in their participation in the global economy, through the transformation of their trade and exchange rate regimes, a large scale re-structuring in the composition and direction of their trade flows, and a re-integration into the world and especially European economy, with prospects of EU membership for at least ten of them (see Kolodko, 2001).

3. A Benchmark for Complete Globalization

In spite of its fast and inexorable progress, globalization is still exceedingly far from completion. Instead of looking at what happened in the last thirty years and projecting it onto possible future paths, let us look at what the world would be like if the globalization process were 100 per cent complete. This is not necessarily likely in our lifetimes, and even if it were, it would not necessarily be desirable, but it does provide a useful insight into what might prevent us from ever getting there, and how we might interpret current events and venture conjectures – better than simple extrapolations – about the near future of globalization processes. The idea underlying this exercise is that globalization needs global governance, that the progress of globalization has already exceeded the governance capacity of existing international institutions, and that this is a major obstacle to the further progress of globalization. Hence the need – if the impetus of recent globalization is to be sustained – to strengthen global governance institutions, far beyond current projects for the reform of international institutions, which are neither radical enough nor broad enough as they are almost entirely limited to international financial architecture.

We can imagine *total or absolute globalization* as the same allocation of resources that would prevail in a world without national borders, run as a competitive, single closed economy or, rather, one of its possible allocations of resources, allowing for the possibility of multiple equilibria.

Such a fully globalized world would require a single global government (whether federal or not, with regional forms of government in what are now sovereign states), with a Ministry of Finance whose powers of taxation and expenditure provide, among other things, for world-wide income re-distribution and global public goods. There would have to be a single world currency and, therefore, a global Central Bank – whose degree of independence from global government might be debated as for any national Central Bank – with the functions of an institute of issue, manager of global government debt and lender of last resort; while the function of financial supervision might be also undertaken by or delegated to an external global agency. There would be global public agencies financing and promoting regional economic development, public authorities taking care of competition or the environment, and various other institutions of global governance.

Trade – all of which would then be internal – and factor movements would be totally unimpeded by policy measures. In such an imaginary world distance continues to be important, including the so-called 'psychic distance' or 'subjective resistance' that differentiates locally produced goods from those produced in more distant locations. Even trade obstacles due to cultural, linguistic or habitual factors might persist – as long as they are not due to the existence of borders. The pull of economic gravity would continue to affect economic transactions over space, indeed would be strengthened by the lack of borders. The agglomeration of production activities would continue, being a feature of economic diversification within a single country as well as across countries. There would continue to exist political links between different parts of the world, including ones of colonial/post-colonial type. Otherwise the world would operate as a single country.

While, as we noted above, there is no operational difference between the two factors that underlie globalization – the reduction of transport costs and that of policy barriers – the two types of trade costs are totally different from the viewpoint of incomplete globalization. Transport costs are inevitable in multidimensional space, but are just as harmless as the existence of a plurality of goods; their reduction appears like any other form of technical progress, which raises the share of exports in world income but does not bring any closer total globalization as defined here. Only a reduction in policy barriers to trade and production factor flows reduces the distance between the achieved degree of globalization and complete globalization.[5]

There can be no doubt whatever that the world as we know it, global as it may seem, is extremely remote from the imaginary world of complete globalization outlined above. First, institutions of global governance are inadequate or missing altogether (Section 4); second, there is a persistence of barriers to trade and factor movements, and especially the recent proliferation of trade blocs (Section 5); third, there are a number of phenomena which remain 'puzzles' difficult to explain in a globalized world (Section 5).

4. Global Governance Institutions

The idea that globalization progress has surpassed the progress of global governance is a recent contribution to the globalization debate. It is embodied for instance in the latest World Bank *Report on Globalisation and Poverty*: 'Both global opportunities and global risks have outpaced global policy' (World Bank, 2000, p. 1). Kolodko (2001) argues that 'Global problems are to be solved by global institutions. The point is [that] such institutions are often lacking, while the number of global problems is increasing' (p. 6). George Soros contends that 'The future of globalised markets will depend on institutions capable of sustaining them' (at a conference at the Institute for International Economics in Washington, October 2001, as reported by *IMF Survey* of 12 November). Bhagwati (2001) calls for 'appropriate governance' of globalization processes, though he does not develop the argument. Further analysis of global governance is needed urgently – not necessarily to promote global governance institutions, which many may find repugnant as 'Big Brother-type' developments and an infringement on local autonomy and liberties, but at least to understand what are the limits of a non-governed globalization, its drawbacks and prospects for the future.

By comparison with the benchmark of complete globalization set out above (in Section 3), the globalization of institutions is a remote prospect.

In place of world government we have various United Nations agencies, without the power of taxation, indeed on the verge of bankruptcy because of member countries' failure or outright refusal to pay their dues; plus groupings/clubs/lobbies of the richer states such as the G-7/8 or the G-24, plus co-ordination agencies such as the OECD. The dominant role acquired, especially after the collapse of the Soviet bloc, by the United States – recently nicknamed the G-1 in the press – falsifies a view of the world as a single 'Empire' (Hardt and Negri, 2001), dominated not by a Metropolis but by multinational companies.

Instead of one world currency we have three major currencies (dollar, euro and yen) floating freely against each other, plus over one hundred other currencies which have proliferated, especially in the last fifty years, as a consequence of independence for many new states. Their exchange rate regimes represent the entire spectrum of possible alternatives; they range from freely floating to hyper-fixed (to a reference currency or a basket of currencies through a currency board or domestic currency replacement including a currency union), via an intermediate range of variously pegged rates (fixed, crawling pegs and bands, with various degrees of government and Central Bank intervention). The 'bi-polar' view has now emerged that such intermediate regimes between hyper-fixed and floating are not sustainable *for countries open to international capital flows*. This is reflected in the actual experience of countries in all groups (developed, emerging, others) moving away from intermediate to extreme regimes (see Fischer, 2001). Neither extreme, however, is completely satisfactory; floating regimes maintain competitiveness at the cost of inflation and volatility; hyper-fixed rates promote stability but raise the cost of failure (see Argentina at the end of 2001).[6] One might agree with Rogoff (2001) that,

> into the foreseeable future, it would not be desirable to aim for a single world currency, and that from an economic point of view, it would be preferable to retain at least, say, three or four currencies [in order to reap the advantages of risk diversification] …

– but even by those standards there are at least a hundred currencies too many for the requirements of a fully global economy.

Instead of a World Central Bank we have a pale imitation of one of its functions by the IMF, which acts as quasi-lender of last resort to sovereign states, including, however, insolvent states that should not be bailed out – creating disincentives for debt resolution – but subjected to 'orderly work-out procedures' (Portes, 1995, 2002). Occasionally, in an emergency such as the immediate aftermath of 11 September 2001, there is some co-ordination among major central banks to provide the liquidity necessary to avoid a major global crisis, but otherwise there is no monetary policy coordination on a world scale. Criticisms of the IMF (reported by IFIAC, 2000) include the following: it exercises too much power over developing countries' economic policies through conditionality, though then fails to enforce conditions; it lacks transparency and accountability; it is used by G-7 governments (read: the US) to further their political ends; it yields few benefits to recipient countries; it encourages non-sustainable pegged exchange rates; it uses defective economic techniques (modeling, forecasting, etc) and theories; it comes into conflicts with other international financial institutions; it is unable to provide liquidity during a crisis. It also performs functions which are alien to a Central Bank, such as providing long term loans at subsidized rates, including loans for poverty reduction. IFIAC (2000) unanimously recommended that (1) the IMF (and the World Bank and regional development banks) should write-off in their entirety all claims against heavily indebted poor countries (HIPCs) that implement an effective economic and social development strategy, and (2) the IMF should restrict its lending to the provision of short-term liquidity, ending long term lending for other purposes. Other recommendations involved restructuring the IMF into a smaller institution with reduced responsibilities, and ending conditionality. Streamlining the IMF along these lines, however, would leave the functions of a World Central Bank even less covered.

Standards for credit regulations – but no actual regulation – are provided by the Basel-based Bank for International Settlements (BIS), acting as a bank for central banks (managing reserves and settlements and promoting central bank co-operation). BIS standards are purely voluntary, ineffective until adopted by each country's legislative or regulatory body.

Instead of development agencies there is the World Bank group and other regional development banks (Inter-American, African and Asian). Their importance declined in the 1980s with the explosion of international financial markets, with private lending and investment dwarfing the multilateral banks credit flows by a factor of 50 (IFIAC, 2000). Frequently raised criticisms include: lending fever and consequent poor performance; skewed lending, mostly (70–80 per cent) to a dozen creditworthy countries that already have access to international financial markets, moreover, subject to government guarantees; loan subsidization; involvement in crisis lending (which is a function of the IMF); large cost to donors (USD 22bn per year); being an instrument of US policy; excessive conditionality; neglect of the environmental impact of financed projects. IFIAC recommendations included re-naming these banks as development agencies; phasing out all resource transfers to countries that already enjoy capital market access; performance related payments; poverty alleviation grants to service suppliers to replace loans and guarantees for physical infrastructure; institutional reform loans but no financial crisis lending; a clear division of geographical areas for the various agencies; concentration on the production of global public goods (See also Gilbert, Powell and Vines, 1999; Gilbert and Vines, 2000).

Lending to transition economies (currently 27) is the responsibility of the EBRD (see their *Transition Reports*, published yearly in November since 1994, and their yearly *Update* in April). It differs from the IBRD in significant respects: it is supposed to invest primarily in the private sector according to commercial criteria. This poses profound existential problems for the EBRD: (1) if it lends only to the private sector on commercial terms, its existence will make no difference; (2) it is a public financial institution whose *raison-d'être* is the inefficiency of public financial institutions; (3) its success in assisting transition can only be judged by the speed of its own demise...

International trade competition is the responsibility of the WTO (ex-GATT). It has a tiny budget, no decision-making role, only providing technical and legal support; it administers the process by which trade rules change and sanctions those rules – too slowly for effective enforcement. (For a radical view of WTO reform, on issues of trade and environment, see DfID, 2000, Ch. 4–6).

The present international 'architecture' and especially financial institutions have come under increasing criticism not only from radical demonstrators in Seattle/Washington/Prague/Davos/Naples/Genoa, but also from leading economists such as the World Bank former chief economist and vice-president, Nobel laureate Joseph Stiglitz (2000), notable for his blistering criticisms of the IMF and World Bank; financiers like George Soros (2000, 2002); government bodies such as the IFIAC-International Financial Institution Advisory Commission appointed by the US government to review most of those entities (see Meltzer Report, 2000); the G-7 Finance Ministers (July 2000), the IMF acting Managing Director reporting on current progress to the IMF International Monetary and Financial Committee (April 2000), or the UK DfID Globalisation Report (2000). The list is not exhaustive (see Nouriel Roubini's website, New York University: www.stern.nyu.edu/globalmacro, and Eatwell 2002).

5. Trade Barriers and Regional Blocs

In spite of the progressive reduction in trade barriers (tariff and non-tariff) in the last thirty years of the 20th century, protectionism is still widespread. Developed countries have low average tariffs, but these are concentrated exactly in the areas in which less-developed countries have a comparative advantage, as in agriculture and in highly labor-intensive manufactures. It is estimated that rich countries' protectionism costs less-developed countries more than USD 100bn a year, which is twice the flow of aid from the North to the South. At the same time in less-developed countries the level of protection is three times higher than in OECD countries and is an obstacle mainly to trade with other less-developed countries; it is estimated that its elimination would bring about another USD 50bn net benefits. Another round of multilateral trade liberalization within WTO could do a great deal to reduce, if not eliminate, these forms of protection, especially if accompanied by a discussion of environmental issues, health standards, and a less strict protection of intellectual property, particularly for pharmaceutical products.

However, 'Political momentum behind the new round of global trade talks has faded, casting a shadow over the agreement to launch it, reached in Doha last November [2001]' (*Financial Times*, 3 May 2002). The decline in world trade by 1 per cent in 2001, in conjunction with weaker growth in world income, instead of encouraging further trade liberalization has revamped protectionism. For example, early in 2002, President George W. Bush could impose overnight a 30 per cent tariff on steel imports, and violate international trade rules by granting a tax break to US exporters. The European Union responded with disproportionate retaliatory sanctions amounting to 100 per cent protection on selected US goods worth USD 4bn. The US farm bill currently [May 2002] under discussion in the US Congress is another bout of US protectionism. The US is also to impose import duties of over 27 per cent on softwood timber imports (worth USD 6bn) from Canada.

The achievement of liberalization of capital flows in all their forms has not been accompanied by that of labor migration. Enormous pressure on labor flows is caused by differences in wage levels that, in 2000, ranged from USD 32 per hour in Germany to 25 cents in India, but does not find a *legal* outlet. 'Compared to 100 years ago, the world is much less globalized when it comes to labor flows' (World Bank 2000, p. 11). Migrations of skilled labor, however, are not only unimpeded but actively encouraged, representing a severe 'brain drain' from less-developed countries (see Commander, Kangashniemi and Winters 2002).

An even more spectacular departure from the complete globalization outlined above in Section 3 is the revival and large-scale proliferation of trade blocs (RIAs or Regional Integration Agreements), especially in the 1990s after twenty years' dormancy, precisely at the time when globalization progressed as a result of post-communist transformations. Thus, instead of gradually becoming a borderless area, the world has been segmented into fenced compartments.

Baldwin (1995) talks of 'domino regionalism'. Frankel and Wei (1998) talk of the 'wild-fire' diffusion of trade blocs. Soloaga and Winters (2001) summarize this phenomenon thus:

During the last 10 years, regionalism has re-emerged as a major issue in the policy agenda. In the Americas, the new Common Market of the South (MERCOSUR, 1991) and the North American Free Trade Association (NAFTA, 1994) were created while old Preferential Trade Agreement (PTAs) like the Andean Pact (ANDEAN) and the Central American Common Market) started a process of renewal in the late '80s and early '90s. In Africa new PTAs were formed on the basis of old ones (e.g., in 1994 the *Union Economique et Monetaire de l'Afrique Occidentale* – UEMOA – was created out of the *Communaute' Economique de l'Afrique Occidentale* – CEAO –, and the Common Market of Eastern and Southern Africa – COMESA – revived and expanded the Preferential Trade Area for Eastern and Southern African States – PTA – and old ones were revamped (e.g., in the early '90s the *Union Douaniere et Economique d'Afrique Centrale* – UDEAC). In Asia, countries in the Association of Southeast Nations (ASEAN) formed in 1992 the ASEAN Free Trade Area (AFTA).

These are only examples: World Bank (2000) talks of a 'veritable explosion of regional integration agreements' in the last fifteen years.

> Nearly every country in the world is either a member of – or discussing participation in – one or more regional integration arrangements. Such agreements have been concluded among high-income countries, among low-income countries, and, more recently, starting with … NAFTA – between high income and developing countries. More than half of world trade now occurs within actual or prospective trading blocs (p. ix).

Moreover, 'In 1999 regional agreements notified to WTO were a greater number than that of its members' (p. 123), to be precise 194 agreements (of which 87 signed after 1990) for about 140 members.

The European Union figures prominently in this picture, with the implementation of the Single Market in 1992, successive rounds of enlargement and deepening, with the European Monetary Union and the introduction of the euro, and the prospective accession of another twelve countries: the European Economic Area, Europe Agreements with accession candidates, the customs union with Turkey, other agreements with Mediterranean countries (see World Bank 2000 and their Table 1.1 for more details on the numerous regional agreements in existence).

There is an official tendency to stress the political objectives and the non-economic dimensions of regional agreements, including national (intra- and extra-regional) security, the strengthening of bargaining power especially for the smaller countries (as in CORICOM, the Caribbean Community), the greater credibility of economic and political reform. Emphasis therefore shifts from the proliferation of agreements to their design, upon which the amount and distribution of desired advantages depend. Such advantages, according to World Bank (2000), depend on the presence of economies of scale and above all on the ability to stimulate competition within the regional market, and on the minimization of incentives to trade diversion rather than creation, discouraging the use of inefficient regional producers. Thus it becomes important to open trade with partners external to the bloc, while simultaneously liberalizing within the bloc.

A corollary of this approach is the recommendation to establish regional blocs made of both less-developed and high-income countries, as the latter tend to have lower barriers, greater opportunities for exploiting comparative advantages and a greater probability of reaching desired political objectives. Agreements between less-developed countries, on the contrary, tend to create additional tensions and problems. Another recommendation is to go beyond tariff reduction and include other trade-promoting policies abolishing non-tariff barriers, such as contingent protection or anti-dumping measures, as well as the construction of joint infrastructure. It is recognized that a greater integration requires an agreement on the distribution of its advantages.

Nevertheless, the World Bank official line continues to be critical of the formation of blocs. These have the merit of allowing member-countries' authorities to explore forms of greater though limited trade liberalization, but in general induce an increase in the real cost of their imports, reduce the technology flow and raise export dependence on particular markets (World Bank 2000). Between the lines one can read a clear negative message.

Already in 1950, Jacob Viner maintained that regional blocs mostly create trade diversion, thus reducing world welfare. However, it is likely that both bloc effectiveness in promoting trade and their presumed efficiency might have been over-estimated. De Melo, Montenegro and Panagariya (1992) find that countries that have followed this integration route have not grown faster than others once investment differences are taken into account. When testing intra-bloc trade 'before and after' years of bloc revamping/creation, Soloaga and Winters (2001) find that, once 'gravity' effects (of trade partners' mutual attraction based on their distance and economic mass) are taken into account, there is 'no statistically significant change in the propensity for intra-bloc trade'. They find convincing evidence of trade diversion only for EFTA and the EU, both for imports and exports.

Should we consider regional blocs as building blocks or stumbling blocks, ask De Melo and Panagariya (1992), or as stepping stones to progress towards multilateralism (Winters 1996)? On the positive side, regionalism to some extent can be regarded as a substitute for liberalization, following the slow progress of the GATT Uruguay Round and the disappointment of the Seattle negotiations (December 1999). There are no countries totally insulated from these processes, everyone takes part in them. Blocs are formed mostly among neighboring countries, already attracted to one another by economic gravity, which means they are unlikely to do much harm in terms of trade diversion. Moreover, these blocs are formed and developed *simultaneously* at the world level (Frankel and Wei, 1998). Several economists believe that it is easier to negotiate trade liberalization between three commercial blocs – Europe, the Americas, East Asia – than multilaterally among over 150 countries. At continental level there should be higher probabilities of obtaining welfare improvement (Krugman 1991; Summers 1991; Frankel and Wei 1998). Within these large blocs, integration between more- and less-developed countries reduces the exclusion effects from which trade blocs usually suffer.

However, there remains a very substantial risk that the formation and enlargement of trade blocs might stop much sooner than universal liberalization. Bloc enlargement raises the incentive to exercise the improved market power vis-à-vis third countries, rather than following a co-operation policy – especially 'given that the dispute settlement mechanism of the WTO is weak at best' (Dimova 2002). Regionalization cannot represent an optimal solution from the viewpoint of economic efficiency, yet '... there is little hope of a convergence of existing trade blocs into one global bloc, thereby *de facto* ushering in free trade' (Dimova 2002).

It seems impossible to understand the formation and growth of trade blocs without reference to the costs and benefits of globalization, and the lack of global governance institutions that might reduce or recompense such costs in a way that is acceptable to commercial partners. The supra-national – though

still regional – governance institutions of trade blocs fill this institutional vacuum and provide a good, perhaps the best explanation of trade blocs' diffusion, otherwise an amazing and contradictory phenomenon. Rather than a brake on globalization, trade blocs complement it, filling a systemic vacuum.

6. Six Puzzles

Obstfeld and Rogoff (2000) raise and discuss six major phenomena in international macroeconomics that appear to be 'puzzles', i.e. they are difficult to reconcile with the progress of globalization:

1. The home-bias-in-trade puzzle: Why do people seem to have such a strong preference for consumption of their own goods?
2. The so-called Feldstein-Horioka puzzle: Why do observed OECD current-account imbalances tend to be so small relative to saving and investment when measured over any sustained period?
3. The home-bias portfolio puzzle: Why do home investors overwhelmingly prefer to hold home equity assets?
4. The consumption correlations puzzle: Why is consumption not more highly correlated across OECD countries?
5. The purchasing power parity puzzle: How is it possible that the half-life of real exchange rate innovations can be only three to four years?
6. The exchange rate disconnect puzzle: Why are exchange rates so volatile and so apparently disconnected from fundamentals?[7]

Obstfeld and Rogoff argue that all that is required to explain these phenomena simultaneously and coherently is a

significant but plausible level of international *trade costs* in goods markets. These *trade costs* may include transport costs but also tariffs, non-tariff barriers, and possibly other broader factors that impede trade (p. 340, emphasis added).

Basically, these *trade costs* introduce a wedge between real rates of return in different countries, and this provides a possible and plausible explanation for the six puzzles.

This ingenious and elegant argument is weak in two major respects. First, in monetary economies with different, mutually convertible currencies, what needs to be equalized is not real rates of return but those rates plus (minus) real exchange rate appreciation (depreciation) with reference to any common currency. Second, since these kinds of puzzles are either absent or much weaker within countries, no matter how large, it must be presumed that the so-called puzzles are related more closely to the policy barriers that we have illustrated in the previous section than to transport costs. Thus lumping the two together into a hybrid category of 'trade costs' is more misleading than enlightening. *The observed phenomena cease to be puzzles in a world characterized by* incomplete *globalization and can be regarded as additional evidence – if it were needed – of such incompleteness.* Financial markets *are still* segmented – though less so now than in 1970; there is a massive gross turnover in foreign exchange markets, but small net flows (the divergence being due partly to hedging); 'National savings tend to remain at home' (Feldstein 2000). In view of globalization incompleteness, the opposite would be puzzling.

7. Globalization Benefits and Costs

Markets are necessary and irreplaceable mechanisms for automatic adjustment, for the mobilization of entrepreneurship and for efficient and innovative change. They also have associated costs in terms of (1) inter-temporal inefficiency, in the form of associated unemployment and fluctuations; (2) adverse impact on the distribution of income and wealth; and (3) possible divergence of market prices from public values (understood as government valuations). The global market is no exception.

In the first instance, globalization is expected to yield the classic benefits of international division of labor, both from 'static' comparative advantages and from the 'dynamic' advantages derived from greater competition and mutual reduction of trade barriers: the impact of trade openness on income per capita is estimated to range from 0.3 to 3.0 per cent for each percentage point increase in trade shares (Frankel 2000). Second, there are benefits derived from capital flows and (increasingly) FDI which, besides providing capital, embodies new technologies, provides management and know-how, and facilitates the export of its production. This may explain the association between trade openness and the growth of *average* per capita incomes (see above, Section 2); the direction of causation is not unambiguous but there is evidence to encourage the presumption that such growth benefits from globalization.

Inter-temporal inefficiency is a recognized feature of any economy where markets for future goods and services (futures or forward markets, as well as markets for 'contingent' goods and services associated with particular uncertain states of the world) are missing, or where in any case markets are 'sequential', i.e. do not close and shut for ever as in the Arrow-Debreu model of general inter-temporal equilibrium, but are repeatedly reopened (see Stiglitz 1995). In the world as we know it, future markets are the exception and exist only for a handful of primary products over a short time horizon and for money and some financial assets. Moreover markets are not just sequential, they actually *never close*: the sun never sets over the global market. In such a world nobody needs to express a demand for, or a supply of, a future good today at a prefixed price: all economic agents act at all times and on the basis not of market prices but of *expectations* of prices and quantities. We live in a Keynesian instead of a neo-classical world. Hence the possibility of self-fulfilling expectations, or wrong expectations, or what Alan Greenspan calls 'irrational exuberance' of markets, or equally plausible irrational despondency and panic, liquidity preference (as in today's Japan), volatility, involuntary unemployment, economic fluctuations.

Financial market integration facilitates not only foreign investment but also capital flight, excessive indebtedness in less-developed countries, financial crises. If there is a presumption that trade and FDI globalization is 'good on average', there must be an equally strong presumption that the unrestricted globalization of short-term capital flows is 'bad on average'. By way of examples we can think of the 1992–3 European ERM crisis, the 1994 Mexican 'Tequila' crisis, the July 1997–January 1999 world-wide crisis in East Asia and other emerging markets, the August 1998 Russian crisis, the Argentinian crisis of end-2001. The ultimate causes of such crises were exchange rate misalignments, mismatch between short-term foreign exchange liabilities and foreign exchange reserves, weakness and poor supervision of national banking systems, and so on; but their depth and diffusion was strictly related to financial markets globalization, at a cost likely to be higher than its advantages of international diversification of risk (see Eatwell, 2002). FDI and (to some extent) equity investments are less volatile than short-term debt, but they can also be liquidated – though at a higher cost.

The second drawback of globalization – as with any market development – is its adverse distributional impact on income and wealth. It is officially recognized that 'Globalization produces winners and losers, both among countries and within them' (World Bank 2001, p. 1).

Losers include those countries which are marginalized – for whatever reason, geographical or political, due to climate or economic policy, weakness of institutions, lack of infrastructure or diffused corruption. Labor and capital operating in sectors that are no longer protected also lose out: it is estimated that China's trade liberalization following WTO membership will raise unemployment by 50 per cent, i.e. by 40 million. Unskilled workers in industrial countries are likely to lose out (though see Wood (2002) for some qualifications due to the diversity of relative endowments in a world with more than two production factors). Even if in the long run everybody stood to gain, in the short run losses may be substantial; the creation of new jobs is slow and delayed whereas losses can be instantaneous.

Three reflections are in order here. First, as long as there are *some* net losers from globalization, it is not enough for there to be positive net benefits *on average*, it is necessary for *all* losers to be compensated for their loss. *Potential* over-compensation of losers by winners is not sufficient to infer a social welfare improvement, *actual* compensation and over-compensation is necessary. Second, even if *everybody* gained from globalization *over time*, some people might lose with respect to what their alternative position *would have been* without it. Such losses, whether absolute or relative to an alternative time path, are easy to imagine: it is enough to think of the trend towards factor price equalization induced by international trade even without factor mobility, or of short term displacement of resource employment patterns. Finally, even if all unambiguously gained from globalization, the overall distribution of net gains might be regarded as unfair, resulting in an adverse change in relative distribution – within or across countries. On a world scale the Gini coefficient (ranging from 0 to 1, with 0 = complete equality) rose from 62.5 per cent in 1988 (in USD PPP) to 65.9 per cent in 1993. In the 1980s the coefficient rose by 0.5 percentage points per year in the UK and USA. The bottom 20 per cent of the world's population received 2.3 per cent of total world USD PPP income in 1988; this proportion was down to 2 per cent in 1993. Overall, the richest 1 per cent of people in the world (50mn) receive as much as the bottom 57 per cent (2.7bn people; see Milanovic (1998), based on worldwide household survey data not yet available for subsequent periods).

Robert Kaplan (2001) describes today's world as bifurcated and uses the image of a stretch limousine driving trough an urban ghetto. Its passengers are western Europe, North America, Australasia, Japan and the emerging Pacific Rim; all the others are outside. In 1999 world average real income per head at purchasing power parity – i.e. the most benign accounting convention that might be used in the measurement of inequality – was USD 7,000; the combined population of 900mn in high income countries had an average income of USD 26,000 whereas 5.1bn people in the less developed countries had average incomes of USD 3,500, of which 2.4bn people had an average of USD 1,900. In 1965–99 average incomes in sub-Saharan Africa fell, while those of the Middle East and North Africa stagnated. Moreover, according to the US Bureau of Census, in the first half of this century, 99 per cent of population increase is likely to take place in the less-developed countries, thus exacerbating current trends.

In Mr Kaplan's dark view, the combined stresses of population, urbanization, environmental degradation and failed development are creating a world of gangster states and states eaten out by gangs, both with a terrifying capacity for anarchic violence (Martin Wolf's review in the *Financial Times*, November 2001).

It follows that globalization must be accompanied by satisfactory mechanisms of world-wide re-distribution not only of current income but also inter-temporally, not only at a national level but also internationally, whereas global re-distribution opportunities are lacking, being left primarily to inadequate unilateral charity. Kolodko (2001) compares the 0.7 per cent of GDP recommended by the UN for transfer from rich to poor countries, with the actual current level of 0.24 per cent, most of which is appropriated not by the intended recipients but by various organizations, intermediaries and consultants.

Power relationships are altered by globalization, within and across countries. Internationally, trading nations increase their power (see for instance India and China). Internally, in theory the power of capital should be reduced by increased competition, but in reality it is strengthened with respect to both labor and national governments, thanks to its greater capacity to move across countries, to sell to the whole world from a single location and at the same time to disperse production stages all over the world. True competition is between governments seeking to attract foreign capital, rather than between capitalists. With the exception of the

USA, no government can adopt anti-cyclical policies any longer. Globalization extends to terrorism and to the fight against it, with equally devastating results.

A further disadvantage of globalization – again, of a kind associated with the existence and expansion of any market – arises from a possible divergence of market prices from social values as expressed by the preferences of democratically elected governments. Opportunities created by globalization include 'social dumping', i.e. competitiveness originating in labor conditions regarded as unacceptable by trading partners (for instance, child labor, though in the longer term its incidence may be reduced by globalization). Such labor conditions can be unacceptable not only by the standards prevailing in partner countries, but also in principle, regardless of where they occur; thus the fact that foreign investors usually pay higher wages than those prevailing locally (as pointed out by Graham, 2000) does not make the practice necessarily acceptable. Globalization opportunities may also be generated by the accompanying environmental destruction in the exporting country, in addition to the exacerbation of environmental problems in the world at large through the enhancement of economic growth associated with liberalization. The protection of intellectual property may impede health care in the poorer parts of the world, as noted above.

Pollution and the depletion of natural resources are simply a transfer, current or deferred, from poorer to richer countries. The decision not to ratify the Kyoto protocol, taken by the president of a country that accounts for 23 per cent of world energy consumption, whose electoral campaign was financed by oil companies, indicates the difficulties of a global solution to environmental problems that of course would exist even without globalization, but which are made much worse by the acceleration and concentration of growth associated with it.

The divergence between market prices and social values as defined above, plus inter-temporal inefficiency/instability and distributional issues, are at the root of widespread and strong anti-global movements. Some of the antiglobalists' arguments seem overblown, such as the emphasis on multinational corporations and their logos (Klein 2001) or debt cancellation. Multinational corporations' turnover being compared to countries' GDP (Anderson and Cavanagh, 2000) is a biased comparison between respectively gross and net magnitudes (as pointed out by de Grauwe, 2002), which also neglects the much broader scope of state and government authority vis-à-vis that of corporations (see Wolf (2002) – although companies large and small may successfully undertake 'state capture' (World Bank, 2002)). Size and its adverse impact on competition matters more than multi-nationality. Regardless of globalization, advertising can and does become a form of pollution that must be regulated and taxed (Meade, 1995), but brands make producers identifiable also for consumers' benefit (see *The Economist*'s leader and special report on brands, 8 September 2001). Some standardization and choice reduction is unavoidable in the process of economic growth, also regardless of globalization; and 'the world that is expected to suffer from cultural uniformity is not so monolithic, defenseless and rigid as it is believed to be' (Baricco, 2002). Cancellation of public creditors' claims towards less-developed countries does not benefit them but their private creditors. Still, even if these particular aspects of anti-global opposition were ignored or rejected, there still remain quite enough claims to justify and sustain anti-global movements and action.

8. Conclusions

Globalization of trade and investment (unlike that of financial markets) can be presumed to yield positive net benefits *on average*. Also, its further though not unlimited growth is probably unstoppable. But there is a sense in which globalization may have 'gone too far' (as suggested by Rodrik (1997) and emphasized by the book's title), in that the development of global institutions is now seriously lagging behind the growth of foreign trade and investment, not to mention financial markets. Like all markets, the global market is a major, if not the ultimate source of economic vitality, but it may have to be tamed (through international regulation, policy coordination, and re-distribution).

Kolodko (2002) asks whether globalization is really as irreversible as it seems: 'We cannot exclude *a priori* a regress from the degree of globalization already achieved' (p.15). Some reversal has already taken place, if only to the tune of a 1 per cent decline in world trade in a sluggish but positively growing world economy in 2001; capital flows trends have also reversed for both FDI and financial investment at the end of the last decade (see the Introduction above). It is too early to judge whether the reversal will be a lasting trend – but it would be foolhardy to rule out this possibility.

The problem is not globalization *per se*, but the lack of agencies and instruments capable of governing it, not only at national but above all at international level, and of means to place them under democratic control. The most important task for global governance is probably that of worldwide distribution. Kolodko (2001) argues that:

> Globalization stands no chance of total success, because it will be unable to win the political support of the inhabitants of the world (to speak of a 'world community' would be premature) as long as the re-distribution channels operate like before. What is necessary is worldwide institutions and a worldwide policy and strategies to rectify the global redistribution system that has evolved thus far (all set in bold in the original; p.18).

It is no accident that world leaders now regard the fight against poverty as an integral part of the fight against terrorism.

Without significantly greater global governance, the net benefits potentially obtainable from globalization are reduced, gross costs and benefits are not redistributed so as to avoid having net losers across and within countries, and any pretence of a presumed superiority of a global world and of a mythical role of globalization in our planet's development is irredeemably falsified. Trade blocs will be revamped or created, with regional government institutions supplementing both the inadequacy of national governments (which cannot re-distribute costs and benefits on a supra-national scale) and that of missing global institutions. It is enough to think of the increasing role of the Brussels and Frankfurt institutions in the governance of the European Union member states. Under these circumstances we can expect further opposition to globalization to become more and more vocal, diffused and powerful, not just by anti-global demonstrators but by no less than the US President, who, with his recent opportunistic protectionism and his successful fight with Bayer over the anthrax vaccine patent, appears decisively to have joined the ranks of the anti-global movement.

Notes

1   Paper presented at the TIGER Institute (Transition, Integration, Globalization Economic Research), 4th International Conference, 'Globalization and Catching-up in Emerging Market Economies', Leon Kozminski Academy of Entrepreneurship and Management, Warsaw, 16–17 May 2002. Acknowledgements for useful comments are due to Conference participants and in particular to Tadeusz Kowalik, Gur Ofer and George Vojta.

2   World Bank (2001) treats globalization and integration as synonyms: 'Integration – or "globalization" – …', p. 1.

3   This is what President George Bush Jr. might have had in mind when he said, in the course of his presidential campaign, that 'Today most of our imports come from abroad…'.

4   Intra-industry trade is measured by the Grubel-Lloyd index, equal to:
     $1 - Sum|Xi - Mi|/Sum(Xi + Mi)$, where Xi and Mi are respectively the exports and imports of the i-th product.

5   Clearly a sufficient degree of transport and communications development is needed to have international trade at all, but for any given level and variation of transport and communications costs, what counts is whether the economy has or has not reached an allocation of resources that might have obtained if the world was a single country.

6   Each of the major international crises since 1994 (Mexico 1994, Thailand, Indonesia and Korea 1997, Russia and Brazil 1998, Turkey 2000, Argentina 2001) involved a fixed or pegged rate regime, whereas countries which did not have pegged rates (e.g. South Africa and Israel 1998, Mexico 1998, Turkey 1998) avoided that kind of serious crisis.

7   This puzzle comes in two versions: the Meese and Rogoff (1983) forecasting puzzle and the Baxter-Stockman (1989) neutrality-of-exchange-rate-regime puzzle; see Ostfeld and Rogoff (2000) for an illustration.

References

Acting Managing Director of the IMF (2000), *Statement and Report* to the International Monetary and Financial Committee on Progress in Reforming the IMF and strengthening the Architecture of the International Financial System, 20 April, Washington.

Anderson, Sarah and Cavanagh, John (2000), 'Top 200: the Rise of Corporate Global Power', Institute for Policy Studies, Washington DC, December.

Baldwin, Richard (1995), 'A Domino Theory of Regionalism', in Baldwin, R., P. Haaparanta and J. Kiander (eds), *Expanding Membership in the European Union*, CUP, Cambridge.

Baricco, Alessandro (2002), *Next*, Feltrinelli, Milan.

Bhagwati, Jagdish (2001), 'Globalisation and Appropriate Governance', Annual Lecture No. 4, UN-WIDER, Helsinki.

Cairncross, E. (1997), *The Death of Distance – How the communications revolution will change our lives*, Harvard Business School Press, Boston Ma.

Commander, Simon, Kangashniemi, Mari and Winters, L. Alan (2000), 'The Brain Drain: Curse or Boon? A Survey of the Literature', Seminar Paper, CEPR/NBER, Stockholm, May.

De Grauwe, Paul (2002), 'How Big Are the Big Multinational Companies?', Leuven University, January.

De Melo, Jaime, Montenegro, Claudio and Panagariya, Arvind (1992), 'Regional Integration, Old and New', World Bank WPS 985, Washington.

Department for International Development DfID (2000), *White Paper on International Development*, London, December.
http://www.globalisation.gov.uk

Dimova, Ralitsa (2002), 'Preferential Trade Areas and Global Trade: Friends or Foes', LICOS, Leuven.

Eatwell, John (2002), 'The New International Financial Architecture: Promise or Threat?', CERF-Cambridge Endowment for Research in Finance.

Feldstein, Martin (2000), 'Aspects of Global Economic Integration: Outlook for the Future', NBER Working Paper 7899.
http://www.nber.org/papers

Fischer, Stanley (2001), 'Exchange Rate Regimes: Is the Bipolar View Correct?', IMF, Washington.

Frankel, Jeffrey (2000), 'Globalisation of the Economy', NBER Working Paper 7858, August.
http://www.nber.org/papers

Frankel, Jeffrey and Wei, S.-J. (1996), 'Regionalisation of World Trade and Currencies: Economics and Politics', in J. Frankel (ed.), *The Regionalisation of the World Economy*, Un. of Chicago Press.

G-7 Finance Ministers (2000), *Report to the Heads of State and Government*, 8 July.

Gilbert, C.L., Powell, A. and Vines, David (1999), 'Positioning the World Bank', *Economic Journal* 109, pp. 598–633.

Gilbert, C.L. and Vines, David (eds) (2000), *The World Bank: Structure and Policies*.

Graham, Edward M. (2000), *Fighting the Wrong Enemy: Antiglobal Activists and Multinational Enterprises*, Institute for International Economics, Washington.

IFIAC (chaired by Allan H. Meltzer) (2000), *Report* submitted to the US Congress and the US Treasury, 8 March.

IMF (1998), 'Open Regionalism in a World of Continental Trade Blocs', WP/98/10.

James, Harold (2000), *The End of Globalisation: Lessons from the Great Depression*, Harvard University Press, Cambridge, Ma.

Kaplan, Robert (2001), *The Coming Anarchy: Shattering the Dream of the Post-Cold War*, Random House.

Kolodko, Grzegorz W. (2001), 'Globalisation and Transformation. Illusions and Reality', TIGER Working Papers Series, No. 1, Warsaw.

Kolodko, Grzegorz W. (2002), 'Globalisation and Prospects for Catching-up in Emerging Market Economies', TIGER-WSPiZ, Warsaw.

Krugman, Paul (1991), 'The Move towards Free Trade Zones', Federal Reserve Bank of Kansas City, Conference Proceedings, Yoming.

McMillan, John (1993), 'Does Regional Integration Foster Open Trade? Economic Theory and GATT's art. 24', in Anderson, Kym and Blackhurst, Richard (eds), *Regional Integration and the Global Trading System*, London, Harvester Wheatsheaf.

Milanovic, Branko (1998), 'True World Income Distribution, 1988 and 1993: First Calculation Based on Household Surveys Alone', World Bank Policy Research working paper.
http://www.worldbank.org/research/transition

Obstfeld, Maurice and Rogoff, Kenneth (2000), 'The Six Major Puzzles in International Macroeconomics: Is there a Common Cause?', in Bernanke, Ben S. and Rogoff, Kenneth, NBER *Macroeconomics Annual 2000*, The MIT Press, Cambridge, Ma., and London.

Portes, Richard (1995), 'Crisis? What Crisis? Orderly Workouts for Sovereign Debtors', CEPR, London.

Portes, Richard (2002), 'Orderly Workouts Redux: New Mechanisms for Restructuring Sovereign Debt', CEEPR seminar paper, London, 16 May.

Rodrik, Dani (1997), *Has Globalisation Gone Too Far?*, Institute for International Economics, Washington DC.

Rogoff, Kenneth (2001), 'Why not a Global Currency?', *American Economic Review*, Papers and Proceedings, May, pp. 243–47.

Soloaga, Isidro and Winters, L. Alan (2001), 'Regionalism in the Nineties: What Effect on Trade?', World Bank, Washington.

Stiglitz, Joseph (1995), *Wither socialism?*, Harvard University Press.

Stiglitz, Joseph (2000), 'What I learned at the World Economic Crisis', *New Republic*, 17 April.

Summers, Lawrence (1991), 'Regionalism in the World Trading System', Federal Reserve Bank of Kansas City, Conference Proceedings, Yoming.

US Congress-Joint Economic Committee, Consultative Commission on international financial institutions (2000), *The Meltzer Report*, Washington.
http://www.house.gov/jec/imf/meltzer.pdf
Viner, Jacob (1950), *The Custom Unions Issue*, New York, Carnegie Endowment for International Peace.
Winters, L. Alan (1996), 'Regionalism versus Multilateralism', WPS 1687, The World Bank.
Wood, Adrian (2002), 'The Puzzling Effects of Globalisation on Unskilled Workers in Developing Countries', Seminar Paper, London Business School.
World Bank (2000), *Trade Blocs*, Washington DC.
http://www.worldbank.org
World Bank (2001), *Globalisation, Growth and Poverty*, Washington DC.
http://www.worldbank.org
World Bank (2002), *Ten Years of Transition*, Washington DC.
http://www.worldbank.org

PART II
ECONOMIC GROWTH IN THE MORE AND THE LESS GLOBALIZED ECONOMIES

Chapter 4

Globalization and Economic Development: Can Sub-Saharan Africa Avoid Marginalization?[1]

Nguyuru H. I. Lipumba

1. Introduction

Globalization has become one of the most politically charged issues in the world. To some it is an extension of the imperialist expansion of old, responsible for the increasing poverty, worsening income distribution and environmental degradation of developing countries. To others it is a panacea for economic development. What is needed for any poor country to attain a high growth of per capita income and join the convergence club is putting in place an institutional framework and adopting policies that promote free international trade and movement of capital. The world economy has experienced remarkable integration since 1950. The last two decades of the twentieth century have witnessed an acceleration of the process of globalization. The driving forces of globalization are technology, tastes and national and international policies (Mussa, 2001). The revolution in telecommunication and information technology has facilitated the globalization of the world economy in which integrated cross-border organization of economic activity, including production, trade, investment, financial flows, information flows and technology transfer is increasing and expanding. The tastes of consumers do not discriminate between goods and services of similar quality that are produced in foreign lands but are cheaper than local products. Government policies have facilitated the removal of barriers to international trade and foreign direct investment.

Not all countries and certainly only a few people in Sub-Saharan Africa (SSA) are participating in the global economy. Many rural Africans depend on subsistence production for their supply of food and housing. Lack of adequate physical and institutional infrastructure has drastically reduced opportunities for rural Africans to participate beneficially in the global economy. National markets in SSA are small and not internally integrated. Poor domestic transport and communication systems make major ports and cities better linked with the rest of the world than with their own hinterlands. Africa is the last frontier of the development challenge.

Is SSA being marginalized in the global economy because of bad domestic policies, or because of unequal and exploitative terms of integration into the global economy? Does globalization offer poor African countries an opportunity to leapfrog several decades of development, if they combine their low wages with basic education, technical skills and export-led growth to take advantage of the rapidly opening global markets? Can globalization be managed to promote pro-poor growth that utilizes abundant labor, generates employment and avoids ruthless growth that increases income inequality and the ranks of the poor?

To promote broad-based growth and development, Africa does not have a choice of disengaging from the global economy. Most countries that have achieved economic development have at least effectively utilized available trade opportunities. Countries that failed to promote exports have fallen behind. The challenge at the national level is to design policies that take advantage of the opportunities offered by the global economy while minimizing the risk of inappropriate exposure to global currents. The development strategy should focus on improving the investment climate for both domestic and foreign investors and increasing the capability of Africans, particularly the poor, to gainfully participate in a market economy.

After this introduction, Section 2 discusses SSA's decreasing participation in the global economy, largely focusing on its decreasing share in global trade and capital flows, particularly foreign direct investment. Section 3 of the paper analyses what the international community should do to assist SSA to integrate into the global economy. Section 4 discusses policies to integrate Africa in the global economy while promoting broad-based development.

2. African Participation in the Global Economy

The marginalization of Sub-Saharan Africa can be observed in the region's decreasing share in world trade. Africa's share in total world exports decreased from an average of 4.0 per cent in 1960–69 to 1.5 per cent in 1990–99. The marginalization of SSA in world trade is largely a product of low growth of output and domestic supply constraints. Growth of output in SSA has been lower than in other regions, particularly East Asia. The share of SSA in world gross domestic product (GDP) decreased from 2.2 per cent in 1960–69 to 1.2 per cent in 1990–99 (see Table 4.1).

Table 4.1: Regional share in world GDP and exports of goods and services (%)

1 (a) Regional share in world GDP

	1960–69	1970–79	1980–89	1990–99
East Asia & Pacific	5.3	4.9	4.6	5.6
High income OECD countries	74.2	73.8	74.2	77.2
Latin America & Caribbean	5.8	6.3	6.0	6.1
Middle East & North Africa	1.3	2.3	2.9	1.8
South Asia	3.4	2.3	2.1	1.7
Sub-Saharan Africa	2.2	2.2	1.8	1.2
World	100.0	100.0	100.0	100.0

1 (b) Regional shares in world exports of goods and services

	1960–69	1970–79	1980–89	1990–99
East Asia & Pacific	2.2	3.0	4.9	7.9
High income OECD countries	71.6	69.9	68.2	68.2
Latin America & Caribbean	5.4	4.3	4.4	4.3
Middle East & North Africa	2.5	5.5	4.1	2.6
South Asia	n/a	0.8	0.8	0.9
Sub-Saharan Africa	4.0	2.9	2.3	1.5
World	100.0	100.0	100.0	100.0

As the output elasticity of trade is usually greater than one, the export share has fallen more sharply than the GDP share. Over 70 per cent of the African labor force is employed in agriculture, and thus Africa should have a comparative advantage in agricultural products. Sub-Saharan Africa continues to produce and export primary products, facing weak world demand and decreasing world market prices. The share of primary products in the value of world trade is decreasing, because of their low income and price elasticities of demand. The share of African agricultural exports in the world total has, however, decreased from 11.8 per cent in 1961 to 3.6 per cent in 1999. The region has lost share in its major agricultural exports; for example, its share of world coffee exports decreased from 29.5 per cent in 1975 to 11.4 per cent in 1999 (Figure 4.1).

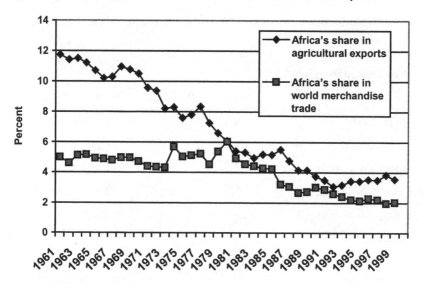

Figure 4.1: Africa's share in world trade

The failure to maintain market share in its major agricultural exports and diversify into other products has contributed to the rapid increase in the number of the poor in the rural areas of Africa.

Sub-Saharan Africa's share in world exports of goods and services continues to be larger than its share in world GDP. Among developing regions, only East Asia has a share in world exports of goods and services that exceeds its share of the world GDP by a larger margin than that of Sub-Saharan Africa. Latin America's share in world GDP is larger than its share in world exports of goods and services. The marginalization of Africa is largely due to the failure of growth and not to a lower share of trade as a percentage of output. The fall in Sub-Saharan Africa's share in global trade is a symptom of the failure to sustain economic growth.

The long-term growth performance of SSA as a region has been disappointing. Per capita income measured in 1995 dollars has hardly grown (only 0.2 per cent per year) over the past four decades (Table 4.2). In contrast, the East Asia and Pacific Region recorded a per capita GDP growth rate of 5.3 per cent per annum over the 1960–99 period. At the average growth rate of 0.2 per cent, SSA will require more than three centuries to double its per capita income while East Asia has been doubling its per capita income every fourteen years. As a result of a high growth rate of per capita income, East Asian countries have been converging towards the high-income OECD countries. Growth of per capita income in SSA has been decelerating. The decade of highest per capita growth was the 1960s. In the past two decades SSA has registered negative growth of per capita GDP. In Latin America, the 1980s is usually considered a lost decade because of the negative growth rate of per capita income that was associated with the debt crisis.

For SSA as a region, both the 1980s and 1990s were lost. Africa has not emerged and joined the convergence club of countries that are growing fast and steadily converging to technological and high-income leaders of the world.

Table 4.2: Regional growth of GDP and GDP per capita (%)

Region	1960–99	1960–70	1970–80	1980–90	1990–99
	Growth of GDP				
East Asia & Pacific	7.2	5.9	6.8	8.0	7.5
High income OECD countries	3.4	5.4	3.4	3.3	2.2
Latin America & the Caribbean	3.9	5.2	5.6	1.7	3.4
Middle East & North Africa	n/a	n/a	n/a	2.0	3.0
South Asia	4.5	4.0	3.4	5.6	5.6
Sub-Saharan Africa	3.0	5.2	3.3	1.7	2.2
World	3.6	5.4	3.8	3.4	2.5
	Growth of GDP per capita				
East Asia & Pacific	5.3	3.4	4.7	6.3	6.1
High income OECD countries	2.7	4.4	2.6	2.7	1.6
Latin America & the Caribbean	1.6	2.4	3.1	–0.2	1.8
Middle East & North Africa	n/a	n/a	n/a	–1.1	0.8
South Asia	2.1	1.6	1.0	3.4	3.6
Sub-Saharan Africa	0.2	2.5	0.5	–1.2	–0.4
World	1.8	3.3	1.9	1.6	1.1

The poor growth performance is also reflected in the volumes of exports. Annual growth of SSA exports has only averaged 2.7 per cent compared to the world annual average of 6.1 per cent, and the East Asia and Pacific region annual average of 9.8 per cent. For small economies, such as those of Africa, growth of exports is necessary for financing imports of capital goods and intermediate inputs needed for the expansion of the production capacity and full utilization of existing capacity, and the tapping of the economies of scale.

Countries that have successfully integrated into the global economy have recorded a high growth of manufactured exports and have increased their share in total exports. In the East Asia region, the share of manufactured goods in total merchandise exports have increased from 25 per cent in 1965 to 45 per cent in 1980 and 81 per cent in 1998, similar to the share of high-income OECD countries.

SSA has continued to depend on primary exports throughout the 1960s to the 1980s. The share of manufactured exports increased in the 1990s and reached 39 per cent, but is still the lowest in all regions except the oil-rich Middle East (Table 4.3).

Table 4.3: Manufactured exports (% of merchandise exports)

	1965	1970	1975	1980	1991	1995	1998
East Asia & Pacific	25.0	32.1	38.9	44.8	72.6	78.9	81.0
High income OECD countries	69.2	73.3	74.1	72.7	78.6	79.3	81.4
Latin America & the Caribbean	8.6	15.9	21.2	19.7	37.1	45.0	48.8
Middle East & North Africa	5.2	6.0	5.6	7.6	14.9	20.3	20.7
South Asia	41.7	48.2	44.6	53.8	72.9	76.3	78.7
Sub-Saharan Africa	17.2	18.8	15.2	12.4	20.2	34.1	38.5
Low & middle income	18.6	24.0	28.3	32.0	55.8	63.3	63.6
World	59.1	63.8	65.8	65.9	74.4	76.9	78.3

Source: World Bank World Development Indicators.

Sub-Saharan Africa is not homogeneous. Trade performance is not uniform across the region (Rodrik, 1998). Botswana and Mauritius have done well but the overall trend in most African countries since 1980 has been falling market shares. The African giants, South Africa and Nigeria, also have lost market shares in world exports. This is largely the result of stagnant economies and export concentration on commodities with falling prices.

African countries have not yet exhausted the potential expansion of agricultural exports, but they also need to diversify away from tropical beverages into manufactured goods without losing their market share of agriculture exports.

2.1.   Capital Inflows to Sub-Saharan Africa

Developing countries as a group experienced a phenomenal increase in resource inflows during the 1990s. Aggregate net resource flows to all developing countries (including economies in transition) increased by a factor of two between 1990 and 1993. The increase of aggregate transfers (net of debt service payments and repatriated profits) was more than five-fold between 1990 and 1993, and more than eight-fold between 1990 and 1997 (see Table 4.4).

Table 4.4: Aggregate net transfers, annual average (USD, billion)

Region	1970–74	1975–79	1980–84	1985–89	1990–94	1995–99
East Asia and Pacific	2.2	3.5	4.5	0.4	37.9	72.8
Europe and Central Asia	0.7	3.6	3.2	-2.9	13.7	33.7
Latin America and the Caribbean	3.2	10.7	1.4	-17.8	15.7	56.6
Middle East and North Africa	-2.5	2.6	2.1	6.1	3.0	1.6
South Asia	1.5	3.0	5.2	7.9	6.7	6.1
Sub-Saharan Africa	1.3	4.5	6.8	8.5	9.8	10.6
All developing countries	6.4	27.8	23.3	2.1	86.7	181.3

Source: Computed using data from World Bank Global Development Finance 2000.

The 1997 Asian financial crisis caused a sharp decrease in net transfers not only to the East Asian region, but also to other regions, including Sub-Saharan Africa.

The capital flows to developing countries became increasingly dominated by private flows. In 1990, private flows accounted for 44 per cent of all aggregate net resource flows to developing countries, and by 1996, this proportion increased to 89 per cent. The Asian financial crisis of 1997 not only decreased aggregate net resource flows but also the share of private capital flows that decreased to 75 per cent in 1999. Aggregate figures for the developing countries mask enormous country-specific and regional differences. The East Asian and Pacific region has been the main beneficiary of private capital inflows, receiving 45 per cent and 35 per cent of all inflows during the 1990–94 and 1995–9 periods, respectively. Latin America emerged from the 1980s debt crisis (when it was transferring resources to the developed countries) and started receiving net resource transfers. SSA received only 2.3 per cent of private capital flows from 1990 to 1994. The share of private capital flows destined to SSA has fallen over time (see Table 4.5).

Table 4.5: Regional shares of private capital flows (%)

	1970– 74	1975– 79	1980– 84	1985– 89	1990– 94	1995– 99
East Asia & Pacific	17.0	14.9	23.3	26.5	45.0	35.0
Europe & Central Asia	5.9	6.9	10.2	15.9	12.0	16.2
Latin America & the Caribbean	66.5	56.7	50.1	19.3	33.9	40.7
Middle East & North Africa	–0.2	12.1	4.9	18.3	2.7	1.9
South Asia	0.8	0.4	3.8	11.9	4.1	2.7
Sub-Saharan Africa	9.9	9.1	7.7	7.3	2.3	3.5
Low & middle income	100.0	100.0	100.0	100.0	100.0	100.0

Private capital flows as a share of total resource flows have been decreasing in SSA but increasing in all other developing regions. The causes of declining shares of private capital inflows to Sub-Saharan Africa include low economic growth and small markets, policy environments that are not conducive to investment, high perceived risk, weak institutions, and debt overhang.

Africa is increasingly dependent on official flows and receives the highest per capita aid compared to all developing regions (Figure 4.2). Aggregate official flows to all developing countries are decreasing in nominal and real terms. From 1994 to 1999, official development assistance to SSA fell by 35 per cent in nominal terms, despite the fact that more countries implemented market-friendly reforms. With the end of the cold war, the United States has drastically reduced development assistance to all countries except Israel, which is a high-income country. It seems only Denmark, Luxembourg, the Netherlands, Norway and Sweden continue to be politically committed to international solidarity of contributing at least 0.7 per cent of their GNP to development assistance. African countries will need to effectively use the decreasing development assistance and increasingly tap global private-capital markets to supplement their domestic savings.

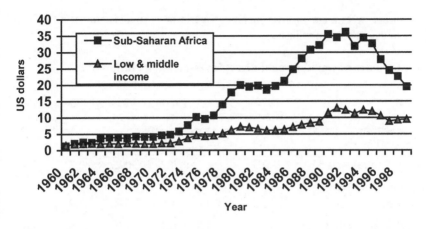

Figure 4.2: **Aid per capita 1960–99**

2.2. Foreign Direct Investment

In the 1990s, there was a dramatic increase in foreign direct investment, mainly in the high-income OECD countries – particularly, the European Union, Japan and the United States. The liberalization of the capital account transactions within the OECD, which began in the 1970s and was largely completed in the first half of the 1980s, laid the foundation for the explosion of foreign direct investment in these countries, mainly in the form of mergers and acquisitions. Developing countries also experienced a surge of foreign direct investment inflows in the 1990s, but this increase has generally bypassed most African countries. Despite the shortage of capital in sub-Saharan countries, capital inflows have been limited. Foreign direct investment is concentrated among the industrialized countries and only a few emerging economies. The share of global foreign direct investment inflows to Sub-Saharan Africa has been decreasing (Table 4.6). The United Nations' *World Investment Report 2001* estimates that in 2000 the developed countries accounted for three quarters of the inward foreign direct investment inflows. In the 1990s, the share of emerging and developing economies has increased from 12.6 per cent in 1990 to 40.4 per cent in 1994, only to decrease to 19.0 per cent in 2000. The whole of Sub-Saharan Africa, however, accounted for only 0.9 per cent of the inward foreign direct investment inflow in 1999, compared to 4.6 per cent and 1.4 per cent in 1972 and 1995, respectively.

From 1990 to 1999, SSA accounted for less than 1.2 per cent of the total foreign direct investment to all developing countries, despite the fact that rates of return on foreign direct investment in SSA averaged 24–30 per cent, compared to 16–18 per cent for all developing countries (Bhattacharya, Montiel and Sharma, 1997; World Bank, 1997). Most of the foreign direct investment was in natural resource extraction, particularly in the petroleum sector. The leading recipients of foreign direct investment inflows include Nigeria and Angola; almost all of it is directed to the petroleum industry.

Table 4.6: Share of world foreign direct investment, net inflows %

	1970–74	1975–79	1980–84	1985–89	1990–94	1995–99
East Asia & Pacific	3.5	3.9	4.9	4.6	13.1	12.7
Europe & Central Asia	0.5	0.2	0.2	0.2	2.3	4.3
Latin America & the Caribbean	11.6	11.9	11.0	5.2	7.9	11.3
Middle East & North Africa	-4.5	1.9	0.1	1.7	1.6	0.6
South Asia	0.4	0.2	0.3	0.3	0.4	0.8
Sub-Saharan Africa	3.4	3.3	1.4	1.3	1.0	1.3
High income OECD countries	83.3	76.7	79.1	84.5	70.8	66.9
Developing countries	14.9	21.5	17.9	13.4	26.3	31.0
World	100.0	100.0	100.0	100.0	100.0	100.0

	1994	1995	1996	1997	1998	1999
East Asia & Pacific	19.3	16.6	16.6	14.4	9.6	6.3
Europe & Central Asia	2.9	5.3	4.4	5.2	3.8	3.0
Latin America & the Caribbean	11.8	9.3	11.8	14.3	10.9	10.2
Middle East & North Africa	1.3	-0.1	0.6	1.1	1.0	0.2
South Asia	0.7	0.9	1.0	1.1	0.5	0.3
Sub-Saharan Africa	1.4	1.4	1.4	1.8	1.0	0.9
High income OECD countries	58.7	63.8	61.1	59.7	72.0	77.9
Developing countries	37.5	33.4	35.9	37.9	26.8	21.0
World	100.0	100.0	100.0	100.0	100.0	100.0

Source: World Development Indicators 2001.

2.3.   Can African Countries Attract Private Capital Inflows?

African countries need to design their development strategies that take into consideration their own realities without falling into the trap of believing that 'open trade and investment policies are the surest ways to achieve economic growth and poverty alleviation.' As Rodrik (2001) has argued for developing countries as a whole, 'Policy makers need to forge a *domestic* growth strategy, relying on domestic investors and domestic institutions.' Policy makers should aim at improving the investment climate facing their own small and medium-scale enterprises rather than providing subsidies and tax breaks to attract foreign investment. At their current level of development, however, foreign capital can supplement domestic savings. Official development assistance is likely to continue decreasing despite major improvements in the economic policies of African countries.

Access to private foreign capital can facilitate the transfer of technology necessary for sustaining economic growth and structural transformation. Foreign direct investment is the appropriate form of capital flow. The key question is what policies are required to attract these flows?

2.4.   Macroeconomic Stability

Most African countries have liberalized their foreign exchange markets and have made their currency convertible for current account transactions. Inflation rates in most countries not experiencing civil wars are moderate and declining, below the 40 per cent threshold considered by Barro (1997) and Bruno and Easterly (1997) to be harmful, and thus not very likely to cause a decrease in long-term growth. At least 30 African countries has had single digit inflation rates in the past 3–5 years. Parallel market exchange rate premiums are disappearing. By 1997 at least 35 Sub-Saharan African countries had exchange rate premiums of less than 10 per cent.

However, many African countries are far from macroeconomic stability, with unsustainable fiscal deficits and an accumulation of external and domestic payment arrears. In many cases inflation control has been achieved by the use of the cash budget under the auspices of the IMF-supervised stabilization program. Many countries, including Côte d'Ivoire and Nigeria, have huge debt payments arrears, which hinder access to commercial bank loans and any possibility of attracting portfolio flows, even to their national stock exchanges.

Despite the extensive liberalization that has been undertaken in many sub-Saharan countries, the continent is perceived as largely economically unfree. The Heritage Foundation/*Wall Street Journal* 1998 Index of Economic Freedom Report concludes that:

> Sub-Saharan Africa remains the most economically unfree – and by far the poorest – area in the world. Of the 38 sub-Saharan African countries graded, none received a rating of free. Only 7 received a rating of mostly free, 25 were rated unfree, and 6 were

rated repressed. Economic freedom in sub-Saharan Africa, in fact, declined in 1997; 11 countries (29 per cent) received lower scores this year, while 9 (24 per cent) improved their scores.

2.5.   Small Markets

Sub-Saharan African countries have very small economies. Compared to the value of GDP of the whole of SSA, China's economy is more than three time as large, Brazil is almost two and a half times as large, Mexico is more than one and half times as large, and India is almost one and half times as large. What would be the long-term economic viability of Mexico if it were divided into 48 independent states, most of them with their own currencies, visa requirements for traveling, and independent trade policies with customs inspection in all major border crossings?

South Africa accounts for around 40 per cent of the Sub-Sahara Africa GDP. Nigeria accounts for another 10 per cent. The remaining 46 countries have a combined GDP of 90 per cent of that of Denmark. Most African countries have GDP levels similar to that of a medium-size European town. The 1998 GDP estimates show that each of the 46 countries had GDP of less than 12 billion dollars. Twelve countries had GDP value of less than one billion dollars. In addition to being small markets, 19 Sub-Saharan countries are land locked. Balkanized Africa cannot attract large inflows of foreign direct investment.

Regional economic integration is necessary for Africa to gainfully participate in a globalizing world. The quest for economic integration has dominated African development thinking and intergovernmental conferences. There is, however, a proliferation of Regional Integration schemes with limited practical achievements. Lack of success in implementing various regional integration schemes did not deter African heads of states from declaring the formation of the African Union in 2001.

Most of Africa's regional integrating schemes followed a model of 'closed' regionalism that aimed at creating trade barriers to the rest of the world. Despite the proliferation of regional integration schemes since the 1960s, intra-African trade accounts for only 10 per cent of total external trade of Africa. Inward looking regional economic integration has failed in Sub-Saharan Africa (World Bank, 2000; Oyejide et al., 1998).

Africa is now increasingly committed to open regional economic integration. President Abdoulaye Wade (2001) of Senegal has argued in his Plan Omega:

At a time when financial markets are globalizing and foreign direct investment is booming and both production networks and trade in goods and services are going transnational, Africa should be plugging into the new global economic deal. Globalization is a major challenge that should be met with a global and comprehensive vision of African development that will speed up the sustainable economic growth of African countries within a perspective of regional integration.

The main stumbling block to open regional integration is poor infrastructure within and among African countries. The New Partnership for African Development has noted that

> [u]nless the issue of infrastructure development is addressed on a planned basis – that is, linked to regional integrated development – the renewal process of the continent will not take off. Therefore, the international community is urged to support Africa in accelerating the development of infrastructure.

Effective regional integration schemes require a convergence of political systems towards democratic governance and their legitimacy within each polity. The African Union in many respects follows the European Union model. African leaders should seriously take into consideration that

> from the very beginning, the model of integration pursued by Europe has gone beyond the economic sphere. It now entails significant political and legal integration – with a directly elected Parliament, a European Court of Justice, and a common legal and regulatory architecture that spans more than 80,000 pages (Rodrik, 2001b).

2.6. Good Governance

The rule of law is the extent to which the country's institutional arrangements effectively provide for the implementation of laws of the land, protect the security of individuals and their property, adjudicate disputes, provide orderly, but not necessarily democratic, succession of power. Political stability and the rule of law have been lacking in many African countries. Both the levels of investment and the efficient utilization of the existing capital stock and labor are affected by the rule of law.

African leaders increasingly appreciate the importance of good governance, at least in their statements. In the New Partnership for African Development they have argued:

> It is now generally acknowledged that development is impossible in the absence of true democracy, respect for human rights, peace and good governance. With the New Partnership for Africa's Development [NEPAD], Africa undertakes to respect the global standards of democracy, whose core components include political pluralism, allowing for the existence of several political parties and workers' unions, fair, open, free and democratic elections periodically organized to enable the populace choose their leaders freely.

The democratization process is gaining momentum in Africa. South Africa is the leading democratic country in the region. Botswana and Mauritius, the best performing economies in the region, have remained democratic throughout their post-independence period. In 2000, there was good news of the peaceful democratic change of government in Ghana and Senegal. The recent election experience in Zimbabwe has unfortunately put a huge question mark over the African leaders NEPAD commitment to organize 'fair, open, free and democratic elections.'

The most appropriate policy for promoting productive foreign investment is to create an environment conducive to domestic saving and investment. The policy priority for attracting growth-promoting foreign investment is to establish macroeconomic stability, a competitive real exchange rate, efficient infrastructure, and 'rules of the game' that promote saving, investment and enterprise, and improving the human capital base. Building institutions that support stable governance and legitimize the state to its citizens is a necessary ingredient in promoting broad-based development.

3.   What Should be Done by the International Community?

3.1.   Debt Relief and Development Assistance

The extending of loans to African countries was largely influenced by cold war rivalry and less by rational economic calculations of the productivity of external borrowing in African economies. The growth of debt was too high compared to the growth of exports. African governments seem to have perceived most of the external loans as grants. Lenders tended to be in the driver's seat. During the 'Cold War period', the supply of loans created its own demand, regardless of the loans' contribution to economic growth.

Among the 42 countries that are classified by the IMF and World Bank as heavily indebted poor countries (HIPCs), 35 are in Sub-Saharan Africa. The implementation of the HIPC initiative has been very slow. Largely as a result of intense pressure from international civic organizations, such as Oxfam and Caford, as well as the anti-globalization 'brigade' that has been tormenting conferences of international institutions, the IMF and World Bank have speeded up the debt relief qualification process for eligible countries. Many of the HIPC debt relief packages were approved only in late 2000. As of March 2002, four countries: Bolivia, Uganda, Mozambique and Tanzania had reached completion point and received large debt relief. Other 21 countries had reached decision point at which bilateral and multilateral donors start reducing debt service payments to enable the eligible countries to commit more resources to measures that can reduce poverty.

For the 24 countries that have benefited, the IMF and World Bank estimate that debt service falling due over 2001–2003 will on average be about 30 per cent lower than the actual payments in 1998–9, averaging 8 per cent of exports – less than a half of what the typical developing country pays – or 12 per cent of government revenue – about half the 1998–9 share.

Oxfam (May 2001) argues that

of the twenty-two countries receiving debt relief, three-quarters will be spending over ten per cent of government revenue on debt this year. Sixteen countries will be spending more on debt than on the health of their citizens, and ten will be spending more on debt than on primary education and health combined. Oxfam is calling for deeper and wider debt relief, and for 100 per cent cancellation of IMF and World Bank debt.

In defense of the enhanced HIPC Initiative, the IMF and World Bank have pointed out that

Before the HIPC Initiative, eligible countries were on average spending slightly more on debt service than on health and education combined. For the first 24 countries that have qualified for HIPC relief, this is no longer the case: all of them are now spending more on social services than debt service, on average more than triple; and all have shown a marked increase in the share of health and education in their budgets under their recent IMF-supported programs.

The IMF and World Bank are opposed to 100 per cent debt cancellation on the flimsy ground that 'debt relief comes at a cost.' As Cohen (2000) has pointed out,

the HIPC initiative is distorted by the fact that – contrary to the Brady deal itself – it lacks all perspective on the 'market value' of the debt which is written down. The appropriate 'market value' is one that takes account of the risk of non-payment: arrears, rescheduling and 'constrained' refinancing of various sorts. The (HIPC) initiative is about ten times less generous than face value accounting would suggest.

The Bretton Woods Institutions have dragged their feet in providing debt relief to poor countries. They first argued that their special privileged creditor status should be protected at any cost, so that they can raise funds in capital markets at low interest rates. Their debt could not be rescheduled, let alone cancelled. It was only intense pressure from developed countries' civil society that led to the HIPC initiative. They oversold the first HIPC initiative as adequate to reduce the external debt of poor countries to sustainable levels, which was not true, and thus the Extended HIPC Initiative was introduced.

Cancellation of external debt per se will not deliver enough resources to implement growth and poverty-reduction strategies. The limited capability of African governments needs to be directed in designing and implementing national poverty-reduction and growth strategies. This means creating delivery capacity for social policy, better expenditure management, and the many other elements of economic, social, political and institutional reform. Scarce technical capacity available in Central Banks and Ministries of Finance is being utilized to prepare phony debt sustainability analyses and compile information for voluminous decision and completion point documents. Poor countries should receive 100 per cent debt cancellation and new development assistance to deserving countries should be in the form of grants.

In The New Partnership for African Development, African leaders have pledged to ensure that the continent achieves the agreed International Development Goals (IDGs), which are:

- to reduce the proportion of people living in extreme poverty by half between 1990 and 2015;
- to enroll all children of school age in primary schools by 2015;
- to make progress towards gender equality and empowering women by eliminating gender disparities in the enrolment in primary and secondary education by 2005;
- to reduce infant and child mortality ratios by two-thirds between 1990 and 2015;
- to reduce maternal mortality ratios by three-quarters between 1990 and 2015;
- to provide access for all who need reproductive health services by 2015;
- to implement national strategies for sustainable development by 2005, so as to reverse the loss of environmental resources by 2015.

The World Bank has estimated that 'it will take on the order of an additional USD 40 to 60 billion a year to reach the Millennium Development Goals – roughly a doubling of current aid flows – to roughly 0.5 per cent of GNP, still well below the 0.7 per cent target agreed to by global leaders years ago.'

Jim Wolfensohn (2002), the World Bank President, has called on rich countries to

commit to matching the efforts of developing countries step by step with a phased-in increase in aid – say an additional USD 10 billion a year for the next 5 years; building to an extra USD 50 billion a year in year five.

It should be noted that USD 50 billion is only a seventh of the subsidies of USD 350 billion a year provided, in rich OECD countries, as farm support that goes mainly to a relatively small number of agribusinesses, many of which are large corporations.

3.2.   A Development Trade Round

Africa can diversify its exports into non-traditional products, including labor intensive manufactured goods and services such as tourism. What is needed is correct policies of moving Africa into the global economy, such as production-oriented trade liberalization, better institutions, investment in infrastructure and human capital, and improved public services and supportive environment for private sector development that can initiate and sustain a rapid growth of non-traditional exports. There is no justification for persistent Afro-pessimism. If governments play their part by investing in infrastructure and make current reforms credible by improving the investment climate and eliminating remaining anti-export bias, labor intensive exports will grow. A book written by African researchers, published by the World Bank (2000), has rightly argued that trade policy reforms should be integrated into an overall business plan for economic diversification that include improved infrastructure, better public services delivery, improved education and technical training, stable exchange rate regimes, broadening fiscal base from trade taxes, and an investment strategy for promoting small and medium-scale enterprises.

Open regional integration can promote export growth and diversification not only by enlarging economic space but also by locking in trade reforms. Inward looking regional integration is simply not viable. To benefit from global trade and protect its own interest, Africa should actively participate in multilateral trade negotiations, preferably in regional blocs and in alliance with other developing countries with similar interest. Africa needs improved market access for its agricultural products, processed products and labor intensive manufactured goods, such as textiles and clothing. Africa should negotiate hard to exclude trade restrictions on developing countries' exports based on labor standards and environmental issues.

Africa should insist on 'dramatic reduction of agricultural subsidies in rich countries – which currently stand at USD 350 billion a year, roughly seven times what rich countries spend on development aid' (World Bank, 2001). The least developed African countries should also insist on special and differential treatment in meeting WTO obligations. As Finger and Schuler (1999) have noted,

> WTO obligations reflect little awareness of development problems and little appreciation of the capacities of the least developed countries. In most cases standards have been developed with little input form the least developed countries, undermining their sense of ownership.

For some African countries, 'implementing WTO obligations would cost as much as entire year development budget.'

4. Policies for Promoting Development in a Globalizing World

Participating in the global economy through trade and attracting investment is important for growth and human development. We have shown that Sub-Saharan Africa's decreasing share in world trade does not result from exporting a smaller share of its GDP, but largely from the failure to attain growth and diversification of exports. The falling export volumes and market shares suggest that the binding constraint on Africa's participation in global trade is domestic supply problems rather than inadequate market access. The first challenge is therefore to increase African capability to supply goods that are in demand in a dynamic global economy.

In the past decade, Africa has implemented far-reaching reforms. Most countries have currencies that are convertible for current account transactions. Overvalued exchange rates are no longer a common phenomenon. Quantitative restrictions have been reduced. The number of tariff categories has been reduced and rates lowered. Average rates are still higher in Africa, largely because of Africa's dependence on import duties as a source of fiscal revenue. With a few exceptions of countries recovering from long-term decline, such as Uganda, reforms have not restored the growth that was attained in the 1960s and 1970s. To revive growth, Africa needs more public and private investment and better institutional arrangements, such as credit to smallholder farmers, to promote fair market interactions and create markets where they do not exist.

To increase domestic supply capacity, African countries must continue with the implementation of market-oriented policies and build institutions that complement competitive markets and address problems of market failures. In order for market-enhancing policies to succeed, it is necessary for the governments to be fully in control of the reform process. Reforms should not be imposed as conditionalities for access to World Bank, IMF and donors' resources (Killick, 1998).

To promote broad-based growth that will drastically reduce poverty in Sub-Saharan Africa requires creating a favorable climate for investment and growth and empowering poor people to participate in that growth. The consensus is that sustained growth, expansion and diversification of exports and reduction of poverty is promoted by:

1. Macroeconomic stability in the form of moderate inflation, a competitive exchange rate, and low, broadly defined fiscal deficits (including public enterprise and other semi- autonomous government-funded institutions);
2. Good governance and strong institutions that promote the rule of law with effective law enforcement, control of corruption and limits to bureaucratic harassment, especially in the administration of regulations and taxes;
3. Sound management of public expenditure and allocation of public resources into priority sectors, such as education, health, infrastructure – particularly roads – and agriculture research and extension;
4. A tax system that is simple to manage, broad-based, with low tax rates, capable of generating government revenue equivalent to at least 20 per cent of GDP;
5. A sound domestic banking system, with an adequate supervisory and regulatory framework, and a growing financial system that provides credit at affordable interest rates, not only to medium and large enterprises but also to smallholder farmers and micro enterprises.

Increasing numbers of African governments are improving their macroeconomic management, but it will take time to build high-quality institutions and a sound banking system, providing credit to most people at affordable rates. Building growth-promoting institutions requires specific understanding of local conditions and constraints, as well as experimentation. The challenge to African leaders is to build institutions that will improve the investment climate, taking into consideration their own cultures and historical experiences.

In order to initiate and sustain broad-based growth of 6–8 per cent, Africa needs gross investment rates of 25–30 per cent, which should be efficiently utilized rather than being used to build monuments. Among less developed countries, Africa has the most inadequate infrastructure. For most countries, domestic tax revenues are insufficient for improving basic infrastructure, including rural feeder roads; restructuring and revamping basic primary education systems; reorienting post-primary education toward technical and science-based training; carrying out primary health care, including setting up a system that will provide vaccination against the most common communicable diseases; building agricultural research and extension capability; and strengthening the legal framework to promote productive investment.

African access to private capital markets is limited. Most countries cannot raise money on the international bond market for long-term financing of infrastructure construction. Private sector participation in the provision of infrastructure services should be encouraged wherever possible. It would, however, be a mistake to have any illusions that the private sector can provide most of the infrastructure and utilities that Africa needs in order to develop. African markets are small and perceived to be politically risky. Private investors want to maximize returns and minimize risks. They will invest in countries that offer public guarantees of high prices and a minimum purchase agreement. Prices sufficient to lure private development of electric power and other utilities are likely to be too high for competitive, new manufacturing industries to emerge. Public investment in roads, rehabilitation of railways, power generation, and water supply will continue to be indispensable. African governments are broke; private investors have limited interest at present, except at government-guaranteed rates of return. Concessionary development finance will continue to be indispensable. Effective participation by Africa in the global economy requires international public support for investment in infrastructure and human development.

The 35 per cent fall in nominal official development assistance to Sub-Saharan Africa between 1994 and 1998, even as more countries are implementing market-friendly reforms is alarming. The World Bank and the IMF argue that economic reforms are working in Africa, while reducing support to the region. Public opinion continues to believe that more money is thrown to Africa without any impact on development and poverty reduction. The crisis in development assistance to a Sub-Saharan Africa that is reforming should be highlighted. If the US Congress fails to take a progressive position and provide its share of finance to multilateral development institutions, African countries that are willing to undertake reforms will find it more difficult to initiate and sustain poverty-reducing growth. Africa has succeeded in selling NEPAD to the international community. African leaders should abide by their commitments in NEPAD of practicing good democratic governance, in order to be taken seriously in a globalizing world.

Note

1   This paper is based on research at MESO supported by the Ford Foundation. I have liberally used my paper on Globalization and Human Development written as background paper for the UNDP Human Development Report 1999.

References

African Union (2001), *The New Partnership for African Development* (NEPAD). http://www.nepad.org

Barro, R. (1997), *Determinants of Economic Growth*, MIT Press, Cambridge, Massachusetts.

Bhattacharya, Montiel and Sharma (1997), 'How Can Sub Sahara Africa Attract More Private Capital Flows?' International Monetary Fund, *Finance and Development*, June.

Bruno, M. and Easterly, W. (1997), 'Inflation Crises and Long-Run Growth', *Journal of Monetary Economics.*

Cohen (2000), *The HIPC Initiative: How Really Good Is It?* OECD.

Finger, J. M., and Schuler, P. (2001), 'Implementation of Uruguay Round Commitments: The Development Challenge', in: B. Hoekman and W. Martin (eds), *Developing Countries and the WTO: A Pro-Active Agenda*, Blackwell, Oxford, Great Britain.

Heritage Foundation/*Wall Street Journal* (1998), *The 1998 Index of Economic Freedom*, Heritage Foundation, Washington, DC / *Wall Street Journal.*

Killick, T. (1998), 'Responding to the Aid Crisis', in: *International Monetary and Financial Issues for the 1990s*, Volume 9, United Nations, New York and Geneva.

Mussa, M. (2000), 'Factors Driving Global Economic Integration', paper presented at Federal Reserve Bank of Kansas City Economic Symposium on The Nature of Globalization, Jackson Hole, Wyoming, 26 August 2000.

Oxfam International (1998), 'Making Debt Relief Work: A Test of Political Will', Oxfam International Position Paper, April.

Oyejide, T.A., Ndulu, B.J. and Gunning, J.W. (eds) (1999), *Regional Integration and Trade Liberalization in Sub-Saharan Africa*, Vols. 1 and 2, Macmillan Press, London.

Rodrik (2001), 'Globalization, Growth and Poverty: Is the World Bank Beginning to Get It?' mimeo.

Rodrik (2001b), 'Trading in Illusions', *Foreign Policy* magazine (March/April 2001).

Rodrik, D. (1995), 'Getting Interventions Right: How South Korea and Taiwan Grew Rich', *Economic Policy*, 20 April, pp. 55–107.

Rodrik, D. (1998), 'Trade Policy and Economic Performance in Sub Sahara Africa', National Bureau of Economic Research Working Paper, Number 6562.

Sachs, J. (1999), 'Helping the World's Poorest', *The Economist*, 14 August.

Sachs, J. (ed.) (1989), *Developing Country Debt and Economic Performance*, vols. 1, 2 and 3, University of Chicago Press, Chicago.

Singer (1950), 'The Distribution of Gains between Investing and Borrowing Countries', *American Economic Review*, May.

Stiglitz, J. (1994), 'The Role of the State in Financial Markets', *Proceedings of the World Bank 1993 Annual Conference on Development Economics.*

UNCTAD (United Nations Conference on Trade and Development) (1998), *World Investment Report 2001.*

UNDP (United Nations Development Programme) (1999), *Human Development Report 1999,* Oxford University Press, New York.

UNECA (2001), 'Compact For African Recovery: Operationalising The Millennium Partnership For The African Recovery Programme'.
http://www.uneca.org

Wade Abdoulaye, 'Plan Omega',
http://www.uneca.org

Wolfensohn, James D. (2002), 'A Partnership for Development and Peace', address at the Woodrow Wilson International Center.
http://www.worldbank.org

World Bank (2000), *Trade Blocs,* Washington, DC.

World Bank (2000), *Global Development Finance,* CD-ROM.

World Bank (2000), *Can Africa Claim the 21st Century,* Washington DC: World Bank.

World Bank (2001), *World Development Indicators,* CD-ROM.

World Bank (2001), *Globalization, Growth and Poverty,* Washington DC: World Bank.

Chapter 5

Globalization and Growth in the CIS

Keith Crane and Zbyszko Tabernacki

Introduction

The purpose of this paper is to assess prospects for economic growth in the Commonwealth of Independent States (CIS) through closer integration into the global economy. The paper first briefly sizes the CIS economies. Subsequently, it assesses the extent of integration of the CIS countries into the global economy and how economic integration has developed over the course of the transition. The paper then analyzes the sources of growth in the CIS since the August 1998 financial crisis in Russia and the role international economic integration has played in stimulating this growth. The paper concludes with an evaluation of the prospects for economic growth in the region over the next several years and the role further integration of the CIS into the global economy will play in this process. Although the paper discusses Russia, it focuses heavily on the other CIS member states. The discussion of Russia is often in terms of Russia's economic importance to the other CIS members, rather than the economic performance of Russia itself.

The Economies of the CIS States

The CIS is a regional economic and political organization set up in 1991 after the collapse of the former Soviet Union. Its membership consists of Armenia, Azerbaijan, Belarus, Georgia, Kazakhstan, Kyrgyzstan, Moldova, Russia, Tajikistan, Turkmenistan, Ukraine, and Uzbekistan. The three Baltic states of Estonia, Latvia, and Lithuania chose not to become members, in part because these states wished to underline the illegitimacy of their annexation by the former Soviet Union. The institution is designed to further political and economic cooperation among member states.

In aggregate, the economic output of the CIS is quite respectable. In 2001, aggregate GDP ran 1,186bn 1995 US dollars at purchasing power parity exchange rates, roughly similar to that of Italy (Table 5.1). However, at market exchange rates, output is much smaller, running just USD 413.2bn in 2001, roughly four-fifths the size of the economy of Brazil. The region is the world's largest producer of natural gas and the second largest source of crude oil. With an aggregate population of 281.3 million people, per capita income runs 4,205 1995 dollars at purchasing power parity exchange rates, placing the region in the ranks of the middle income developing countries. The region is not a wealthy one. Per capita incomes are far less than in the countries of Central Europe, let alone Western Europe, although on average they are similar to those in the Balkans.

By a number of measures, the CIS is a very disparate group. Russia is by far the largest member as measured by geographic size, population, and economic output. Russia accounts for 65 per cent of aggregate CIS GDP at purchasing power parity exchange rates and 75 per cent at market exchange rates. Russia is also one of the richest members of the CIS, with a per capita GDP in 2001 of 5,353 1995 dollars at purchasing power parity exchange rates and USD 2,142 at market exchange rates, the highest in the CIS. In terms of population, Russia accounts for 51.3 per cent of the CIS total.

Ukraine is firmly in second place in the CIS in terms of the size of its economy and population. Its GDP accounts for 11.5 per cent of the CIS total at PPP exchange rates and 8.5 per cent at market exchange rates; its population represents 17.4 per cent of the whole. Ukraine is substantially poorer than Russia, with a per capita income of 2,791 1995 dollars at PPP exchange rates, 52 per cent of Russia's, and just USD 796 at market exchange rates, 37 per cent of Russia's.

Three other economies, those of Belarus, Kazakhstan, and Uzbekistan, also contribute appreciably to aggregate CIS GDP: 5.8, 4.1 and 5.6 per cent, respectively. Kazakhstan and, according to official figures, Belarus, are among the richer members of the group with per capita incomes in 1995 dollars at purchasing power parity exchange rates of 3,270 and 6,789, respectively. The very high figure for Belarusian per capita GDP is suspect because of the many statistical problems with Belarusian economic data. At market exchange rates, incomes are USD 1,411 in Kazakhstan and a more realistic USD 1,151 for Belarus. Uzbekistan is much poorer. At market exchange rates, per capita income in Uzbekistan was just USD 444 in 2001.

The remaining seven countries have very small economies and are generally much poorer than the larger countries. In aggregate, in 2001, their GDPs ran just 7.6 per cent of the CIS total and ranged between 6.4bn and 20.6bn 1995 dollars at purchasing power parity exchange rates and between just USD 1.2bn and USD 6.0bn at market exchange rates. Their populations vary between 3.8 million in Armenia and 7.8 million people in Azerbaijan. Per capita incomes are much lower than Russia's, running between 989 1995 dollars at purchasing power parity exchange rates in Tajikistan to 3,824 in Turkmenistan. Although many of these smaller states were the first to recover following their transition recessions, the depth of their economic declines was so steep in the early 1990s, that, at least according to official figures, none of these countries are near to achieving pre-independence levels of output. For example, Armenia, Azerbaijan and Kyrgyzstan reported growth rates in GDP ranging from 6.3 to 8.0 per cent in 2001 and have enjoyed fairly rapid growth since the mid-1990s, but GDP is still less than 75 per cent of pre-independence levels in all three countries. In contrast, the larger, slow reforming or non-reforming countries of Belarus, Turkmenistan, and Uzbekistan claim that GDP is now at or nearing pre-independence levels.

The CIS Economies and Global Integration

The CIS economies have undergone enormous ructions in trading relationships since independence. First, immediately preceding and following independence, the CIS states had to adjust to the collapse of trade with Central and Eastern Europe, especially members of the Council of Mutual Economic Assistance (CMEA). Prior to its dissolution, the Soviet Union traded very heavily with the CMEA countries. Although valuation of this trade is difficult because it was conducted through bilateral trade agreements and was priced in transferable rubles, an accounting unit, trade with the CMEA is estimated to have accounted for at least half of total Soviet trade in the late 1980s.[1] In contrast to exports to Western Europe, the Soviet Union's other major trading partner, which primarily consisted of raw materials and energy, Soviet exports to the CMEA included substantial exports of manufactured products, especially machinery. Once the members of the CMEA began to settle trade in convertible currencies at market prices, trade in machinery and manufactured goods collapsed. We estimate that valued in dollars, in aggregate, Soviet exports to formerly socialist countries fell from USD 41bn in 1985 to just USD 16bn in 1991. Soviet exports of machinery to formerly socialist countries fell from USD 6.3bn in 1986 to just USD 1.3bn in 1991.[2] Because all the members of the CIS had participated, at least indirectly, in this trade, its collapse had a very negative impact on their economies.

Second, and more important, the collapse of the former Soviet Union disrupted supply relationships among all of the CIS member states. The value of pre-independence intra-CIS trade is difficult to quantify because of the distorted prices employed under central planning. Rough estimates of these transactions between Russia and the other former Soviet republics for 1990 and 1991 are very large. We have roughly estimated the dollar value of Russian exports to the other republics in 1990 at USD 76.9bn and imports at USD 52.9bn.[3] In 1991, exports fell to an estimated USD 57.6bn and imports to USD 29.6bn. However, the dollar value of this trade is difficult to compute because it was valued in rubles, which were depreciating rapidly during this period, and because relative prices remained highly distorted for a number of years after the CIS states began their move towards creating market economies.

After 1991, the CIS member states began to collect trade data. A number of countries only included trade settled in dollars in their figures, excluding barter arrangements and trade valued in rubles. Other countries, most notably Kazakhstan and Ukraine, continued to include in these figures at least some trade conducted on the basis of barter or trade agreements that stipulated deliveries in physical quantities. The use of barter was partially dictated by liquidity and payments problems, as initially enterprises had no foreign currency holdings. Most transactions were valued in rubles, but the very high rates of inflation during the period made transactions settled in rubles highly risky, leading to agreements that stipulated physical quantities. Barter also contributed to cash avoidance, as enterprises were free to value bartered goods as they saw fit for tax purposes.

Consequently, the aggregate figures for the CIS countries are not always readily comparable with each other or with our estimates of pre-independence trade flows. However, even these data show that intra-CIS trade fell in the first years after independence (Table 5.3). Total intra-CIS exports dropped from USD 36.5bn in 1992 to USD 30.3bn in 1994. Total intra-CIS imports dropped from USD 40.1bn in 1992 to USD 33.2bn in 1994. (Theoretically, exports and imports should net out to zero, but customs, insurance and freight, invoicing discrepancies, and statistical errors result in a substantial intra-CMEA trade deficit.) Even after inflation rates declined and exchange rates stabilized in the second half of the 1990s, intra-CMEA trade has failed to recover: intra-CMEA exports were lower in 2000 than they were in 1994.

The decline in intra-CIS trade in the 1990s stemmed from a number of factors. One, in many instances, the final product was not competitive. Soviet-era agricultural equipment, trucks, and many types of machinery no longer had markets, especially in the volumes that were manufactured under the centrally-planned system because buyers could purchase better quality used vehicles from West European markets and because traditional buyers no longer had the necessary funds as the state no longer had the wherewithal to channel investment funds to the factories and state and collective farms that had been the main purchasers of these products. The inability of CIS enterprises to find buyers for these products forced a reduction in output and a concomitant fall in demand for imported inputs.

Two, enterprises that managed to find markets for their products began to develop alternative sources of component supplies. Initially these enterprises, especially those that assembled more complicated products such as machinery, stuck to their traditional supply networks. However, after the collapse of the ruble zone in 1992–3, these enterprises could no longer easily make payments to each other. More importantly, after the demise of the centrally dictated price system and as enterprises were forced to survive on their own without benefit of government subsidies, enterprises began to concentrate on generating positive cash flows. At that point in time, purchasers evaluated whether it would be cheaper to purchase from alternative suppliers or produce components internally. As many had substantial surpluses of labor and unused capacity, many chose to produce internally. In addition, higher transport costs have rendered a number of CIS suppliers uncompetitive. By design and happenstance, supply relationships in many industries in the former Soviet Union were very dispersed. In the Soviet era, plants were often sited for political reasons: to provide employment in less developed regions, to please an important Communist Party functionary, or at the behest of the military so as to keep important plants far from the Soviet Union's borders. Once the old, centrally-dictated supply relationships began to fall apart and providers of transport services such as trucking companies and railroads had to recover more of their costs, enterprises no longer had an incentive to bear the high transportation and logistics costs of such a dispersed supply network. Consequently, inter-CIS trade fell.

Some intra-CIS trade survived initially because enterprises were able to offload costs on other economic participants. Manufacturing plants were able to slash their variable costs in the early years of the transition. They stopped paying taxes, wages, utilities, and often failed to pay their suppliers or engage in routine maintenance. However, over time, workers sought alternative means of making a living, suppliers would no longer ship, and delayed maintenance and the failure to invest had severe consequences for factory operations. Many of these enterprises have suffered a slow economic death over the past decade, foretelling the eventual disappearance of these types of transactions.

The declines in intra-CIS trade of the 1990s have left their mark. All of the CIS countries except Moldova and Turkmenistan now export more to the Far Abroad (countries other than members of the CIS) than to CIS member states (See Table 5.2). As of 2000, 80 per cent of aggregate CIS exports went to the Far Abroad. Earlier in the transition, the CIS, especially Russia was the primary export market for most of the CIS countries. In 1992, over four-fifths of Armenia's exports and more than two-thirds of Kazakhstan's went to the CIS. As of 2000, three quarters of Armenia's and Kazakhstan's exports went to the Far Abroad.

Despite these disruptions in traditional trade relations, by 2001, trade as a share of GDP in many of the CIS states was very substantial, in general running over 60 per cent, 147 per cent in the case of Tajikistan. For a number of countries, including Tajikistan, the high ratios of trade to GDP are more a reflection of the very low value of their GDPs at market exchange rates than the strength of their export sectors. Many of the currencies are very weak. Their market value is far below their value at purchasing power parity exchange rates. However, some of the relatively high trade to GDP ratios of the larger CIS economies reflect the recent dynamism of their export sectors. In Kazakhstan, Russia and Ukraine, for example, the share of trade (exports plus imports) as a share of GDP computed at market exchange rates ran 77.8, 60.0 and 95.2 per cent, respectively, in 2000, high even by the standards of wealthier West European economies (Table 5.4).

In all three of these larger countries, exports as a share of GDP are relatively large, 50.1, 42.1, and 46.2 per cent, respectively, in 2000. In contrast, exports as a share of GDP in the smaller, poorer economies are often quite low, running just 15.5 per cent for Armenia and 10.9 per cent for Georgia in 2000. The low share of exports in GDP in these countries reflects the difficulties the smaller countries have encountered in finding markets for their products in the rest of the world. Most of the smaller countries rely on just a few commodities for their exports. For example, Armenia relies on cut diamonds for 35 per cent of its exports, Kyrgyzstan counts on gold for 46 per cent, Uzbekistan is reliant on cotton for a quarter, and Tajikistan depends on aluminum for 40.7 per cent of its exports. Much of the rest of their productive sectors serves the domestic market only.

Exports from CIS member states began to recover in the mid-1990s, but for the smaller CIS countries, the emerging patterns of trade are far different than those immediately following the collapse of the former Soviet Union. Trade in manufactured goods, which accounted for the bulk of pre-independence exchanges, has yet to recover. Where light manufacturing has experienced some rebound, it often involves textiles, clothing, and shoes for domestic consumption, or in the case of Moldova and Ukraine, for export to West European markets. Exports of commodities, especially crude oil, non-ferrous and precious metals, and cotton have gained in importance. These exports generally go to the Far Abroad. The major exports that continue to go to CIS markets have been intermediate industrial goods such as alumina, copper ore, chemical intermediaries, or wood, that are shipped to large processing plants, primarily in Russia. The purchasers then frequently export the final product to West European markets. Output of industrial intermediates has fueled the rise in industrial output in Kazakhstan, Russia, and Ukraine of the past two years.

Although the above three categories of exports (labor-intensive consumer goods, energy and raw materials, and industrial intermediaries) are the primary areas of growth in CIS exports, including those from Russia, two other export categories bear mention. First, because of infrastructure constructed during Soviet times, many of the electric power grids and pipeline networks in the region cross borders. As a consequence, many of the republics are heavily dependent on their neighbors for electric power, natural gas, or refined oil products. These items are very important in inter-CIS trade. Two, as markets have gained a greater role in the CIS, a number of countries have begun to develop market-based industries that cater to consumer demands in the CIS. This is most apparent in the Caucasus and Moldova, where exports of food products, alcoholic beverages, and other consumer goods to Russia and other large CIS markets have been on the rise. Although these regions were traditional producers of these products and had recognized brands during the Soviet period, privatized enterprises are now more aggressively marketing and exporting these products and enjoying some success with these activities.

The shift to more market-based trade has started to generate solid increases in exports. Aggregate CIS exports rose at an average annual rate of 6.5 per cent between 1994 and 2000. However, all of this growth was in trade with the Far Abroad, intra-CIS exports fell slightly during this period. Despite a 39.5 per cent increase in Russia's exports in 2000, export growth in the non-Russian CIS between 1994 and 2000 has been almost as strong as Russia's, running 6.2 per cent per year over the entire period. Even countries like Belarus, Kyrgyzstan, and Uzbekistan have enjoyed substantial export growth since 1994. Export growth has been an important factor in the rapid economic growth rates enjoyed by most CIS countries in the past two years.

Import growth has been determined by exports and the availability of foreign financing. After solid growth between 1994 and 1998, imports plummeted 26.4 per cent in 1999, the year after Russia's financial crisis. Russian imports dropped 33 per cent that year, but almost all other CIS countries also experienced drops in imports in 1999. Russia's default had repercussions across the CIS, triggering declines in the currencies of almost all the other CIS countries. The effects of the depreciation of exchange rates in most CIS countries extended into 2000, as imports, although up 16 per cent from the 1999 low, were still 15 per cent lower than in 1998. Imports and the real effective exchange rates continued to rise in 2001.

CIS suppliers account for a much larger share of imports than they do of exports. They provided 41 per cent of total imports in 2000 even though CIS buyers took only 20 per cent of CIS exports. This anomaly stems from Russia's very large trade surpluses, virtually all of which stem from trade with the Far Abroad. CIS suppliers remain important sources of fuels and electric power, industrial intermediates, and some consumer goods, including food and beverages. However, the Far Abroad has been the most important source of CIS imports since the very early 1990s. Western Europe is a major supplier of investment goods and machinery; East Asia has become an important source of consumer goods and in some instances, industrial components. A joint venture controlled by South Korea's Daewoo in Uzbekistan has precipitated substantial imports of automotive components from South Korea. Turkey is an important trading partner for almost all the CIS countries, including Russia and Ukraine. Turkey exports buses and machinery as well as consumer goods. The United States, historically an important supplier of grain and oil seeds to the former Soviet market, has seen this market fall sharply. However, Western agricultural exporters had been able to substitute exports of meat, including chicken, for feed grains by the mid-1990s. In light of the very small size of their economies, the CIS countries appear to enjoy very appreciable gains in economic welfare from this trade.

In aggregate, the CIS has run very large trade surpluses with the rest of the world since the ruble crisis of 1998. The aggregate surplus peaked at USD 65bn in 2000, 18.8 per cent of aggregate CIS GDP; it shrank in 2001. The large surpluses have been solely due to the energy exporters. Russia's and Kazakhstan's combined trade surpluses exceeded the entire CIS surplus. Azerbaijan and Turkmenistan, the other two large energy exporters, also have had very large merchandise trade surpluses. The external balances of the other countries have been more mixed. The non-energy exporters have generally not run large trade surpluses along the lines of the energy exporters. Tajikistan, Ukraine and Uzbekistan posted surpluses in 2000, but most of the other countries ran trade deficits, some of which were quite large. For example, Armenia, Georgia, and Moldova ran trade deficits equivalent to 12 to 31 per cent of GDP in 2000. These three countries have been recipients of substantial inflows of foreign aid, lending from multilateral financial institutions, and, in the case of Armenia and Georgia, remittances from abroad, enabling them to finance these large deficits.

The very large aggregate trade surplus has translated into a substantial aggregate CIS current account surplus. In 2000, the aggregate current account balance for the CIS was USD 47.4bn, 13.8 per cent of aggregate CIS GDP at market exchange rates. The surplus was almost entirely due to Russia, which ran a surplus of USD 46.3bn by itself. Although the aggregate surplus declined sharply in 2001, it still remained substantial, over 10 per cent of aggregate CIS GDP, again due to Russia. Despite the large aggregate current account surplus, a number of the smaller countries, most notably Armenia, Georgia, Kyrgyzstan, Moldova, and Tajikistan, have been running substantial, eventually unsustainable, current account deficits. Current account deficits for these five countries ranged from 6 to 15 per cent of GDP in 2000, large by international standards.

Those countries that ran substantial current account deficits were able to do so because of external financing from international financial institutions or bilateral credits provided or guaranteed by foreign governments. The IMF and World Bank, in particular, have provided a very significant share of total financing for the smaller CIS states over the course of the transition. These loans have been crucial for all the smaller states. Since August 1998 none of these countries has had access to significant commercial credits. Although external financing is also an indicator of global economic integration, it is not a stable one as lenders are at liberty to cut off borrowers at any particular point in time. Thus, the heavy dependence of the smaller countries on external finance from official sources to fund their very large current account deficits is not a good sign.

In aggregate, CIS debt has actually fallen since 1999, as Russia and Ukraine have paid down some of their foreign debt. However, the smaller countries have added to theirs. Because of substantial current account deficits in the smaller CIS states, foreign debt levels, another indicator of international economic integration, have been rising in these countries. Foreign debt levels exceed 100 per cent of GDP in Kyrgyzstan, Moldova, and Tajikistan. Almost all of this debt has been provided by foreign governments, either through direct loans or guarantees, or international financial institutions such as the IMF and World Bank. Of the government debt, a substantial amount is owed to other CIS countries, especially Russia, primarily for unpaid energy deliveries. Although debt service levels often remain relatively low because many of the loans have been offered at concessional interest rates, the relatively high level of debt is a threat to the long-term health of these smaller CIS countries.

Direct foreign investment as a share of GDP, another indicator of international economic integration, varies greatly in the CIS, from 110 per cent in Moldova to 12 per cent of GDP or less in the case of Belarus, Russia, Ukraine, and Uzbekistan (Table 5.4). Of the larger countries, only Kazakhstan has an appreciable amount of FDI in relation to the size of its economy: 44.5 per cent in 2000. Per capita FDI ranges from USD 25 in Tajikistan to USD 545 in Kazakhstan. It was just USD 160 in Russia in 2000, in contrast to Hungary, where it was USD 2,134. Despite the relatively low levels of per capita FDI in the CIS, companies controlled by foreign investors are the biggest exporters in a number of countries. For example, Armenia's cut diamond exports are processed by Belgian, British, and Israeli firms. A Korean company, Daewoo, has a controlling interest in UzDaewoo, an automobile producer, one of Uzbekistan's three largest exporters, Kyrgyzstan's major exporter, the Kumtor Gold Mine, is controlled by a Canadian company. Two-fifths of Azerbaijan's oil exports are pumped by the Azerbaijan International Operating Company, an international consortium of 10 companies, including BP and Unocal.

In aggregate, foreign direct investment in the CIS has not risen much since 1998, primarily because of suspicions about the business climate in Russia and Ukraine. However, there have been some substantial increases in FDI in the smaller countries because of sales of state-owned assets and in Azerbaijan and Kazakhstan because of foreign investment in oil production.

In short, according to a number of indicators, the CIS countries have made impressive strides towards becoming much more integrated into the global economy since independence in 1991. Export to GDP ratios are respectable by international standards and trade to GDP ratios are substantial. Exports have been increasing at more than 6 per cent per year since 1994 and, after collapsing in 1999 following the Russian default, imports are rising as well.

On other accounts, the CIS countries do not score as well. Foreign direct investment in most countries is relatively low, both on a per capita basis and in proportion to GDP. On the other hand, in some countries gross debt to GDP ratios are quite high, more than 100 per cent of GDP. The region is also subject to large external imbalances. Trade and current account surpluses in Kazakhstan, Russia, and Turkmenistan were very large in 2000, in part because of capital flight. Current account deficits have been unsustainably large in some of the smallest CIS states, threatening substantial economic adjustments in these countries in the near future.

Economic Growth in the CIS and International Economic Integration

Rising exports from the CIS since 1998 have been accompanied by a sea change in economic performance in the region. Although a few of the smaller CIS countries enjoyed very respectable growth rates in the mid-1990s, until 1999 none of the larger economies reported appreciable gains in output. Russia reported its first year of dynamic growth that year as output rose 5.4 per cent. Until the year 2000, the best that Kazakhstan had done was 2.7 per cent growth in 1999. Ukraine had suffered nothing but declines in output.

The last three years have been entirely different for these three countries and have restored the faith of those of us who have argued that the larger CIS countries should be able to generate some of the same increases in output and efficiency that had been experienced in Central Europe and the smaller former Soviet republics earlier in the transition from central planning to market economies. Over the course of the last three years, the turnaround in the three largest CIS economies has been spectacular. In 2000, GDP rose 9.0 per cent in Russia, 9.6 per cent in Kazakhstan, and 5.8 per cent in Ukraine. Growth slowed slightly in Russia in 2001 to 5.0 per cent. But the other two economies reported some of the fastest growth rates in the world. Kazakhstan enjoyed an estimated 13.2 per cent increase in GDP in 2001 and Ukraine, which finally reported an upturn in GDP in 2000, grew an estimated 9.0 per cent. By the end of 2001, the Russian, Ukrainian, and Kazakh economies had cumulatively increased output by 20, 15, and 26 per cent, respectively, over the previous three years. Kazakh government officials are even starting to compare their performance to that of Hungary's, the current economic leader in Central Europe.

What is going on in these economies? Exports have been an important source of economic growth. Kazakhstan and to a lesser extent Russia benefited from higher world market prices for oil in 2000 and 2001. Both countries are also producing more oil, although only in Russia's case is higher output unambiguously tied to the effects of higher oil prices. In Kazakhstan, investment decisions made in earlier years have led to increased output. In Russia, higher oil prices are stimulating investment in the oil sector as Russian companies are reopening wells that had been shut-in and are developing new fields. Both Kazakhstan and Russia also benefited from relatively high world market prices for non-ferrous metals in 2000, although like in the case of oil, prices have since fallen. As ferrous and non-ferrous metals account for a quarter of Kazakhstan's exports, price increases have had a tangible impact on the country's terms of trade. Higher profits by metal exporters triggered investment in these sectors as investors put money into mines and smelters.

However, higher prices for oil and metals are only part of the story. Ukraine, where growth has been more rapid than in Russia and almost as dynamic as Kazakhstan's, is a net energy importer. Terms-of-trade losses from higher oil prices have been appreciable in 2000 and 2001. On a macroeconomic level, growth in all three countries has been fostered by a combination of competitive exchange rates and declining inflation, which has been made possible by sensible monetary policies and prudent budget management. All three countries are currently registering surpluses on their central government budgets. Any latent financing needs are primarily being met through privatization revenues.

Some of the increase in tax revenues, and hence better budgetary performance, has been triggered by profits and better tax payment discipline at large, formerly state-owned enterprises. These companies are taking the lead in integrating the larger CIS economies into the global economy. They have been able to take advantage of the sharp declines in real effective exchange rates after the Russian financial crisis in August 1998. Between 1997 and 1999, the real effective exchange rate fell 44 per cent against the dollar in Russia and Ukraine. In Kazakhstan the decline was less severe: the real effective exchange rate fell 30 per cent from peak to trough. In all three countries, the decline in the real effective exchange rates contributed to a substantial boost in the competitiveness of commodity exports, especially steel, non-ferrous metals, and chemicals.

Despite the sharp depreciation of the exchange rates, except for Russia, inflation never got out of control as it did in the early 1990s. December-on-December inflation peaked at only 25.8 per cent in Ukraine and 18 per cent in

Kazakhstan in 1999, despite the sharp declines in their currencies. In Russia, on the other hand, year-on-year inflation hit 84.5 per cent in 1998, but even there the Central Bank of Russia was able to rein in inflation in 1999 as the December-on-December rate fell to 36.7 per cent. The ability of the central banks in these countries to forestall another bout of very high inflation was crucial for the economic rebound as enterprise managers could focus on improving productivity rather than shuffling payments to push losses due to inflation off on their suppliers.

A sharp real effective depreciation of the local currencies in the context of a fairly benign inflationary environment would have had no effect on growth unless enterprises had responded to these signals. The key difference between 2000 and 1992 has been the creation of a species of transition capitalism in the CIS, in which enterprises pursue profits, not output. As in Central and Eastern Europe, small businesses are playing a key role in this process, accounting for most of the value added generated in a number of industries. Across the CIS, retailing, wholesaling, construction, and road transport are almost exclusively private sector activities, in which small private businesses dominate.

However, much of the increase in output, especially in industry, is being generated by large domestically owned companies. In contrast to Central Europe where subsidiaries of Western companies have played an important role in driving growth, the larger CIS companies are owned by locals or investors from other CIS countries. The state frequently owns smaller portfolio stakes in these companies, but the majority shareholders are firmly in charge. These companies, created out of the remnants of formerly state-owned enterprises, have undergone substantial management changes after the shift in ownership from the state to the private sector. The new owners are focused on cash flow. They insist on getting paid, in contrast to past managements, who let traditional customers run up substantial bills, and in return failed to pay their own suppliers. They also have had an eye for investments with substantial rates of return. The very large increases in investment in Ukraine in 2000 and 2001 and in Russia in 1999 and 2000 were primarily financed by private CIS capital. Even in Kazakhstan, wealthy Kazakh investors are becoming an increasingly important source of investment funds.

These individuals and the senior managers they employ are responsible for the construction of expensive dachas on the outskirts of major cities. They are also constructing modern corporate headquarters buildings in Moscow and now, more frequently, in Almaty and Kiev. Somewhat like successful Asian entrepreneurs, these individuals have a penchant for diffuse, opaque ownership schemes. Similar to their Asian counterparts, the new owners are skillful in hiding profits and moving them to safe locations abroad. Like some Asian entrepreneurs, investment decisions are made by a small group of individuals, usually the owners, at the top of the company. Gut instinct and political analysis often play as important a role in decision-making as financial analysis, although there is a mounting respect for financial skills. Over the past three years, these wealthy entrepreneurs have also shown an interest in acquiring businesses outside their original areas of interest, in the process creating unwieldy conglomerates.

In contrast to a number of Asian entrepreneurs who have had decades to acquire wealth and sources of capital, many of the new entities are actively looking for portfolio or strategic investors from abroad. The absence of functional banking systems in any country in the CIS outside of Kazakhstan and the collapse in foreign financing after the Russian financial crisis have compelled these corporations to rely on retained earnings and depreciation allowances to finance investments, although a rudimentary corporate bond market is rapidly reemerging in Russia. However, many of the larger companies are beginning to again seek finance from abroad. Although outside of Kazakhstan foreign direct investment plays a very modest role in the CIS economies, over the next few years, cross-border flows of investment are set to rise sharply. Initially, these flows often involve investments by other companies or investors from the CIS. In Ukraine, Russian, and, to a lesser extent, Kazakh investors dominate the energy sector. However, as the recovery continues, Western multinationals will play a rising role in the region as marketing, financial, and technological expertise become even more important than capital. In short, continued strong growth in these three economies will depend on inflows of foreign capital and expertise, integrating these economies more closely into that of the rest of the world.

However, the weak financial sectors of Russia and Ukraine will constrain growth in the coming few years. In both countries, financial intermediation remains very underdeveloped. Broad money as a share of GDP runs just 22.1 per cent in Russia and 18.6 per cent in Ukraine. Unfortunately, recent growth in financial intermediation has not been matched by improvements in the allocation of capital or creation of a solvent financial system. The Central Bank of Russia remains firmly unconvinced of the importance of supervising banks, evaluating credit risks, and having banks lend on a risk-weighted rate-of-return basis. *Sberbank*, the largest bank in Russia and the only one to which the government provides a guarantee on deposits, is busy lending to bankrupt Russian companies now that the federal government no longer needs its deposits. It is targeting credits to 'strategic' companies, most of which will not be able to service their loans, and lending at negative real interest rates. In Ukraine, the financial system is also grossly underdeveloped. As in Russia, state-controlled banks hold almost all deposits and account for most assets, many of which are shaky. As shown by the experiences of the Central and East European states, lax financial controls will store up problems for the future, culminating in a collapse of the banking system.

The financial sectors can improve, especially with the involvement of foreign banks. In contrast to Russia and Ukraine, Kazakhstan is developing a modern banking sector. Private banks, especially *Kazkommertsbank*, which holds over a quarter of the entire industry's assets, are well run and focused on making money through their lending operations. In addition, foreign banks are playing an expanding role in the economy. Of 44 banks operating in the country, foreign investors hold strategic stakes in 16.

Slow Reformers Begin to Hurt

While Kazakhstan, Russia, and Ukraine appear to have cobbled together economic systems in which the private sector is finally generating growth, in part by opening their economies to the rest of the world, two of the three members of the CIS that have been most loath to use markets had a poor year in 2001 and face difficult prospects in 2002 and 2003. Belarus, Turkmenistan, and Uzbekistan remain reluctant to reform. Of these countries, Belarus and Uzbekistan are struggling: both are posting slower growth and are attempting to reduce high rates of inflation. Turkmenistan has avoided the same fate due to higher exports of natural gas.

Official statistics still show that both the Belarusian and Uzbek economies are growing. In 2001, GDP in Belarus was up an estimated 3 per cent, but this compares to growth of 5.8 per cent in 2000. The reason for the slowdown in Belarus has been tougher Russian policies on payments for exports to the country. Over the course of the transition, Belarus has survived by trading Soviet-designed machinery for Russian raw materials, which it then processes for sale in West European markets. This strategy worked well in 2000 when Belarus ran a USD 1,548m trade deficit with the CIS, all with Russia, while running a USD 441m trade surplus with non-CIS countries. These proceeds were used to service Belarus's USD 1.2bn foreign debt. In 2001, exports to the CIS (including Russia) were up 7 per cent while imports were down 10 per cent as Russian energy producers took a tougher line with their Belarusian customers. The decline in the CIS trade deficit squeezed Belarusian aggregate demand.

Although tougher Russian payments conditions are a factor in the economic slowdown in 2001, most of Belarus's problems are of its own making. The misallocation of resources to poorly performing collective farms and state-controlled enterprises has reduced living standards. High rates of inflation have heightened commercial uncertainty and slowed growth. For the past five years, Belarus has posted some of the highest inflation rates in the CIS. December-on-December, Belarusian inflation hit 251 per cent in 1999 and was still over 100 per cent in 2000, although it finally declined to an estimated 34 per cent in 2001. The decline in 2001 reflects tighter fiscal and monetary policies. However, government decisions to limit increases in administratively controlled prices to less than cost-recovery levels have also played a modest role. These constraints impose financial and efficiency costs on the economy as utilities fail to generate enough revenues to cover their costs.

Tougher payments conditions from Russia and the quest to reduce inflation are forcing the Belarussians to begrudgingly adopt more market-oriented economic policies and to open the economy more to global forces. The exchange rate has been unified and the ruble is now tied to the Russian ruble through a crawling peg within a fairly wide band. The government has also asked the IMF for assistance. The IMF is monitoring economic policy and developments.

The Uzbek economy is rocky as well. Although growth in GDP has been in the 4 per cent range for the past four years, growth in aggregate demand sank to an estimated 2.3 per cent in 2000 as the current account deficit had to shrink because of external financing constraints. In 2000, Uzbekistan suffered from the financial problems of Daewoo Motor, a major Korean investor that has since gone bankrupt. But the economy has also suffered from lax quasi-fiscal policies because of government price controls on utilities. Export taxes and government-mandated marketing boards have reduced incentives to farmers of cotton and other field crops. Although Uzbekistan has made strides on privatization, especially of small businesses, remaining government price controls have slowed economic growth and are storing up additional adjustment costs in the years ahead.

Smaller CIS Economies Struggle with Budget and Current Account Deficits

While the larger economies are enjoying rapid growth, much of which has been export-led, some of the smaller former Soviet republics are having difficulties controlling their external imbalances. Many of these economies are so tiny that even modest movements in trade or current account balances can easily derail growth. Tajikistan enjoyed estimated growth in GDP of 10.3 per cent in 2001, following an 8.3 per cent increase in 2000. However, rapid growth has come courtesy of a widening current account deficit that is estimated to have exceeded 11 per cent of GDP in 2001. Like Kyrgyzstan and Moldova, Tajikistan will need continued IMF support to sustain growth as no private lenders will provide loans to cover its substantial current account deficits.

Moldova's new Communist government is also having difficulties with the IMF. Although Moldova was on track to post its first decent year of growth since independence in 2001, an estimated 5.2 per cent, the government is out of compliance with its IMF program and received no funds from the IMF. As Moldova ran another large current account deficit and no other entity is willing to provide funds, the government's posture threatens growth and the country's creditworthiness for 2002. The current account deficits are very large as a share of GDP, running 9.3 per cent in 2000 and an estimated 7.6 per cent in 2001. Thus, unless the government moves ahead with reductions in implicit subsidies through price controls and with more rapid privatization, Moldova's period of stronger growth may quickly come to an end.

After rapid growth of 5.0 per cent in 2000, Kyrgyz economic growth continued in 2001 as GDP rose an estimated 6.7 per cent. However, like Tajikistan and Moldova, growth has been accompanied by large current account deficits of 14.4 and 5.9 per cent of GDP in 1999 and 2000, respectively. Government reluctance to tighten fiscal policy is at fault. The government has been financing some of its expenditures and support for loss-making enterprises by printing money. This policy and a sharp fall in the value of the som after the August 1998 Russian financial crisis boosted December-on-December inflation to 40 per cent in 1999. Inflation is now falling sharply, but Kyrgyzstan's large current account deficits and disputes with the IMF make another currency crisis very possible.

Georgia and Armenia face similar problems. Georgia's current account deficits have been very large, 8.7 per cent of GDP in 2000 and an estimated 9.8 per cent in 2001. The country generally has good relations with Western governments; but relations with international financial institutions are rockier, even though continued economic growth is dependent on the provision of external finance. In 2000, growth in GDP slowed to just 1.8 per cent as Georgia continued to have difficulty recovering from the 1998 Russia crisis. After reporting growth of over 10 per cent in 1996 and 1997, growth has averaged just 2.7 per cent between 1998 and 2001. Growth accelerated to an estimated 6.0 per cent in 2001, but at the expense of a widening current account deficit. Armenia has enjoyed more rapid growth than Georgia in recent years, 6.0 per cent in 2000, but it too has large current account deficits, running well over 10 per cent of GDP. Maintaining access to foreign financing remains key to continued growth.

Eventually, all of the small CIS countries will have to reduce their current account deficits. The key to achieving this goal while maintaining growth is, of course, increasing exports of goods and services. Here, to a great extent, Russia will be a key factor. Although non-CIS countries have become more important export markets than the CIS for almost all the CIS countries, value added from exports to the CIS is generally much higher than to non-CIS countries. A substantial share of exports to countries outside the CIS involves piece work or processing (such as cut diamonds in the case of Armenia) where domestic value added is fairly low. In addition, Armenia and Georgia benefit from substantial remittances from citizens working in Russia. Thus, solid growth in surrounding countries, especially Russia, would be very helpful for maintaining growth.

Fortunately for these smaller countries, Russia and Ukraine should indeed enjoy very solid growth in aggregate demand over the next few years, a projected 5.9 and 5.8 per cent, respectively, in 2002. Despite the rising importance of non-CIS countries as export markets, rising aggregate demand in Russia and Ukraine will contribute to growth in the smaller CIS countries both through imports of more traditional manufactured and agricultural products and through the provision of jobs for Armenians, Georgians, and Moldovans in the more dynamic economies of Moscow and Kiev.

This said, the most important determinant of medium-term growth will be continued access to multilateral funding. Although the Bush administration now appears likely to support more IMF lending for economies in trouble, all of these countries have been put on notice that fiscal policies, market reforms, and privatization need to be implemented quickly, if this funding is to continue.

Globalization and the Outlook for Future Economic Growth

As highlighted above, the former Soviet republics, especially the three large economies of Russia, Ukraine, and Kazakhstan, have recently enjoyed a period of solid economic growth, their first since independence. A species of transition capitalism has taken root in most of these countries and has begun to result in rising incomes and GDP. Over the next few years, this system should be healthy enough to continue to push output upward. Going forward, Russia and Ukraine are poised for a few years of solid growth, punctuated by problems in the financial sector. Both small businesses and the large formerly state-owned enterprises controlled by local entrepreneurs are in a position to increase output, wages, profits, and employment by improving efficiency and tapping markets in the rest of the world as well as at home.

However, in the case of Russia and Ukraine, because of the failure of their governments to open their financial systems to outside investors, their domestic financial systems are still dominated by institutions with very limited abilities or desires to effectively evaluate credit risks. Within a few years, borrowers will default and the Russian and Ukrainian governments will have to cover the losses by issuing bonds. In the interim, the misallocation of capital will slow growth. This gloomy scenario could be forestalled if Russia and Ukraine would permit foreign banks to freely enter their markets. Russia's and Ukraine's reluctance to permit foreign competition in the financial sector reflects the outcome of an alliance between nationalistic politicians and domestic banks. In both countries, the lack of competition from foreign-owned banks is severely retarding the development of a modern financial sector, a development that will be necessary for sustained, rapid growth.

The oil economies of Azerbaijan and Kazakhstan will continue to enjoy a period of very rapid growth as the development of new fields and opening of pipelines boosts output and exports to international markets. Currently, Kazakhstan appears to be handling its oil wealth more effectively than Azerbaijan as many non-oil sectors are thriving. However, in both cases on-going investments in expanding energy output assure a period of very buoyant growth made possible by foreign investment and rising energy exports to markets in the Far Abroad.

We project much slower growth in Uzbekistan and a recession in Belarus as these countries go through a difficult period in which they will have to unify their exchange rates, reduce subsidies to loss-making enterprises, and watch as their domestic industries restructure as the governments find they must dismantle barriers to international trade and investment. In our view, it is unlikely that the presidents of either country will cease interfering with markets and will attempt to slow this adjustment process. Consequently, both countries face a period of slower growth than in other countries in the CIS.

Balance-of-payments problems threaten sustained growth in the smaller CIS countries. Although Tajikistan, and possibly Kyrgyzstan, may receive more balance-of-payments support and assistance because of their proximity to Afghanistan, most of the smaller CIS countries are running very large current account deficits, financed by lending from international financial institutions and Western governments. Most of these governments have either had difficulty in meeting fiscal targets agreed upon with the IMF because of institutional failings in terms of tax collection, or have been reluctant to pursue these targets because of opposition from key domestic political groups. In most instances, the governments have eventually agreed to make institutional and policy changes needed to near the original targets. Based on past performance, however, all of the smaller countries will oscillate between periods of rapid growth and widening current account deficits and slower growth or recession and narrowing deficits. Despite these problems, we project growth rates in the range of 4 to 7 per cent in the coming years, under the assumption that official lending will not be cut off.

To summarize, the relative economic success and failure of the various CIS republics indicate that those countries fortunate enough to have economic sectors capable of selling into the global economy have enjoyed the best economic performance in recent years. In addition, sectors that have attracted foreign direct investment have performed better than those that have not. However, virtually all of the CIS countries have made impressive strides in becoming more integrated into the global economy since independence in 1992. Over the nest few years, they are poised to enjoy a period of solid growth drive by expanding trade in goods and services, and much more substantial inflows of foreign direct investment, especially in the larger economies of Russia, Ukraine, and Kazakhstan.

Notes

1   *Trade and Finance Review for the Soviet Union*, PlanEcon, 1991.
2   Ibid.
3   *Trade and Finance Review for Russia*, PlanEcon, May 1995.

Tables

Table 5.1:   The gross domestic product of the CIS in 2001 (in USD billion)

	GDP at PPP exch. rates	GDP % of CIS Total	GDP at market exch. rates	GDP % of CIS total	GDP Growth %	GDP % Previous Peak
Armenia	12.1	1.0	2.0	0.5	6.3	74.5
Azerbaijan	18.4	1.6	5.2	1.3	8.0	63.4
Belarus	68.8	5.8	11.7	2.8	3.1	90.4
Georgia	11.7	1.0	3.2	0.8	6.0	40.3
Kazakhstan	48.6	4.1	21.0	5.1	11.6	77.3
Kyrgyzstan	12.2	1.0	1.4	0.4	6.4	70.4
Moldova	8.9	0.8	1.5	0.4	5.2	36.3
Russia	772.2	65.3	309.0	75.0	5.0	69.1
Tajikistan	6.4	0.5	1.2	0.3	8.1	53.6
Turkmenistan	20.6	1.7	6.0	1.4	12.7	97.7
Ukraine	136.8	11.6	39.0	9.5	8.5	43.5
Uzbekistan	66.6	5.6	11.1	2.7	3.8	100.4
Total	1183.2	100.0	412.2	100.0	5.7	66.3

Table 5.2:   Economic and demographic data for the CIS, 2001

	Population thousands	Population % of CIS total	Per Capita GDP in USD at PPP exchange rates	Per capita GDP in USD at market exchange rates
Armenia	3803.7	1.4	3176.2	538.4
Azerbaijan	7771.1	2.8	2372.4	665.1
Belarus	10129.4	3.6	6788.7	1150.9
Georgia	5376.4	1.9	2181.3	601.5
Kazakhstan	14865.1	5.3	3270.6	1411.3
Kyrgyzstan	4936.2	1.8	2461.9	292.5
Moldova	4362.5	1.6	2034.9	333.0
Russia	144246.0	51.3	5353.2	2141.9
Tajikistan	6440.7	2.3	989.1	181.5
Turkmenistan	5398.0	1.9	3824.3	1103.5
Ukraine	49001.8	17.4	2791.0	795.9
Uzbekistan	25015.0	8.9	2660.7	444.1
Total	281345.9	100.0	4205.4	1465.0

Table 5.3: CIS trade (in USD million)

| | Exports | | | | | | | |
	To CIS 1992	Total 1992	To CIS 1994	Total 1994	To CIS 1998	Total 1998	To CIS 2000	Total 2000
Armenia	126.5*	156.2*	158	216	81	221	73	298
Azerbaijan	730	1484	274	637	232	606	235	1745
Belarus	1709	2903	1478	2510	5160	7070	4453	7380
Georgia	77	87	117	156	107	190	136	330
Kazakhstan	3315	4769	1874	3231	2100	5436	2380	9140
Kyrgyzstan	209	285	223	340	231	514	207	505
Moldova	304	471	405	565	429	632	280	477
Russia	11229	53605	14541	67542	15300	74200	14800	105565
Tajikistan	74	185	263	559	192	586	369	779
Turkmenistan	624	1533	1651	2176	152	614	1282	2465
Ukraine	17600	21374	7800	13900	4200	12600	4500	14600
Uzbekistan	554	1424	1519	2549	901	3218	1172	3265
Total	36551	88276	30302	94380	29085	105886	29887	146548

*1993

continued overleaf

Table 5.3 – continued

Imports

	From CIS 1992	Total 1992	From CIS 1994	Total 1994	From CIS 1998	Total 1998	From CIS 2000	Total 2000
Armenia	168.1*	254*	206	394	230	902	173	885
Azerbaijan	607	940	486	778	405	1077	376	1172
Belarus	1878	2721	2091	3066	5554	8549	6001	8487
Georgia	159	176	268	327	303	915	222	700
Kazakhstan	7315	7885	2177	3561	2002	4350	2615	5052
Kyrgyzstan	326	396	209	436	441	842	299	555
Moldova	336	506	476	659	440	564	253	793
Russia	5987	42971	13551	50518	13600	59100	13400	44862
Tajikistan	107	240	264	686	460	725	559	674
Turkmenistan	416	446	686	1691	500	1137	605	1728
Ukraine	22100	24319	11400	16500	7900	14700	8300	14000
Uzbekistan	731	1654	1394	2603	916	3125	1126	2947
Total	40129	82506	33207	81219	32749	95985	33927	81855

*1993

continued on opposite page

Table 5.3 – continued

Balance of Trade

	CIS 1992	Total 1992	CIS 1994	Total 1994	CIS 1998	Total 1998	CIS 2000	Total 2000
Armenia	−41.6	−97.8	−48.0	−178.4	−149.7	−681.9	−100.3	−587.6
Azerbaijan	122.6	544.1	−211.7	−141.2	−172.5	−471.0	−140.3	572.8
Belarus	−168.5	182.5	−613.0	−556.0	−394.0	−1479.0	−1547.5	−1107.0
Georgia	−82.4	−88.9	−151.1	−171.7	−195.4	−725.0	−85.3	−370.3
Kazakhstan	−4000.0	−3115.3	−302.9	−330.4	98.7	1086.2	−234.9	4087.4
Kyrgyzstan	−117.0	−111.0	14.3	−96.0	−210.1	−327.9	−91.6	−50.1
Moldova	−32.0	−35.0	−71.0	−94.3	−11.1	68.1	27.0	−315.4
Russia	5242.0	10634.0	990.0	17024.0	1700.0	15100.0	1400.0	60703.0
Tajikistan	−33.3	−54.7	−1.0	−127.0	−267.8	−138.8	−190.4	104.8
Turkmenistan	208.3	1087.0	964.9	485.0	−347.9	−523.0	677.2	737.5
Ukraine	−4500.0	−2945.4	−3600.0	−2600.0	−3700.0	−2100.0	−3800.0	600.0
Uzbekistan	−176.1	−229.8	124.7	−53.6	−14.4	93.5	46.6	317.3
Total	−3578.0	5769.7	−2904.8	13160.4	−3664.2	9901.2	−4039.5	64692.4

Source: Statistical Yearbook of the Commonwealth of Independent States, Moscow.

Table 5.4:   Indicators of economic integration in 2000

	Total Trade % of GDP	Exports % of GDP	Imports % of GDP	Trade Balance % of GDP	Cur a/c Balance % of GDP	Foreign Debt % of GDP	Cumula- tive FDI % of GDP
Armenia	61.6	15.5	46.1	−30.6	−14.7	44.9	28.8
Azerbaijan	59.6	35.6	23.9	11.7	−3.4	23.7	76.3
Belarus	135.3	62.9	72.4	−9.4	−1.4	9.9	10.5
Georgia	34.2	10.9	23.2	−12.3	−8.7	51.6	27.1
Kazakhstan	77.8	50.1	27.7	22.4	5.9	68.7	44.5
Kyrgyzstan	81.2	38.7	42.5	−3.8	−5.9	136.0	30.2
Moldova	97.7	36.7	61.0	−24.3	−9.3	125.7	110.3
Russia	60.0	42.1	17.9	24.2	18.5	67.0	9.2
Tajikistan	146.6	78.6	68.0	10.6	−6.3	121.6	16.4
Turkmenistan	95.2	56.0	39.2	16.7	11.5	54.5	22.1
Ukraine	90.6	46.2	44.3	1.9	1.9	31.4	12.1
Uzbekistan	45.1	23.7	21.4	2.3	−0.1	33.9	6.2
Total	66.4	42.6	23.8	18.8	13.8	60.2	13.2

Source: Statistical Yearbook of the Commonwealth of Independent States, Statistical Committee of the CIS; International Financial Statistics, International Monetary Fund.

Chapter 6

Reform, Growth and Slowdown: Lessons from Chile

Rodrigo Vergara

1. Introduction

About three decades ago the Chilean economy began a process of deep economic reform. In the 1960s and early 1970s Chile had a closed economy with heavy state intervention. Import tariffs were on average 105 per cent with a high variance – ranging from 0 per cent on some products to 1000 per cent on others. Copper represented more than 80 per cent of total exports. Price distortions were enormous with absolutely no link between domestic relative prices and international prices.[1]

Government intervention was not only related to heavy regulation, taxes, tariffs, price controls, minimum wages, subsidies and the like. The state had also a significant weight in the economy in terms of ownership. It controlled all public utilities, copper companies and many other enterprises. Hachette has estimated that in 1973 the state owned 600 companies, which represented about 40 per cent of total Chilean GDP (in terms of value added). A massive process of expropriation was implemented in the early 1970s, which also produced uncertainty about property rights.

In such an environment it is not a surprise that investment, saving and growth were very modest. Industry was based on an import substitution strategy with no incentives to create new firms, innovate and improve efficiency. As there was uncertainty about property rights, there were no incentives to invest. Chile was a stagnant economy, not very different from most Latin American economies. On the other hand, inflation was high (it reached its peak of 500 per cent in 1973). But high inflation (two digits) was, at that time, considered a normal state of things.

In the mid-1970s Chile started its process of economic reform. A group of mostly Chicago-educated young people took over the economic program of the dictatorial government and decided to implement radical (by the standards of those days) free-market economic reforms.[2] This was done in the midst of an economic crisis, which was a consequence of both the collapse of the previous economic system and a world economic slowdown (with a significant impact on Chile's terms of trade) as a consequence of the oil shocks.

At the beginning the results were impressive. After the recession of 1975, the economy grew 6.8 per cent on average during 1976–81. But then, Chile suffered the worst recession since the great depression. GDP fell 16 per cent in 1982–3 and unemployment climbed to 30 per cent of the labor force. Two causes have been mentioned to explain this recession. First, the world economic recession of the early 1980s. The huge increase in international interest rates, induced by the very tight monetary policy in the United States, had a devastating effect over Chile and the rest of Latin America. Second, there were clearly some policy mistakes that contributed to the magnitude of the recession. In particular, there was not enough banking supervision. The crisis hit banks, which went under. The banking crisis made things much worse. On the other hand – from a macroeconomic perspective – the authorities watched passively a massive real exchange rate appreciation and huge current account deficits (in 1981 the current account deficit reached 14.5 per cent of GDP) without taking any measure to correct these.

In 1984, Chile started a long period of economic growth, not seen before in its history. Its economy grew at an average rate of 7 per cent a year for fifteen years (Table 6.1, Figure 6.1). This was an outstanding achievement which produced a massive change in the standards of living of the population (Table 6.2 shows social indicators).

Unfortunately, this economic boom period seems to be over by now. For the first time in a decade-and-a-half, Chile had a recession in 1999. GDP fell 1.1 per cent that year and, although growth resumed in 2000, it has not come back to its high levels since then. Again, external factors had something to do with this economic slowdown. The Asian crisis and the decline of external capital flows to emerging economies had a negative impact over Chile. But there were also internal causes. Indeed, at some point Chileans thought that the process of reforms had been completed and there was nothing else to do but just wait and grow. One of the main theses of this paper is that the reform process is a continuous one. It is true that at the beginning the most visible and obvious reforms are carried out. But if countries stop reforming (or modernizing), at some point growth will go back to a more modest level. This is not to say that countries can grow forever at 7 per cent. We all know that there is a natural convergence process. But at the per capita GDP level that Chile has at this moment, there is no reason to think that the economic slowdown is just due to the natural convergence process.

The purpose of this paper is to draw lessons from the Chilean economic reform process. These lessons are divided in two groups. First, lessons from the initial period of reform. The paper discusses what could have been done differently and what can be learned by countries currently embarked on this type of reforms (the so-called first generation of reforms). Second, lessons from the latest period, when an economic slowdown has occurred. Here we put more emphasis on the so-called second or third generation of reforms.

The paper is organized as follows. The second section contains an analysis of the major reforms that Chile has undertaken in the last three decades, an overview of the results and some practical lessons. In the third section, the slowdown of the late 1990s is analyzed in terms of productivity growth. We analyze productivity growth for a number of countries and draw some conclusions for Chile and other emerging economies. Finally, section four presents the conclusions.

2. Economic Reforms in Chile

The reforms initiated by the new economic authorities in the mid-1970s covered many areas. It is not the purpose of this section to make a comprehensive analysis of each reform, but to mention some of them, their main results and lessons. Specifically, we will talk about the public sector reforms, trade liberalization, financial sector reform, pension reform and central bank independence. There were many other areas in which significant reforms took place, such as education, health, regulation of public utilities, infrastructure, etc. All of them were very important in producing the so-called golden age of economic growth in Chile. However, for reasons of space it is not possible to include all of them in this paper.[3]

2.1.   Public Sector Reforms

Public sector reforms can be divided into three types of reform:

* rationalization of public spending
* privatizations
* tax reform.

Rationalization of public spending A chronic problem of Chilean economic policy had been the large and persistent budget deficits. The basic problem was, of course, the lack of fiscal discipline, which collapsed in 1971–3, when on average the budget deficit of the non-financial public sector was 23.4 per cent of GDP. The peak was reached in 1973 at 30 per cent of GDP. Hence one of the basic measures was to adjust public spending in basically three areas: public investment, public sector wages and the elimination of most of the subsidies implicit in the operations of the state-owned companies. In 1974 the deficit was reduced to 5 per cent of GDP and in 1976 there was a surplus of 2 per cent of GDP.

However, the problem with the budget was not only the lack of fiscal austerity, but also a complete chaos in the administration of public spending. Indeed, there were no clear responsibilities in terms of spending, and in practice no one knew exactly what was going on with the public finances. In 1975, the new organic law on the 'financial administration of the state' was approved. According to this, only the executive branch is responsible for proposing the budget for the year (the estimates of both revenues and spending) and Congress cannot increase spending.

Table 6.1: Chile main macroeconomic indicators, 1974–2001

	1974	1975	1976	1977	1978	1979	1980	1981	1982	1983	1984	1985	1986	1987
1. GDP growth	1.0	-13.3	3.2	8.3	7.8	7.1	7.7	6.7	-13.4	-3.5	6.1	3.5	5.6	6.6
2. Unemployment rate (annual average)[a]	n/a	14.9	12.7	11.8	14.2	13.6	10.4	11.3	19.6	14.6	13.9	12.0	12.3	11.0
3. Gross fixed capital formation (% real GDP)	18.9	16.7	13.8	15.2	16.5	17.7	20.9	23.2	15.8	13.7	16.3	17.7	17.1	19.6
4. National saving rate (% nominal GDP)	n/a	9.5	16.9	13.8	15.3	16.7	19.3	14.2	4.9	6.9	6.5	7.8	11.5	17.3
5. Current account deficit (% GDP)	0.5	6.4	-1.4	3.9	6.8	5.6	7.1	14.5	9.0	5.5	10.8	8.6	6.7	3.6
6. Real exchange rate (1986=100)[b]	n/a	n/a	n/a	57.1	68.1	70.2	60.8	52.9	59.0	70.8	74.0	90.9	100	104.3
7. Inflation (CPI, Dec.-Dec.)	369.2	343.3	197.9	84.2	37.2	38.9	31.2	9.5	20.7	23.1	23.0	26.4	17.4	21.5
8. Fiscal balance (central government, % GDP)	-5.4	-2.0	4.0	0.4	1.6	4.8	6.1	0.8	-3.4	-3.0	-4.3	-2.6	-2.1	-0.2
9. Terms of trade (1986=100)	225.9	121.4	132.6	122.3	120.9	134.7	132.7	122.3	112.1	114.3	107.6	99.9	100	109.8
10. Real (in UF) interest rate on 90-days deposits	n/a	n/a	11.6	15.5	17.5	14.4	8.4	13.1	12.0	7.8	8.4	8.2	4.1	4.3

	1988	1989	1990	1991	1992	1993	1994	1995	1996	1997	1998	1999	2000	2001
1. GDP growth	7.3	10.6	3.7	8.0	12.3	7.0	5.7	10.6	7.4	7.4	3.9	-1.1	5.4	2.8
2. Unemployment rate (annual average)[a]	9.9	8.0	7.8	8.2	6.7	6.5	7.8	7.4	6.5	6.1	6.3	9.8	9.2	9.1
3. Gross fixed capital formation (% real GDP)	20.8	24.5	24.2	22.4	24.7	27.2	27.4	30.6	31.0	32.2	32.2	26.9	26.6	26.5
4. National saving rate (% nominal GDP)	22.3	23.3	23.2	22.3	21.5	20.9	21.1	23.8	21.2	21.6	21.2	21.8	21.9	20.5
5. Current account deficit (% GDP)	1.0	2.5	1.6	0.3	2.3	5.7	3.1	2.1	5.1	5.0	5.7	0.1	1.4	1.4
6. Real exchange rate (1986=100)[b]	111.2	108.6	112.7	106.4	97.6	96.9	94.2	88.9	84.7	78.2	78.0	82.3	86.0	96.5
7. Inflation (CPI, Dec.–Dec.)	12.7	21.4	27.3	18.7	12.7	12.2	8.9	8.2	6.6	6.0	4.7	2.3	4.5	2.6
8. Fiscal balance (central government, % GDP)	0.2	1.3	0.8	1.5	2.3	2.0	1.7	2.6	2.3	2.0	0.4	-1.5	0.1	-0.3
9. Terms of trade (1986=100)	125.9	124.3	116.5	116.0	112.3	108.6	122.2	139.8	121.6	123.6	116.8	115.5	114.8	104.8
10. Real (in UF) interest rate on 90-days deposits	4.6	6.8	9.4	5.4	5.3	6.4	6.4	5.9	6.9	6.4	9.5	5.9	5.2	3.7

n/a – not available

[a] Change in methodology in 1992

[b] An increase in the index means depreciation of the local currency

Source: Central Bank of Chile.

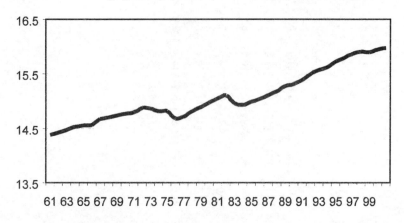

Figure 6.1: log GDP

Source: Central Bank of Chile.

Table 6.2: Chile – social indicators

	1970	1999
Life expectancy at birth (years)	64	75
Death probability before one year of age (%)	8.2	1.0
Illiterate population (%)	11	4.6
Drinking water (%)	66	99
Telephone lines (per 1,000 inhabitants)	37	207
Automobiles (per 1,000 inhabitants)	16	83.4

Source: Central Bank of Chile.

It only can approve the proposal of the executive or, if it considers that public spending is too high, propose its reduction. All public debt issue must be approved by the Budget Office and has to be in line with the approved budget. There is some flexibility in the allocation of resources within the different areas of the state, but there is an absolute ceiling for public spending provided for by the budget.

This new institutional framework established clear responsibilities in the administration of the budget and allowed the government to control spending.[4]

Privatizations There were three rounds of the privatization process in Chile. The first (1974–83) was aimed at returning the assets that had been expropriated to the previous owners. It involved for the most part farms and some industries. In addition, the government privatized enterprises that had been acquired by the state during the government of President Allende. These included mostly industrial enterprises and banks. In this first phase state-owned enterprises were reduced in number from 596 in 1974 to 48 in 1983. However, as the enterprises that remained in state hands were bigger than those privatized, their total value added was only reduced from 39 per cent of GDP to 24 per cent of GDP (Table 6.3).

This first phase ended abruptly with the 1982–3 crisis. Several companies that had been privatized, including the largest two banks, failed, and the government took them over. As mentioned in the Introduction, one of the factors behind the banking crisis was very lax banking regulation and supervision.[5]

In 1985, the second round of privatization was launched. This included the privatization of public utilities plus the re-privatization of companies that had returned to government hands during the crisis. The share of state-owned enterprises in GDP in terms of value added declined to 13 per cent in 1989. There exists a substantial amount of literature regarding this second round of privatization. Some authors claim that this process was a total success, while others maintain that it lacked transparency and that the privatized companies could have been sold at a much higher price. What is clear, in any case, is that these companies have invested heavily since privatization and that the services provided to the consumers have improved significantly.[6] They have been among the most dynamic companies in a very dynamic environment.

The third round began in 1990 and comprised basically infrastructure (through concessions) and water companies. By 1998 the share of public enterprises in GDP had fallen to 9 per cent. Currently, the most important state owned enterprises are CODELCO, a copper company, a state owned bank and the oil company.

Table 6.3: Public sector reform. Privatization of public enterprises

	1973	1983	1989	1998
Value added (% of GDP)	39	24	13	9

Source: Hachette (2001).

Tax reform Chile has had two major tax reforms in the last three decades. In 1975, the value added tax was introduced at a flat rate (currently 18 per cent) and with very few exceptions (most importantly education and public transportation). Currently about 50 per cent of tax revenues come from the value added tax.

The second major tax reform came in 1984, reducing drastically the corporate income tax (currently at a flat rate of 16 per cent) and integrating this tax with the personal income tax. This means taxes paid at the corporate level are credited towards one's personal income tax.

Hsieh & Parker (2001) show that the reduction in the tax rate on retained profits contributed to the Chilean investment and growth boom. Bennett et al. (2001) argue that the tax structure had a positive and significant effect on saving. Additionally, tax evasion in Chile, estimated at around 22 per cent of potential tax revenues, is the lowest in Latin America and not very different from many developed countries (see Barra and Jorrat, 1999).

2.2.   Trade Liberalization

In 1974, Chile initiated a unilateral strategy of trade liberalization. The strategy consisted in reducing tariffs independently of what other countries did, so as to converge on a low and flat rate. By 1979 that rate was 10 per cent (Table 6.4). After the crisis of the 1980s, there was some attempt at protectionism and tariffs increased marginally. However, starting in the mid-1980s the process of tariff reduction was resumed. Currently the average tariff is 5 per cent. However, as Chile signed in the 1990s several bilateral free-trade agreements, tariffs remain low but are not uniform.[7]

The effect of trade liberalization has been a significant increase in exports, which went from USD 1 billion in 1970 to close to USD 18 billion currently (Figure 6.2), despite the fact that the prices of main export products (especially copper) have declined in real terms.

The other major effect has been a diversification of exports. The share of copper in total exports declined from 76 per cent in 1970 to 38 per cent in 2001, while non-traditional exports have increased their share in total exports from 10 per cent to 38 per cent (Figure 6.3).

Table 6.4: Average tariffs

1973	105%
1979	10%
1991	11%
2000	5%

Source: Central Bank of Chile.

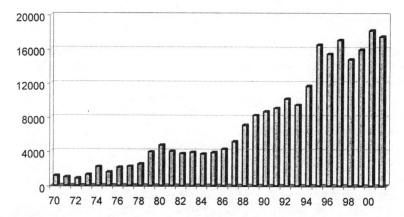

Figure 6.2 Total exports (USD millions)

Source: Central Bank of Chile.

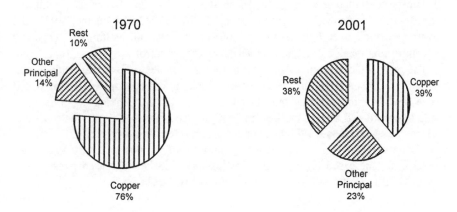

Figure 6.3 :   Composition of exports

Source: Central Bank of Chile.

2.3.   Financial Sector Reform

In the mid-1970s, Chile initiated a process of financial liberalization. State-owned banks (with one exception) were privatized. Interest rates, previously set by the government, were liberalized. Reserve requirements were lowered. The scope of banking business was widened. Banks became involved in a variety of business activities, which they had never performed before. People who did not have any banking experience became bankers. At the same time they were owners of major companies in the country. As supervision was very lax, they used banks to lend to their own companies.

On the other hand, although the government liberalized the market, it soon became clear that it would protect the depositors if a bank failed. Indeed, in 1977 a major bank failed and the government backed all deposits. This, of course, created a serious moral hazard problem.

At the beginning everything looked very well, except that interest rates remained high during the whole period. In the early 1980s the world recession and domestic policy mistakes produced a slowdown in economic activity. Profits declined and it became difficult to serve the debt with the banks. Companies rolled over and asked for more credit in a situation which could be described as distress borrowing. As the owners of banks were the same as the owners of the companies, old credits were rolled over and new credits were granted. On the other hand, depositors continued lending to banks on the premise that there was an implicit state deposit insurance. Everything collapsed in 1982–3. In January 1983, the government took over four banks and four other financial institutions. About 50 per cent of total bank credit came under government control.

The cost of the banking crisis was enormous.[8] The lesson was that banking was not like any other sector in the economy. Banking supervision was strengthened and a new banking act was introduced in 1986. Today, banking supervision in Chile is considered one of the best in emerging economies. Despite the recession and slowdown of the late 1990s, the banking sector remains very strong.

Financial deepening, as measured by the ratio of various monetary aggregates to GDP, has increased significantly. For instance, M3 has increased from 14 per cent of GDP in 1970 to 48 per cent of GDP in 2001 (Table 6.5).

Table 6.5: Financial liberalization (% of GDP)

	M3	M7
1970	14%	n/a
1980	25%	24%
1990	28%	54%
2001	48%	89%

Source: Central Bank of Chile.

2.4. Pension Reform

In 1981, Chile adopted an individual capitalization pension system. This means each person saves a certain percentage of his/her salary (with a ceiling) for his/her retirement in an individual account. The funds in an individual account are administered by a private company. Individuals can freely move their funds among different private companies if they think that their funds are not properly administered. These companies are regulated and supervised. For instance, there are restrictions as to the composition of their portfolio, so that a specific level of diversification is enforced.[9]

Pension funds have increased persistently over the previous two decades and currently approach USD 35 billion, or more than 50 per cent of GDP (Table 6.6 and Figure 6.4).

Private pension funds have been key players in the growth of the financial sector in Chile, especially in the development of the long-term market. Chile is one of the very few emerging economies that have a long-term market denominated in their own currency. Bonds and mortgages with maturities of twenty years and more are the norm. Without the pension system it would have been difficult to achieve this level of development. It is also important to mention that private pension systems of the Chilean type have been adopted in a number of Latin American and Eastern European countries.

Table 6.6: Pension reform. Basic data (December 2001)

Total fund	USD 34,307m
Number of affiliates	6,427,391
Annual Real Return (July 1981 – December 2001)	10.70%

Source: Central Bank of Chile.

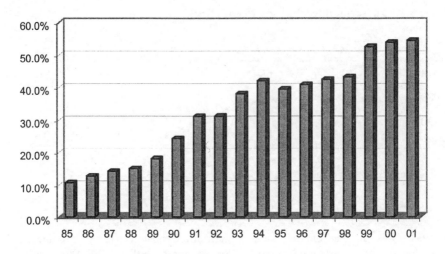

Figure 6.4:   Pension fund (% of GDP)

Source: Superintendencia de AFP.

2.5.   Central Bank Independence

Chile had a long tradition of high inflation, even longer than most Latin American countries. That is why in 1989 a new law giving independence to the Central Bank was adopted. According to this new act, the board of the Central Bank consists of five members nominated by the president and approved by the senate. Each one has a 10-year term. Every two years one of the board members is changed. They are independent of the government (cannot be removed from their position). The Ministry of Finance has the right to participate in the board meetings but does not have any voting power.

The Central Bank's record in keeping down inflation is impressive (Figure 6.5). After the high inflation rates of the early 1970s, inflation in Chile remained in the 20–30 per cent range. The new autonomous central bank decided to implement inflation targets, starting in 1991. The purpose was to bring about a persistent and gradual decline in the inflation rate. As seen in Table 6.7, inflation targets have been met every year since 1991, with minor exceptions, such as 2000, when inflation at 4.5 per cent was somewhat above the 3.5 per cent target. The reason for this difference was the increase in the price of oil.[10]

Since 2000, a permanent target has been set (rather than on a year-to-year basis as was the case previously), which corresponds to a range between 2 and 4 per cent.

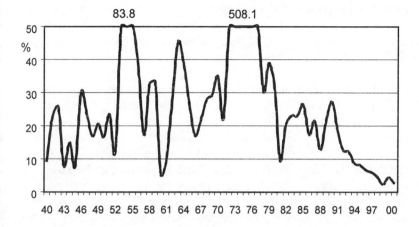

Figure 6.5:   Inflation rate (Dec.–Dec.)

Source: Central Bank of Chile.

Table 6.7: Inflation target (IT) and actual inflation (AI) (%)

Year	IT	AI
1991	15–20	18.7
1992	13–16	12.7
1993	10–12	12.2
1994	9–11	8.9
1995	9.0	8.2
1996	6.5	6.6
1997	5.5	6.0
1998	4.5	4.7
1999	4.3	2.3
2000	3.5	4.5
2001	2–4	2.6

Source: BCCH.

2.6.   Main Lessons of the Reforms

From the Chilean experience, it is possible to derive several lessons for reforming countries. Among them, are the following:

- Reforms pay off. The results in Chile were impressive. When things stabilized after the crisis of 1982–3, the Chilean economy entered a golden period. Growth averaged 7 per cent for the next fifteen years, savings and investment boomed, unemployment fell and inflation was reduced to a 2–4 per cent level.
- It is important to be patient. In the case of Chile, high growth began just after the initial reforms. However, the crisis of 1982–3 showed that there had been some policy mistakes that needed correction. These corrections were implemented and high growth resumed, but this time for a much longer time. Being impatient and reversing the reforms when it seems that they are not working is the wrong reading of the situation. In the case of Chile, after the crisis the direction of reforms was maintained and they even deepened. For instance, banks and companies that returned to state hands after the crisis were soon after re-privatized.
- Financial regulation and supervision is key. Chile disregarded this issue in the first phase of reforms and paid dearly for it. It then corrected it with a new banking law and strengthened supervision.
- Public sector adjustment is essential. It would have been impossible to attain the outstanding economic performance that Chile achieved for many years without heavy fiscal adjustment. And this was done right away, with no delay.
- Tax and pension reforms are key in promoting investment and saving. The tax reform is associated with creating a favorable environment for investment, while the pension reform is instrumental in developing a long term capital market.

3.   The Economic Slowdown: The Role of TFP[11]

The crises that swept through Asia in late 1997 brought Chile's economic boom to an abrupt halt. Having grown at an average rate of 7.3 per cent per year in 1984–97, the Chilean economy has expanded by less than 3 per cent a year since then. So what happened?

One answer, often put forward by the authorities, posits significantly worse external conditions as the basic explanation. As Chile is a small open economy, when the world economy slows down, the demand for its exports declines, leading to lower export prices and volumes. If the price of oil rises at the same time, this small open economy, which imports nearly all the oil it consumes, will suffer even more. Things will become still worse if net capital flows to emerging economies suddenly dry up. Moreover, the argument follows, the proof of the strength of the Chilean economy is precisely the fact that it is still growing (although at low rates).

This marks a difference from the previous external crises, which always produced an internal recession.

As documented in Beyer and Vergara (op. cit.), the problem with this explanation is that in the previous decade-and-a-half there were periods in which external conditions were no different from those prevailing in recent years and the economy was growing at much higher rates. Hence, although external conditions have clearly worsened, this provides only a partial explanation for the weak performance of the Chilean economy.

Chile's golden age in terms of economic growth was explained by a strong expansion in total factor productivity (TFP). This, in turn, is explained by the productivity effects of the reforms implemented in the 1980s and early 1990s. To some extent these have now been exhausted. Accordingly, what Chile now needs to reinvigorate economic growth is a new wave of reforms in areas were it has fallen behind – areas relating mainly to the 'microeconomic foundations' of growth, namely institutions and their efficiency and efficacy. Another way to put it would be to say that new microeconomic reforms are needed to enhance the efficiency of the use of available resources.

If we view economic growth not as a linear process but rather as one marked by sporadic productivity shocks that lead to high growth for a period, before fading in convergence until the next productivity boost, then Chile would currently be in a phase in which the most recent productivity shock is contributing its last ammunition. If this is the case, the country needs a new shock to kick-start a new period of rapid economic growth. Of course this new boost could be luck – discovery of oil or a significant positive terms-of-trade shock, for instance. But, as luck is random, I prefer to consider a new productivity shock arising from economic policy initiatives aimed at improving economic efficiency. Improvements in these areas are likely to produce a new surge in economic growth in Chile. Furthermore, the deterioration in external conditions increases the need for policies to boost the country's currently sluggish growth rate.

3.1. Total Factor Productivity in Chile

Table 6.8 presents data on TFP growth in Chile over the last two and a half decades. TFP is measured as the residual GDP growth that is not explained by labor or by capital accumulation. There are no input quality adjustments. A productivity boom occurred in the second half of the 1970s in the wake of the first wave of structural reforms; this was followed by the crisis of the early 1980s. Recovery began in the mid-1980s, when there was a second productivity boom (associated with a second wave of reforms) which reached its peak in the first half of the 1990s. In the second half of that decade, productivity growth slowed down once more, and over the last four years (1998–2001) TFP growth has been nil.

These calculations clearly show that the key difference between this latest period (1998–2001) and the previous fourteen years of high economic growth (1984–97) is TFP growth. As Table 6.8 shows, capital's contribution to growth has been around 2.5 percentage points since the mid-1980s (1986–2000) and has not changed in recent years. On the other hand, labor's contribution to growth averages 1.3 points, but the share it accounts for has been declining in recent years. This is explained by a significant increase in unemployment since 1998. Finally, as mentioned above, TFP rose from two to three percentage points before falling back to a figure close to zero.

Table 6.8: Chile – components of economic growth

	GDP growth	Contribution of:		
		TFP	Labor	Capital
1976–80	6.8	3.2	2.4	1.2
1981–5	–0.1	–2.3	1.2	1.0
1986–90	6.5	2.2	2.0	2.2
1991–5	7.5	3.3	1.4	2.8
1996–2000	4.6	1.6	0.5	2.5
1998–2001	2.8	0.3	0.1	2.4

Source: Roldós (1997) and own estimates.

3.2.   *TFP as an Explanation for Growth: Cross Country Evidence*

But is TFP an important source of economic growth? Or if you prefer, is economic growth affected by the quality of policies and institutions? To answer this question, a very simple exercise in growth accounting for the period 1980–2000 is needed. This consists of estimating the unexplained rate of GDP growth after controlling for investment and increases in employment. The data of the IMF collected in the International Financial Statistics is used. The labor share in GDP is supposed to be 0.6. Assuming a stock of capital that is 2.5 times output and a depreciation rate of 5 per cent, this implies an average rate of return of capital of 11 per cent, a reasonable return for the entire physical capital stock. Since there are no consistent data on employment for the sample, population data are used. TFP is the result of solving the following equation:

$$\text{TFP}_t = \hat{Y}_t - (r + \delta)I_t - s_L \hat{L}$$

meaning that TFP is the result of subtracting net investment weighted by the gross rate of return of capital (δ is the depreciation rate) and the rate of growth of labor weighted by the labor's share in GDP, from the rate of growth in GDP.

There is no doubt about the importance of TFP as an determinant of growth. Figure 6.6 draws the relationship between TFP and the rate of economic growth for the period between 1980 and 2000. Two thirds of the variance in growth rates is explained by variations in the rate of TFP growth. Of course this observation doesn't mean that factor accumulations do not play a role in explaining the differences in economic growth among countries. Since our estimations do not correct for human capital, it could be argued that our calculations for TFP exaggerate its actual importance. However it would be surprising if the inclusion of human capital reduced significantly the importance of TFP.[12] Chile shows a high rate of TFP growth that explains a significant portion of GDP growth. Here it is possible to notice the impact of the many reforms that have transformed Chile from a very closed and over-regulated economy into an open and competitive economy. To repeat these high rates of TFP growth is precisely the challenge for Chile and, as the same graph shows, this is not an easy task. Many countries do have rates of TFP growth close to zero and indeed some do have negative rates of TFP growth.

To confirm the role that TFP plays in economic growth, I have analyzed country data on average growth in 10-year periods (1981–90 and 1991–2000). Since TFP is obtained for 107 countries, this allows the analysis of 214 periods. The top 10 per cent and bottom 10 per cent of the periods in terms of economic performance are chosen. Then the importance of TFP in explaining the differences in the rate of growth of GDP is compared. As Table 6.9 shows, more than 80 per cent of the difference in growth rates is explained by differences in TFP growth.

The difference in the rate of growth in GDP among countries is explained almost exclusively by the differences in the rate of growth in TFP. Factor accumulation plays a relatively modest role. Beyer and Vergara (op. cit.) confirm this conclusion with other types of exercises. For instance, they rank countries according to per-capita income in 1980 (the first year of this analysis) using the Penn tables. They find that for both rich and poor countries, TFP differences are by far the major explanation of the rates of growth in each group.

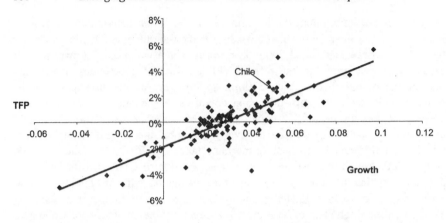

Figure 6.6:   TFP and growth: average growth 1980–2000

Table 6.9:   The sources of growth: countries with highest GDP per capita

		Output	Factor accumulation	TFP
Highest periodic growth rates	Mean	4.57	3.48	1.09
Lowest periodic growth rates	Mean	0.50	2.79	−2.29
Difference in mean		4.07	0.69	3.38

3.3.   TFP, Policies and Institutions

There is a large body of literature (for example, Easterly, 1993, and Krueger, 1990) pointing out that bad economic policies may affect economic performance heavily. A related strand in the literature targets the role that institutions play in the process of economic growth   (for example, North, 1990). At the same time the discrepancies in levels of income and rates of economic growth among countries are far beyond the differences in factor accumulation. Therefore, it is worthwhile to explore in more detail the links between the rate of growth of TFP and economic policies and institutions. Of particular interest is the role that microeconomic policies play in this story. The simple hypothesis that we are considering is that differences in the quality of these policies play a significant role in the rate of growth of TFP.

In the previous sections it was shown that countries that are unable to grow tend to exhibit negative rates of TFP growth. The differences in factor accumulation play a minor role in the variation of growth rates across countries. On the other hand, it is easy to verify that countries differ significantly in their economic policies and institutions. Moreover, these differences tend to persist in time. For example, changes in the effectiveness of government, in the legal system or in the quality of educational systems take a very long time to be put in effect and they remain broadly similar over considerable periods of time.

The positive or negative effect of policies and institutions on TFP may also last for very long periods of time. An inefficient government bureaucracy, for example, may hinder permanently efficiency gains. On the other hand, a state reform that substantially improves the efficiency of the state bureaucracy may generate an increase in the economic efficiency of an economy almost continuously. The same thing can be said of a once-and-for-all improvement in the quality of education. The increases in productivity associated with the entering of the 'new' school graduates into the labor force will last until there is a complete replacement of the 'old' labor force. This may occur even if the schooling level of the new labor is the same as that of the old labor force.

One of the problems faced by the empirical work on this subject is the lack of data on much of the economic policies and institutions we are interested in. However, in the last two decades there has been a systematic effort by different institutions trying to collect reliable data on the quality of economic policies and institutions. One problem is that much of the data relies on subjective measures of the quality of institutions. Another problem is that different indicators tend to be highly correlated within each data set. Probably this is not surprising, since most of the high-quality policies and institutions come in a package. So a country with a good regulatory framework probably has simultaneously a highly qualified bureaucracy and at the same times low levels of corruption. The reverse is true in the case of countries with a bad regulatory framework.

Gallego and Loayza (2001) consider four areas in which Chile could improve: quality of education, technological adoption, microeconomic restrictions and quality of governance. In the first three areas Chile is still far from the leaders, while in the fourth its position is good. The authors run a cross-section regression of growth depending on these and other variables and estimate that if Chile were to upgrade these four variables substantially, growth could increase by more than 2 per cent.

Beyer and Vergara (op. cit.) find that major gains in economic growth for a country like Chile may come from an improvement in its educational systems. Reasonable and reachable improvements may increase the rate of growth in Chile by 0.6 percentage points. Further gains are possible if the country's regulatory framework is improved. Although the country's policies are market friendly, they are less than optimal. Increasing government efficiency and more investment in R&D may produce additional gains in economic growth. Taking these results together, it is possible to conclude that reasonable changes in the country's policies and institutions may increase Chile's rate of growth by 1 to 1.5 percentage points.

3.4.   Main Lessons

The main lesson that can be obtained from the latest period of economic slowdown in Chile is that economic reform is a continuous process. Countries that think that they have done all necessary reforms, risk returning to a low-growth scenario. A dynamic world makes it necessary to be alert to changes and to be ready to upgrade institutions and policies all the time. Chile is in a better position than most Latin American countries. Chile made the reforms earlier, has a stable macroeconomic environment (low inflation and budget deficit) and a better climate for investment. This is the reason why it is still growing, although at a much lower rate than in the previous decade, while many of its neighbors are in recession. However, to come back to high growth rates, the dynamic reform process has to be resumed. This does not mean the first generation of reforms, which are already in place and have been successful, but rather a later generation of reforms aimed at improving the quality of human capital and of institutions. Having, on average, perhaps the best institutions in Latin America is not enough to grow at 6–7 per cent again. The good news from the Chilean point of view is that there is a growing consensus that new reforms should be implemented. The authorities have been involved in a process directed at identifying and implementing them. If this process is successful, sooner rather than later, high growth will resume.

Perhaps this kind of discussion can be seen as something too distant from the reality of many Eastern European and former Soviet Union countries that are in the first phase of reforms, still facing the costs of these reforms or just starting to see the benefits. But as time goes by, they will realize that long-term growth requires a process of long-term reforms.

4. Conclusions

This paper analyzes the economic reform process that Chile has undertaken since the mid-1970s and draws lessons from this experience. Three decades ago Chile initiated a process of comprehensive economic reform. At that point in time Chile was a very closed economy with heavy government intervention. An import substitution and directed industrialization strategy (a way of picking the winners) – advocated by the ECLA (Economic Commission for Latin America) – had been adopted by Chile (and most Latin American countries) starting in the 1940s. The new economic authorities changed the economic model completely. Prices were liberalized, tariffs reduced, state-owned firms were privatized; there was a fiscal adjustment, a tax reform, a pension reform, financial liberalization and so on. Education, health, and other reforms in many areas were implemented, all with a free market orientation. Chile was the first country in Latin America to adopt this type of model, but in the late 1980s and early 1990s many countries followed the same path.

The results were a great success. In the mid-1980s, Chile entered what was later called the golden age of its economy. Between 1984 and 1997, Chile grew at 7 per cent on average per year, investment and saving boomed, inflation was reduced from around 25 per cent to a 2–4 per cent range, unemployment was significantly reduced and the number of people living under the poverty line fell from more than 40 per cent in 1987 to about 20 per cent in the late 1990s. However, these results took time to arrive. Indeed, just after the initial reforms in the mid-1970s, the economy boomed, but a few years later, in the early 1980s, it was in a deep recession. There were external and internal reasons for this recession. The latter included lax banking regulation and supervision. The cost of the banking crisis was huge and the lesson clear: financial liberalization has to come hand in hand with a proper financial regulation and a strong supervisory agency.

The Chilean experience also teaches us to be patient. Often the reforms take time to show their effects. Most likely, benefits come after the costs. However, in the end the balance is very positive. Chile, from a long-term perspective, is an example of a very successful reform process. The consensus on this matter in the country is so strong that the model was maintained in democracy despite the fact that it was implemented under a dictatorship.

Unfortunately, the golden age seems to be over. This year (2002) will mark the fifth consecutive year of modest growth in Chile (about three percent per year). Although, this is not low compared to other Latin American countries, it is quite low when compared to Chile's recent attainments. This rather modest performance has opened the debate on what must be done to return to a high-growth path. Chile's economic success in the last years is associated to the application of sensible economic policies and the existence of a sound institutional environment. This paper suggests that if the country is able to keep and improve these policies and institutions, an additional period of high growth may be assured. The reform process can never be considered finished. In a dynamic world, countries that are not constantly upgrading their institutions and policies will sooner rather than later experience a slowdown in economic growth.

Notes

1   See Harberger, 2001.
2   One of the most hotly discussed issues in Chile's economic reform has been the combination of an authoritarian government and a free market economic program. This was not usual for Latin America, where most military governments were also very interventionist in terms of economic policy. Fontaine (1992) describes this combination as the 'original sin' of the Chilean economic reform process. He argues that when, in 1990, the free market model was adopted by the new democratic authorities, the sin was expiated and the model became legitimized (1992).

3   For a comprehensive analysis of the whole process of economic reform in Chile, see Larraín and Vergara (eds) (2001).
4   See Larraín and Vergara (2001).
5   The owners of the failed banks were at the same time the owners of the failed companies. Loans from the banks to these companies surpassed all legal limits.
6   Hachette and Luders (1992).
7   In the case of countries with which Chile has signed free trade agreements, tariffs are zero for many products. There are also a few agricultural products that carry high tariffs.
8   Eyzaguirre and Larrañaga (1990) estimate the total cost at about 25 per cent of the 1990 Chilean GDP.
9   There are at least two reasons why it is reasonable to regulate these companies. First, the funds amount to mandatory saving. This means each individual is required by law to save in one of these companies for his/her retirement. In this sense, there is a sort of responsibility of the state regarding the prudent administration of the funds. Second, there are explicit state guarantees.
10   In Chile the target is headline inflation rather than core inflation.
11   This section is based on Beyer and Vergara (2001).
12   Indeed, for a smaller sample and the period 1970–91, Beyer (1997) corrects for human capital accumulation finding that, on average, TFP felt 0.48 percentage points, the decrease ranging from 0.04 to 1.01 percentage points.

References

Barra, Patricio and Jorrat, Michael (1999), 'Estimación de la Evasión Tributaria en Chile', Documento de Trabajo, SII, June.

Bennett, Herman, Loayza, Norman and Schmidt-Hebbel, Klaus (2001), 'Un Estudio del Ahorro Agregado por Agentes Económicos en Chile', in F. Morandé and R. Vergara (eds), *Análisis Empírico del Ahorro en Chile*, Banco Central de Chile, Santiago.

Beyer, Harald and Vergara, Rodrigo (2001), 'Productivity and Economic Growth: The Case of Chile', paper presented at the Fifth Annual Conference of the Central Bank of Chile *The Challenges of Economic Growth*, November, Santiago.

Beyer, H. (1997), 'Sources of Economic Growth: a Cross Country Comparison' paper presented at the Western Economic Association, Seattle.

Easterly, William (1993), 'How Much do Distortions Affect Growth', *Journal of Monetary Economics*, 32 (2).

Eyzaguirre, Nicolás and Larrañaga, Osvaldo (1990), 'Macroeconomía de las Operaciones Cuasifiscales en Chile', Working Paper, ILADES/Georgetown University, Santiago.

Fontaine, Arturo (1992), 'Sobre el Pecado Original de la Transformación Capitalista Chilena', in Levine, Barry B. (ed.), *El Desafío Neoliberal*, Norma, Colombia.

Gallego, Francisco and Loayza, Norman (2001), 'The Golden Period For Growth in Chile: Explanations and Forecasts', paper presented at the Fifth Annual Conference of the Central Bank of Chile *The Challenges of Economic Growth*, November, Santiago.

Hachette, Dominique (2001), 'Privatizaciones: Reforma Estructural pero Inconclusa', in Larraín, F. and Vergara, R. (eds), *La Transformación Económica de Chile*, Centro de Estudios Públicos, second edition.

Hachette, Dominique and Luders, Rolf (1992), *La Privatización en Chile*, Cinde.

Harberger, Arnold (2001), 'Memorandum Sobre la economía Chilena', written in 1956, in Larraín, F. and Vergara, R. (eds), *La Transformación Económica de Chile*, Centro de Estudios Públicos, second edition.

Hsieh, Chang-Tai and Parker, Jonathan A. (2001) 'Taxes and Growth in a Financially Underdeveloped Country: Explaining the Chilean Investment Boom', mimeo, Princeton University, June.

Krueger, Alan (1990), 'Government Failures in Development', *Journal of Economic Perspectives*, 4 (March).

Larraín, Felipe and Vergara, Rodrigo (eds) (2001), *La Transformación Económica de Chile*, Centro de Estudios Públicos, second edition.

Larraín, Felipe and Vergara, Rodrigo (2001), 'Un Cuarto de Siglo de Reformas Fiscales', in Larraín, F. and Vergara, R. (eds), *La Transformación Económica de Chile*, Centro de Estudios Públicos, second edition.

North, Douglass C. (1992), *Institutions, Institutional Change and Economic Performance*, Cambridge University Press, Cambridge.

Roldós, Jorge (1997), 'El Crecimiento del Producto Potencial en Mercados Emergentes', in Morandé, F. and Vergara, R. (eds), *Análisis Empírico del Crecimiento en Chile*, Centro de Estudios Públicos, Santiago.

PART III
ONE WORLD, DIFFERENT PATHS
OF DEVELOPMENT

Chapter 7

The Dual-Transformation of China: Past 20 Years and 50 Years Ahead

Gang Fan

China has been one of the world's fastest growing economies in the past 20 years and has also achieved remarkable progress in the institutional transformation towards a market system. However, at the same time, people have kept asking throughout those 20 years, just as they do at the present moment, (1) where China is heading or transiting to, both in the next step and in the long-term perspective, and (2) whether China is likely to collapse due to any of the current economic, social and political problems.

This paper is an effort to answer these two questions.

The Complexity of the 'Dual Transformation' Process in China

China differs from Eastern European countries because it is a low-income, rural-society-based developing country. At the same time, China differs from other developing countries, like the Southeast Asian economies, because it is a 'transition economy' sharing with Russia and Eastern European countries many similar problems, such as state-owned enterprises and government control. And China is a big country with a population of 1.2 billion, which makes any problem tougher and more difficult to handle.

This argument means that while other countries may be facing one set of problems, related either to 'development' or 'transition', China faces two at the same time. It is simultaneously undertaking to transform the rural economy into a modern society and the planning economy into a market system. It is this dual nature that makes the transformation process in China more difficult, as the two sets of problems complicate and amplify each other. For instance, the legal reform in China involves not only changing one kind of laws or rules into another, but also a process of building up the whole concept of the 'rule of law' and the whole set of accompanying institutions, starting from the initial condition of a rural society with a specific, 'medieval' legacy of Chinese history. After the laws have been set down on paper, a large body of court interpretations needs to accumulate to get these laws firmly established in practice.

Such a dual nature of the problems faced by the economy determines the time horizon of the dual transformation: it will unavoidably take China a long time to build up an orderly, functioning market system. The past twenty years have been only the first phase and it will be no surprise if we take another 20, 30, or 50 years to fulfill our objectives. In general, institution building is a long-term process anyway. Seventy years may not be too much for a transformation from a 'medieval' society to a modern market economy, compared to how much time Western countries have taken since the 17th century and bearing in mind that China did not benefit from colonialism.

Such a historical, long-time perspective is necessary to understand the current situation. Hard problems are so easy to find that they are hardly newsworthy, because the country is and will remain beset by all kinds of adversities for a long time. The real news should be changes – for better or for worse – which have come about since yesterday, and development trends for tomorrow. The question should not be whether China has problems, but whether China can develop quickly enough to close the gap to the advanced market economies. The banking sector, for instance, is poorly developed, but just 5 years ago, all the state-owned banks were not yet really banks, merely serving as government departments for financial resource reallocation. The corruption stories are disgusting, but the very fact that you can read about such stories (even if just selected ones) in official newspapers constitutes progress in many respects. A picture carried by major Western media of a garbage-collecting family with a monthly income of USD 50 is depressing and touching, but the most important thing was missing from the report: namely, that the family used to earn probably as little as USD 5 only yesterday, before they moved out from their home village in the mountains. The overall political stability that has puzzled many observers is fundamentally based on the fact that most interest groups in society have become better off in many respects over the past 20 years and still have expectations for a further improvement, no matter how difficult their current situation is. It should not be a puzzle at all if we look at it from a historical perspective.

The State Sector Reform and the Development of the Non-state Sectors

It has been pointed out by many commentators that the most serious economic problem in China is the situation of state-owned enterprises (SOEs). Inefficient SOEs have increasingly hampered economic growth. Unemployment among former state employees is the major cause of local-scale social unrest. The mounting non-performing loans owed by SOEs to state banks have caused a credit crunch that contributes to the on-going deflation. And the SOE reform does not seem to have achieved real progress in most of the large-sized SOEs. These problems have led some analysts to claim that China was (and is) on the verge of collapse and its economic growth would soon stop.

It seems puzzling, therefore, that China has not collapsed and growth continues and will continue in the foreseeable future.

The key to understanding this puzzle is that economic growth in China is now mostly supported by the non-state sectors (NSS), rather than the state sector. The non-state sectors, which consist of private companies, self-employed persons, share-holding corporations, joint-ventures with foreign investment, and community-owned rural industries, a great part of which are actually private undertakings, now contribute 74 per cent of the industrial output, 62.2 per cent of the GDP, and has attained an over-100 per cent increase in employment (See Tables 7.1 and 7.2). This means that even though the state sector's problems have become worse and worse, the importance of SOEs has been decreasing in view of the overall economic growth and development of market economy.

Table 7.1: Main indicators of the development of the NSS (%)

Year	Share in total industrial output	Share in newly-employed labor	Contribution to fiscal revenue	Share in fixed investment	Share in retail sales
1978	22.4	28	14.1	–	45.4
1980	24	36.4	23.3	18.1	48.6
1984	23	–	23	33.9	–
1990	45.4	39.5	28.7	33.9	60.4
1992	51.9	50.2	28.7	32	58.7
1994	62.7	58.9	28.6	43.6	68.1
1996	71.5	65.6	–	47.6	72.8
1997	68.4[a]	201.5[b]	–	47.5	76.7
1999	71.8[a]	564.0[b]	–	46.6	–

[a] Data have been adjusted for certain types of ownership (China Statistical Yearbook 2000, p. 409).

[b] The figures reflect the change of the statistical definition of employment in various sectors: from 1997 onward, all employees working in a reformed enterprise (a former SOE) are no longer counted as state-sector employees, but included in the non-state sector. The statistics also reflect the fact that the state sector is laying off, and the non-state sector is increasingly employing. See also Table 7.2.

Source: 1978-96 from China Reform Foundation, 1997, p. 219; the remaining years from China Statistical Yearbook 2000.

Table 7.2: Contributions to the increase of non-farming jobs by state and non-state sectors respectively

Year	Total increase of non-farming jobs (millions of persons)	New employment of state sector as % total increase	New non-farming employment of non-state sector as % total increase
1990	37.28	6.38	93.62
1991	8.33	38.18	61.82
1992	14.10	15.96	84.04
1993	24.03	1.29	98.71
1994	11.66	25.21	74.79
1995	21.83	2.15	97.85
1996	17.02	–1.00	101.00
1997	1.97	–101.52	201.52
1998	4.28	–464.02	564.02

Source: China Statistical Yearbook, 2000.

The most important feature of China's 'gradual' or 'incremental' approach to institutional transformation so far has been the development of the market-oriented non-state sectors, not the reform of the state sector.[1] The low level of industrialization and nationalization (never reached 20 per cent in terms of the proportion of state employees in the total labor force) allowed China to rely on its vast rural and 'non-state' labor force to expand the new sector first without reforming the old sector for a while. In comparison, Russia did not enjoy this 'luxury', because without releasing all the resources from the state sector, the new system would hardly have got started[2] (Sachs and Woo, 1993).

The reform of SOEs has long been delayed, compared with the 'radical approach to reform' in some other countries. But one of the key elements of the 'incremental approach to reform' is that the development of new sectors and changes of economic structure should create and improve the conditions for the reform of the old sector:

- The growing competition from the non-state sector brought down the monopolistic profits of SOEs and pushed them into the corner of financial difficulties. Without such difficulties, no one would like to accept the reform programs.
- The jobs created by the non-state sector prepared the ground for the 'mass lay-off' in the state sector. The overall economic growth supported by the growth of the non-state sector also allows the government to mobilize some resources

to compensate the unemployed state workers. As a result, over 15 million state employees have been laid off in the past 5 years, without causing major social instability.

- Because of the growing private capital and entrepreneurial capacity, the 'reform' takes a form closer to 'taking-over' than to merely 'dismantling'. As the non-state companies are not yet big enough to take over large-sized SOEs, privatization has been mainly restricted so far to small and medium-sized SOEs, except for a few cases of a joint-venture between large SOEs and foreign investors. Some reports show that in certain regions over 70 per cent of small SOEs have been privatized one way or another, including employee and management buyout and conversion into so-called 'employee share-holding company' as the first step of reform.

Although many large SOEs are not yet ready to be reformed, the conditions will be surely improving with the further development of the non-state sectors.[3] The recent reform policies adopted by the central government have not only reconfirmed the direction of 'restructuring the property rights', but also introduced some more concrete steps towards the 'diversification of ownership' by offering 'executive stock options' and a further reduction of state holding in the listed companies, which were previously un-tradable.

The Dynamic Evolution of the 'Objective Model' of the Transformation

Some questions may emerge from the above discussion of reforms about where China's economic system is heading and what is the real meaning of the officially declared reform objective of 'socialist market economy'.

To answer such questions, it may be useful to look back at how the official line was drawn at various points during the past 20 years. Box 7.1 shows that the official 'objective formula' has kept changing and evolving (in the same direction) constantly over the past 20 years, from 'planned economy supplemented with some market elements' in 1979 to 'socialist market economy' with the withdrawing of SOEs from most 'competitive industries' and the introduction of 'mixed ownership'.

From this point of view, it does not seem very meaningful to spend too much time to clarify 'what is' the current official objective. A more useful exercise is to analyze when, why and in what direction the objective changes. Such an analysis reveals that nothing is left to chance and the logic of political economy prevails. For instance, a major policy shift took place in 1993, when the words 'socialist market economy', replacing the 'planned economy', were first adopted by the 'Reform Decisions' of the Central Committee of the Chinese Communist Party (CCP). This move followed the previous year's announcement that the share of the non-state sector in the industrial output had exceeded for the first time 50 per cent (see Figure 7.1). In 1996, the state industrial sector as a whole suffered its first ever 'net loss'. Then, in the following year, the CCP adopted the policies of 'diversifying ownership' and 'developing private sector together with the state sector'. Then, in 1998, the Constitution was amended by adding the provision that 'Private ownership enjoys equal protection and promotion as state ownership'. In short, the definition and contents of 'socialist market economy' change over time according to the changing circumstances. With the further growth of the private sector and private business community, which serves as the main basis of the economic prosperity and social stability, the Communist Party has recently started to invite private 'millionaire' businessmen to join the Party (see Box 7.1). There is no doubt that the official 'objectives' will keep changing in the same direction.

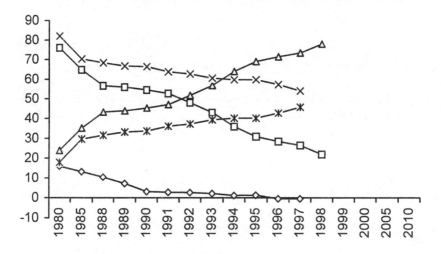

Figure 7.1 Political Economy Dynamics of China's Transition

It may be correct to say that the lack of clear-cut reform objectives is a major weakness of the Chinese transformation. But talking only about 'what is achievable and acceptable' without specifying a 'final destination' may have its pragmatic virtues and save a lots of political costs.

Box 7.1: **The gradual evolution of the official 'Formula' of reform objectives since 1978**

Time	Formulation of reform objectives
1978 – Oct. 1984	Planned economy supplemented with some market elements
Oct. 1984 – Oct. 1987	Planned commodity economy
Oct. 1987 – June 1989	'The state regulates the market and the market regulates enterprises'
June 1989 – 1991	'Organic integration of planned economy and market regulations'
1992	A share-holding system and a (newly started) security market can function under socialism
Oct. 1992	Socialist market economy
1994	'Corporatization of SOEs and reform of property rights'
1997	Developing the state sector together with all other kinds of ownership; 'holding on to large SOEs while letting small ones go to the market'.
1998	Constitution amendment: private ownership enjoys equal promotion and protection
Oct. 1999	SOEs withdraw from competitive industries; diversification of ownership of corporate and 'mixed ownership'; executive stock options for SOEs.
July 2001	'Three representative functions of the Party'; permission for owners of private and individual enterprises to be Party members; further development of various ownership forms.

Source: various official documents of the CCP Central Committee.

Can the Reform and Growth Continue for another 20 Years? Pitfalls and Ways-out

Why '20 years'? First of all, the destruction of an institution is easy and can be accomplished overnight, but institution-building takes time. For a country like China, it may take much longer to build up modern market-based institutions, including all that is required by the rule of law. Second, it may take 20–40 years for China to finish its industrialization process, during which more than 400 million rural laborers will have to find new jobs in non-farming sectors in the current global environment of technological revolution and over-supply.

There are many obstacles and potential explosive issues which may cause crises or a 'collapse' and stop the process of transformation and economic growth. Some major economic problems include, among others:

- huge non-performing loans and financial risks
- large numbers of the unemployed and social unrest
- income disparity in general, and
- regional disparity in particular
- rural poverty
- challenges of globalization
- corruption and government reform.

The discussion of these issues will show that despite the great difficulties in dealing with the problems, there are still some ways out.

The Financial Risk

China is now notorious for its high percentage of non-performing loans (NPL) in its state banking system. The official estimate of the NPL/total credit ratio in the major state banks was about 26 per cent in 2000, and 24 per cent in 2001, equivalent to about 25 per cent of the GDP. If we add the NPL transferred to the Asset Management Companies (AMC), which were specially designed to deal with the NPL, the total NPL/GDP proportion might be estimated at as much as 40 per cent. This may be one of the highest ratios in the world.

In some sense, a domestic financial crisis has continued in China since 1996. Indeed, the high level of non-performing loans owed by SOEs to the state banks has caused a sort of credit crunch since 1996. The monetary authorities and the banks have had to tighten the financial discipline and to take risk control as their first priority. As a result, the volume of new credits to SOEs has been reduced and some kind of monetary contraction has ensued that contributes to the on-going deflation since October 1997. It is the high level of non-performing loans and the insolvency of the banks, in comparison with some other Asian countries, that lead people to believe that a financial collapse in China is highly probable in the near future.[4]

But some elements necessary to make a correct judgment of China's financial situation and a valid prediction of a crisis are missing here.

One of the major reasons for China's high-level NPL is that the government shifted all its fiscal responsibilities for SOEs to the state banks in the mid-1980s. Since that time, the government has provided neither equity investment, nor subsidies for SOEs, all the needs of which have been met by the state banks instead, in the form of loans. From this point of view, the non-performing loans owed by SOEs to the state banks are actually quasi-government deficits. But at the same time, it is a serious mistake not to take into account the situation of the government budget in the assessment of overall financial risks. The reality is that while the NPL level is extraordinarily high compared to other countries, including some Southeast Asian economies, China's government debt has remained extraordinarily low by world standards. At the end of 2000, it was only equivalent to less than 14.5 per cent of the GDP. Such a comprehensive picture[5] (see Table 7.3) explains why China still enjoys some financial stability despite the high-level NPL and why the Chinese government is still able to mobilize resources to stabilize the economy, including the use of debt-financing as an expansionary fiscal policy instrument to deal with the deflation. It also explains why China remains capable of keeping the growth and reform going.

Table 7.3:   Financial risk indicators in Chinese economy

2000	%
NPL over GDP – official statement	25
Liability of AMCs over GDP	16
Government domestic debt over GDP	14.5
Total foreign debt over GDP	15
Current balance of the social security system	0
Overall national contingent liability	**70.5**
GDP growth rate	8
Budget deficit as % of GDP	2.8
Interest rate on government bonds (1 year)	2.4
Growth rate of budget revenue (3-year average)	19
Current account balance USD billion	20.5
Capital account balance USD billion	1.9
Total short-term foreign debt over GDP	1
Foreign exchange reserve, USD billion (until Sept. 2001)	200.1
Inflation rate	0

Meanwhile, China's external balance remains quite manageable, too. Both the current account and capital account are in surplus, and the foreign exchange reserve has risen to USD 220 billion by now. Foreign debt has been well serviced so far, and the short-term debt over GDP ratio is also extraordinarily low, amounting to just 1 per cent. In addition, China's capital account is not opened yet, and the portfolio investment is minimal. Therefore, it seems safe to say that there will be no financial crisis in China in the foreseeable future, similar to those which occurred in some Asian countries in 1997–8.

The solution to the NPL problem and the way to ensure eventual financial stability will depend, of course, on the reform of SOEs and the banking sector, which will take as long to accomplish as will the whole economic transformation. The good news is that some kind of consensus has been reached among policy makers and bankers at all levels, who all agree that strenuous efforts are needed to stop the growth of NPL.

Unemployment

To avoid confusion and misjudgment of the problem, it should be noticed that there are three kinds of unemployment and under-employment in China.

First, the **unemployment of urban labor**, reflected by the official 'urban unemployment rate' (about 3.5 per cent of urban labor force in recent years). It is mainly accounted for by newcomers to the urban labor force, by people in transition between jobs, and by people who have been laid off in the private sectors. The formally registered urban unemployed are covered by an unemployment insurance managed by the social welfare department of the government.

Second, the **rural under-employment**. There is a total of about 600 million rural laborers, of whom 200 million have become engaged in non-farming activities (about 100 million have already settled in cities), and 70 per cent of the rest are actually underemployed, cultivating very small plots of household land. However, the rural people are never considered as totally unemployed, because every rural inhabitant is entitled to a piece of farming land, small though it may be. Therefore this group should be categorized as 'under-employed'. The high level of underemployment drives rural people out (of rural areas or of agriculture), in search for better-paid jobs in other places and other industries. If they find such jobs, they are better-off; if not, they may return to their land as the last resort, to get a livelihood (or find 'security'). But the employment of rural people has never been the responsibility of the government. They have never been covered by any government-run social-security program, either, even under the previous socialist welfare system. From this point of view, rural under-employment is in principle not a short-term political issue, and the rural people in fact do not expect the government to solve their job problems.

In the long run – in, say, 40 years – bearing in mind the population growth, a total of 400 million rural laborers may have to be reallocated to non-farming industries. Otherwise, the increasing urban-rural income disparity may cause great social instability.

Third, the **laid-off former state employees**. This is a real political problem by nature. The laid-off state workers had been guaranteed employment for life by the government under the previous, implicit or explicit, socialist 'social contract'. The reform put them out of jobs. But so far the laid-off state employees are protected under some special arrangements as they retain a special status of 'off-post workers' (*Xia-gang Zhi-gong*). With this special status, they are entitled to receive a certain minimum payment (higher than the unemployment insurance payment), re-training programs and several job offers during the 2–3 year period after being laid off. In 1997–2001, more than 23 million state workers became laid off. But so far the problem seems manageable in terms of social stability, as the laid-off people are protected relatively well by the government. Under the best scenario, their number might drop to 20 million in the near future. But no one assumes this should happen overnight.

While the figures pertaining to the first two kinds of unemployment (under-employment) may change with the macro-business cycles, the third one is mainly an institutional issue, independent of the cycles – some people must be laid off simply because the reforms proceed. More importantly, the first two kinds of unemployment do not seem very troublesome politically, whereas the mass lay-off may pose a danger to social stability.

But it should be noticed that, with the changed overall economic conditions, the lay-offs have become politically more acceptable in the past years:

- The SOEs concerned are already troubled by financial difficulties and many of them are unable to pay the workers anyway. Most worker protests in the past years have been caused by the delay (6 months, 10 months, etc.) in wage payment. Without much hope for improvement, people realize more and more clearly that the SOEs are no longer reliable as a guarantee of employment and income growth. In short, staying with SOEs becomes less and less attractive a choice.

- Meanwhile, after 20 years of development, the non-state sector now provides many more jobs. The possibilities of finding a new job in the non-state sector (or just simply becoming self-employed) and getting better paid are both increasing, assuming that overall growth continues. In other word, to leave the SOE sector increasingly becomes a viable alternative.

- The lay-off package for the workers normally enables them to keep some benefits they enjoyed in the SOEs. The government has increased the expenditures on the so-called 'Urban Reemployment Centers' in the past two years and consequently has improved the financial situation of the unemployed.[6]

In conclusion, it seems that China can still manage mass lay-offs involving 3–5 million employees each year in the near future, without running the risk of major social unrest.

The real problem for China, however, is how to create jobs for the 400 million rural laborers in the coming decade. Obviously, this is tantamount to the question of whether China can continue its growth for the next 40 years.

Income Disparities

The increasing income disparity between groups, regions and rural vs. urban populations has become a major economic and social problem since the beginning of the reform. Consequently, increasing concerns and complaints are voiced about all these disparities, although they have not as yet given rise to major conflicts or social unrest. But the following facts should be kept in mind:

1. The starting point of China's economic and social transformation was an over-equalized society under the former socialist regime. The introduction of the market system means in itself an enlargement of income differentials, without which the old system would still prevail in China. From this point of view, the disparity is introduced deliberately and is seen as a good thing. For example, there must be lay-offs and there must be a relative decrease of the state employees' income, in order to reform SOEs and develop the private sector at the same time.
2. In the past 20 years, a large majority of the population, including most inhabitants of poor rural areas, have been better off in real and absolute terms, although the relative position of some groups may have deteriorated. This situation is fundamentally different from the case when a large proportion of the population is worse off in absolute terms. The groups who end up being worse-off are mainly older state employees over 40–45 years of age. They have been laid off and find it especially difficult to get new jobs. However, as a generation who remembers the shortages and hunger of the 1960s and 1970s, they seem more tolerant to the current difficulties (compared to the younger generations, who benefit the most from the reform and growth), because of the feeling of overall improvement. Even so, they still strongly oppose the reforms and succeed in slowing down their pace.
3. With a population of 1.2 billion inhabitants, most of whom still live in the countryside, hoping for better income jobs in non-farming industries, China's wage level for the blue-collar workers could remain very low for a long time. At the opposite end of the spectrum, with the growth of the financial market and high-tech industries, a small group of white-collar people may soon catch up with the international income standards. Therefore, the problem of income disparity may be a long-lasting one. China has to face it, as long as it intends to achieve economic development. It is hard to expect from the government to do much about it, if it is committed to the market-oriented reform and economic growth.

The key policy issue here is not how to make a government 'income policy' narrow the gap, but how to ensure that the majority of the population are better off in absolute terms, while sustaining the overall economic growth. In this regard, the further promotion of labor intensive industries, together with the development of 'high-tech' branches, could be the right policy to increase the income of the vast majority across the board.

Regional Disparity and Mass Migrations

As a result of rapid opening up and growth of the coastal regions, regional disparity becomes one of the most sensitive political issues in China.

The problem should not be exaggerated, however. The decentralization of the government and the increase of regional economic differences do not necessarily lead to attempts at a 'split-up', as speculated by some observers.[7] China is now much more integrated than ever, as the market forces bring benefits to all. The poor regions are more dependent on the rich regions' labor market, capital flows, and technology transfers; and the rich ones (like Guangdong) rely more than ever on the markets and resources of the other areas. Every region has its own reasons to complain about the 'disparities' one way or another. But it is clear that having an integrated national market is in everyone's interest.

Meanwhile, there are other factors that contribute to narrowing the gap in per capita income between regions.[8]

* As the living standards and labor costs (as well as land costs) have continued to grow in coastal regions for the last couple of years, investment, both foreign and domestic, has started to move inward to central China, along the Yangtze River. Growth rate in those regions (such as Anhui and Hubei) has already exceeded that of the coastal regions in the previous 3 years.
* The government has started to increase fiscal transfers to and investment in the interior regions, although still on a very limited scale. Recently, the central government has announced a plan of further 'exploration' of the West that would be a major part of the Tenth Five-year plan for 2001-2005.
* Migrations play an important role. People have started to move out of poorer regions to richer regions, looking for better-paid jobs. A working population of over 200 million has migrated to such places as the coastal cities. In the long-run, migration may be the only way for some regions to increase their per capita income, given the resources and the geographical conditions. It can be expected that China will experience even larger mass domestic migrations and the population map will be significantly changed as the economic transformation proceeds.

In conclusion, it seems that regional disparity is not a serious obstacle to continued economic growth and neither is it a major potential source of social instability.

Rural Development and Urbanization

China has experienced an over-supply of grain in recent years, so the voices asking 'who will feed China' have been fading. However, the low productivity of agriculture and low rural population income will remain challenging problems both at present and in the near future.

The key issue here is that there are too many people working on the small cultivable area and, therefore, the ultimate solution to the problem is nothing else but industrialization and urbanization, which move people out of the land. Studies show that the marginal product of labor in agriculture is almost negligible and only the reduction of the number of people who rely on the land as their source of income can make the use of modern technology feasible in China's agriculture. And only an increase of farmland area per head can bring a meaningful increase of per capita income in the agricultural sector.

The rural industries in the past 20 years have played an important role in improving the income level of rural people and supporting the overall economic growth. As a result, the industrialization of the Chinese economy progressed significantly: non-farming employment[9] as the percentage of total labor force was up to 54 per cent by the end of 1997. More than 100 million rural laborers have found new jobs in non-farming sectors. This process has been slowing down in recent years, demonstrating its limitations, as it has not been accompanied by urbanization. At the end of 1998, only 32 per cent of the total population lived in cities and towns. Such a disproportion between industrialization and urbanization is one of the major bottlenecks for further growth.

The government is adopting policies to speed up urbanization. More large cities or groups of cities are to be built in the coastal areas. However, in the foreseeable future, China's agriculture will remain highly labor-intensive and the increase of rural income will be very limited.

Challenges of Globalization

There has been a growing consensus among the Chinese people that globalization is a process you have to participate in or you would be marginalized. People have realized that the opening-up has been actually one of the main pushes for domestic reforms and it is the only way to 'catch up'. The opening-up process will continue and accelerate with or without China's WTO accession.

On the other hand, people have learned from the Asian financial crisis that the opening-up and globalization are full of risks and bring about great challenges. To a country handicapped by serious domestic institutional problems, an over-speedy opening up could be devastating. Therefore, domestic reforms and market liberalization should be pursued together in a compatible way and a 'premature market liberalization' should be avoided. It can be predicted that further opening of the Chinese market will continue to be, generally, a gradual process in order to minimize the costs. Nothing dramatic or radical should be expected. In particular, the financial market opening and the capital account convertibility of foreign exchange will not happen soon.

With the WTO accession, China may be able to enjoy a high level of foreign direct investment (over USD 40 billion per year now, but hopefully over USD 60 billion by 2003) in the near future. The trade surplus will be declining due to the deflation pressures on the international market and the further opening of the Chinese market. It may not be a bad thing because the previous high-level balance-of-payments surplus and foreign exchange reserves are actually not economically efficient for a developing country like China. But in the foreseeable future, China's international accounts will remain balanced and no debt crisis should be expected.

Corruption and the Government Reform

There has been some progress in the government reform in recent years: the restructuring of the administration has been under way since 1998; the anti-corruption campaign has been hiked up; the village election is now the nation-wide practice; and the People's Congress now plays a greater role as a balance to the powers of the administration. But there is no doubt that China's economic transformation requires further acceleration of government reforms.

A great part of the corruption problem is tied to the existence of large state-owned economic sectors, and not only the government bureaucracy and political structure. Therefore, the privatization of SOEs and reforms of other state-owned institutions will be among the key factors to reduce corruption.

The on-going development of the private sector and the fast growth of the middle class are laying down the foundation for the political transition towards a constructive, rather than destructive, democracy.

Very importantly, there seems to be a consensus among most Chinese people that China should under no circumstances go back to the chaos or civil wars which stopped its development in the past century. For most people, nothing is more important than the continuation of economic prosperity and the catching up on the international market. The fear of civil wars and social chaos will bring some last-minute compromises among conflicting groups. This, plus the perception of being better off than in the past, are the essential foundations of political stability.

And the examples of relatively peaceful and gradual transition to a constructive democracy in some Newly Industrialized Asian Economies (such as Korea and Taiwan) make people confident that China may be able to do the same too.

Conclusion

The Chinese economy obviously faces many problems and difficulties, each of which could lead to some kind of crisis or 'collapse'. When China enters a new stage of development and transition following the WTO accession, many scenarios could apply with equal probability. But according to the analyses above, it seems unlikely that China is headed for a financial crisis, political turmoil or vast social unrest in the near future. The government still has some room for policy maneuver, both financially and politically. Growth will continue at a level lower than before, but still as high as 7–8 per cent. The reform will go on in all aspects, although still in a gradual manner. No dramatic changes are expected in the next 5 years, but the gradual accumulation of small evolutionary steps can be very meaningful. However, the question remains, of course, the same: is the progress at the present stage sufficient to lay down the foundation for further development, or is it too small to avoid a crisis at the next stage?

Notes

1   FAN, Gang (1994), 'Incremental changes and dual-track transition: understanding the case of China', *Economic Policy*, Great Britain, December.
2   Sachs, Jeffrey and Wing Thye Woo (1994), 'Structural Factors in the Economic Reforms of China, Eastern Europe and the Former Soviet Union,' *Economic Policy*, April.
3   The author once wrote in a syndicate article, published in some European newspapers, that 'in some sense, a West Germany is emerging in China in the process of reforming East Germany'.
4   See Nicholas Lardy, 1998, 'China's Unfinished Economic Reform', Brookings Institute.
5   We may define the sum of government debt, NPL, and total foreign debt as the 'government comprehensive liability' for China, being an indicator of the financial risk of the economy. An international comparison based on a similar calculation for Southeast Asian countries shows that China's overall liability is not too bad (about 50 per cent), as compared with 73–114 per cent in the other countries. See FAN Gang, 1999.
6   In 1998, a new program was introduced by the central government, i.e., the 'Urban Re-employment Center'(URC). The key new element of the URC is that the lay-off and re-employment should be financed by 3 parties, i.e., the central government, the local government, and the company, instead of only the company as before. This apparently has improved the situation of the laid-off people. According a Ministry of Labor report, the percentage of workers who got paid in time increased to 97 per cent in 1998 from the previous year's 12 per cent.
7   We do not discuss ethnic factors in this paper.
8   It should be noticed that part of the problem of regional disparities is institutional. For example, the slow growth of the Northeast regions has been mainly due to the concentration of SOEs in those regions. From this point of view, the problem will not be solved until the reforms advance.
9   This includes the workers in rural industrial enterprises and rural self-employed non-farming individuals.

References

Byrd, William A. and Qingsong Lin (1990), *China's Rural Industry: Structure, Development, and Reform*, Oxford University Press.

China Reform Foundation (1997), *'Soft Landing' of the Chinese Economy* (in Chinese), Yuandong Publishing House of Shanghai.

Fan, Gang (1994), 'Incremental changes and dual-track transition: understanding the case of China', *Economic Policy*, Great Britain, December.

Fan, Gang (1996), *The Political Economy of China's Gradual Reform* (in Chinese), Yuandong Publishing House of Shanghai.

Fan, Gang (2000), 'The Dynamics of China's Transition—Growth of the Non-state Sector and Reform of the State Sector', in Wang, Xiaolu and Fan, Gang (eds), *Sustainability of China's Economic Growth*, Economic Science Press.

Fan, Gang (2001), *Follow-up Analysis on China's Macroeconomic Variables* (in Chinese), National Economic Research Institute, Beijing.

Fan, Gang and Woo, Wing T. (1996), 'State Enterprise Reform as a Source of Macroeconomic Instability: The Case of China,' (Fan and Woo) *Asian Economic Journal*, Vol. 10, No, 3. November 1996, pp. 207–24.

Lu Wen (1999), *On TVEs' Tendency of Leaving Agriculture* (*Guanyu Xiangzhen Qiye Li'nong Qingxiang Yanjiu*), Ministry of Agriculture, Beijing.

Ma Hong and Wang Mengkui (1999), *China Development Studies*, Selected Research Reports of DRC of the State Council, China Development Publishers, Beijing.

Sachs, Jeffrey and Woo, Wing Thye (1994), 'Structural Factors in the Economic Reforms of China, Eastern Europe and the Former Soviet Union', *Economic Policy*, April.

State Statistical Bureau, various years, *China Statistical Yearbook*, Beijing.

State Statistical Bureau, various years, *China Township and Village Enterprise Yearbook*, Beijing.

Xia Xiaolin (2000), 'Sustained Growth of the Chinese Economy and the Non-State Sector', in Wang, Xiaolu and Fan, Gang (eds), *Sustainability of China's Economic Growth*, Economic Science Press.

Statistics:

China Statistical Yearbook, various years, China Statistic Press.

China Financial Statistics Yearbook, 1987, 1994, China Financial Press.

China Statistics of Fixed Investment, various years, China Statistical Press.

China Statistics of Industrial Economy, various years, China Statistical Press.

Chapter 8

Is Catching-up Possible in Europe?

Daniel Daianu[1]

Introduction: The Scarcity of *Catching-up* in Modern Economic History

As is generally known, the EU accession of Central and Eastern European countries is predicated upon the fulfillment of economic and political preconditions. Less known, however, is that whereas political criteria, for most of the candidates, are considered less of a problem, economic criteria still pose significant difficulties. In this sense, although there are large differences amongst accession (transition) countries, it is nonetheless true that quite a few of them suffer from spreading poverty and diminishing *social cohesion*, high inflation and fragility of financial systems, worsening social indicators, weak public administration etc., all of which should indeed cause serious worry as to their ability to achieve 'real' convergence[2] and cope with competitive pressures inside the EU. Real convergence would, in simple terms, boil down to a rapid increase of income per capita, that is to say, to economic catching-up.

In the current debate on EU enlargement, there is an apparent mythical hypothesis/belief that if the set of preconditions set by Brussels are fulfilled, rapid and sustained economic growth would ensue, which would allow the newly admitted countries to catch up economically in the not too distant future. An encapsulation of this thesis is the expression: 'A well functioning competitive market economy', which would be able to withstand competitive pressures inside the EU. Those who accept this thesis are ready to point out to the experiences of Ireland and Spain in Europe, in particular, and to, a lesser extent, Portugal. But the evidence in this regard is not so conclusive. Thence, I will argue, in this paper, that taking for granted the above hypothesis can be misleading, unless the possible sources of growth are examined in a thorough and open-minded way.[3]

There is glaring evidence around the world which should make us more cautious about the chances of economic catching-up. Angus Maddison's magisterial work[4] on long-term dynamics in the world economy is telling in this respect. As a matter of fact, these dynamics exhibit, essentially, divergence between rich and poor countries. The only exception is the rise of a cluster of Asian countries after the Second World War. Catching-up with the rich countries, or 'beta-convergence', as some economists call it, is very rare; more frequent is convergence inside clusters (groups) of countries, or what is called 'sigma-convergence'. However, Central and Eastern European countries (CEECs) are interested primarily in beta-convergence, that is to say in catching-up with the richer countries of the EU. Such a convergence would supposedly mitigate possible tensions between the richer and the poorer countries of an enlarged EU (against the backdrop of regional aid accounting for much of the EU budget).

Worldwide experience shows that economic catching-up (beta-convergence) requires high saving and investment ratios, constant upgrading of educational standards and of the work force, steady improvement of competitiveness, and tolerable social strain (i.e. a high degree of social cohesion); and first and foremost, it requires a steady and rapid improvement in what economists call total factor productivity,[5] which relies on a steady and fast increase of labor productivity. And it is not clear at all that the 'magic' words of reform (liberalization, privatization, opening) are sufficient to provide the definitive solution. As regards proper institutions, which should be conducive to rapid and sustained growth, arguably, these cannot be constructed or improved at will.[6]

This paper aims at raising the awareness of an issue which is more complicated to deal with than it is conventionally assumed.

The Current Debate on the Sources of Economic Growth (Development)

The debate on the sources of economic growth (potential for catching-up) is often inadequately reflected in the operational frameworks used by governments and aid agencies. This is, to some extent, not surprising, since there has always been a delay between theoretical developments and applied science. But there are stark facts, which should be kept in mind, and several pieces of compelling evidence:

- Policies aimed at fostering growth in developing countries seem to have fared quite poorly, in many respects, in the last couple of decades – a time of firm application of the main tenets of the 'Washington Consensus'.[7] According to a foremost development economist, William Easterly (until recently on the World Bank staff), during 1980–98, average per capita income growth in developing countries was practically 0.0 per cent (!), as compared to 2.5 per cent during 1960–79.[8] I would add that this discrepancy becomes even larger when singling out the economic performance of some Asian countries – which, as an increasing number of economists would concede, did pursue export orientation, but also implemented measures which often were at odds with the 'orthodox' policies;[9] these countries shaped their own, particular, strategies. As Easterly also points out, 'the increase in world interest rates, the increased debt burden of developing countries, the growth slowdown in the industrial world, and skill-biased technical change may have contributed' to this stagnation.[10] Easterly also stresses the inability of governments' policies worldwide to make good use of incentives for growth. This state of affairs begs a simple question:

why is it so difficult to use incentives in order to foster sustained growth?[11] Easterly goes on, 'We economists who work on poor countries should leave aside some of our past arrogance. The problem of making poor countries rich was much more difficult than we thought.'

- Mainstream (neoclassical) theory has still to explain why divergence is so much prevalent in the world economy.[12] Moreover, endogenous growth models[13] and economic geography models have reinforced misgivings about the unqualified optimism on the distribution of benefits of free trade and free capital movements. Hence, a natural question arises: is opening (integration) to the outer economy advantageous, irrespective of circumstances?

- There has been an insufficient attention paid to the reality of asymmetries and informational problems in the functioning of both domestic and international markets, and to the key role of institutions. Partially, this is mirrored by the talk regarding 'second-generation reforms', 'good governance' and 'reinvigorating the state's capabilities'. But as Dani Rodrik remarked, 'The bad news is that the operational implications of this for the design of development strategy are not that clear', and 'There are many different models of a mixed economy. The major challenge facing developing nations is to fashion their own particular brands of mixed economy'.[14] In this respect, he stresses the key role of institutions of property rights, conflict management and law and order. This search for country-specific solutions does not clash with the need to use so-called 'best practices', but one should equally acknowledge that 'best practices' are not always clear. In this context, one has to give a fair hearing to Mauro Guillen, who argues that globalization should not be understood as encouraging 'convergence toward a single organizational pattern' and that '...organizational outcomes in the global economy are contingent on country-specific trajectories'.[15] The implication is that variety[16] does matter and adds value!

- The issue of asymmetries acquires particular salience in the international economy, where there is an increasing disenchantment with the distribution of trade gains[17] and the functioning of financial markets. In this respect, one has to stress both the distribution aspect of trade (which relates to the rules of the game and to the way in which industrial countries defend their own markets),[18] as well as the institutional dimension.

- Prominent voices argue that the world community needs new arrangements, new institutions, which should be capable of addressing the problems of world governance.[19] For instance, it is disconcerting to see that the efforts initiated in the field of financial markets reform, by the Financial Stability Forum, in 1998, subsided. As Larry Summers astutely pointed out, world integration demands financial integration, but, as the 1920s and the 1930s century prove, recurrent financial crises can lead to world disintegration.[20]

To sum up: the current debate on development economics has rediscovered several of its old issues and, in this context, it reemphasizes the existence of externalities, multiple equilibria, bad path-dependencies, vicious circles and 'underdevelopment traps', all of which pose numerous challenges to public policy. For, it is increasingly obvious that public policy (at the national and the international level) has a role to play in order to address *coordination failures*. This is because 'There may be a social equilibrium in which forces are balanced in a way that is Pareto improving relative to one in which the government's hands are completely tied – and certainly better than one in which the private sector's hands are completely tied'.[21] In this context, one needs to underline the importance of good institutions, of proper structures for public and corporate governance, which condition the overall performance of the economy. It is, therefore, increasingly clear that the wide variety of economic performance in transition countries has to be related to the different functioning of institutional set-ups.

Some European Union Evidence

The European Union provides some evidence on the possibility for convergence. I refer in particular to the EU admission of poorer European countries in the 1970s and the 1980s. Ireland joined the EU in 1973, when its per capita income was 59 per cent of the EU average. By 1998, Ireland had caught up, with a per capita income that was slightly over the EU average.[22] By contrast, Greece's experience is less encouraging: its income per capita, as compared to the EU average, went down from 77 per cent at the time of joining the EU (in 1981), to 66 per cent in 1998. But the Irish growth was due to a very special set of circumstances, which can hardly be replicated elsewhere. 'Without those special circumstances, all the macroeconomic stability in the world could not have achieved economic growth rapid enough to promote convergence'.[23] And even this growth needs to be seen in a proper perspective when distinguishing between GDP and GNP dynamics.[24]

A recent study finds convergence inside the EU and between the latter and the USA.[25] Figure 8.1 illustrates two things. One is that the European Union as a whole has been converging towards the level of per capita income in the United States; this may be the result of fast economic reconstruction after the Second World War, and of the ensuing benefits of EU integration. Second, the lower income members of the Union (the so-called cohesion countries, to indicate their eligibility for the EU Cohesion Fund)[26] have been closing up the gap that separated them from the EU average.

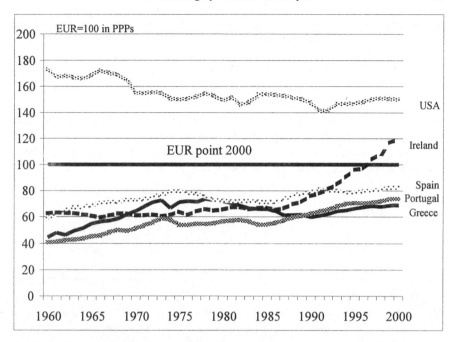

Figure 8.1: Per capita GDP at PPS,[27] 1960–2000

Source: European Commission data, quoted in Carmela Martin, Fr. Velazquez
and B. Funck, op. cit., p. 10.

However, the evidence provided by this study needs to be qualified. Similarly
to Ben David (2000), the study indicates that the cohesion countries were
converging towards the EU average income per capita even before entering the
Union; and that was also the case during that period with member countries
belonging to the European Free Trade Area. Strikingly, Ireland's big advance in
convergence – in the 1980s – took place a decade after its accession into the EU,
which points to certain national policies, which fostered growth – specially in the
field of education and attracting foreign direct investment. As Carmela Martin, Fr.
Velazquez and B. Funck highlight, income convergence is closely associated with
labor productivity convergence; and the rise in labor productivity is determined by
how a country benefits from the international diffusion (transfer) of technology, by
the 'ability to harness technological spillovers' (op. cit., p. 16). The heavy inflow
of foreign direct investment in Ireland seems to explain this country's rapid growth
in the last couple of decades, and to have compensated for the lesser domestic
research and development efforts. Clearly, the build-up of human capital
(education) matters a lot, and infrastructure also plays an important role. The
authors talk in this respect about certain absolute 'thresholds' in public

infrastructure and communication and transport networks, which are needed to take advantage of technological spillovers.

Here are some final comments on the evidence of catching-up in Western Europe. One is that there are significant differences between the earlier decades and the current international environment. First, the earlier decades were a time of more rapid growth in Europe, in general. Second, the earlier candidate countries did not have to overhaul massive industrial sectors (as the transition countries have had to do) and benefited from already existing basic institutions of a market economy. And last but not least, there are areas inside the EU member countries which continue to lag behind substantially.[28]

The Case of Central and Eastern European Countries

Macroeconomic Dynamics

For most of the past decade, policy makers in transition countries have been concerned with the construction of the main building blocks of the new economic system. Institutional disarray (*disorganization*),[29] and the effects of the collapse of the former COMECON trade area, brought about the first transformational recession and high inflation in the early 1990s. Macroeconomic stabilization, privatization, opening, formed their main policy thrust in the early years of transition. Table 8.1 illustrates the collapse of output in these economies at the start of the transition period.

But even so, one can easily discern a major difference between macroeconomic dynamics in CEEC and in the CIS countries. In Central and Eastern Europe inflation was brought down much more rapidly and output recovery started earlier. What lies behind this difference? A World Bank study remarks that 'while initial conditions are the dominant factor in explaining the output decline at the start of transition, the intensity of reform policies explains the variability in output recovery thereafter'.[30] I would argue that initial conditions and geography played a major role during all this period, and that bad path dependencies have evolved in the meantime. Figure 8.2 shows the different evolution of per capita income in the two groups of countries under discussion, and Table 8.2 shows the improvements in labor productivity in industry, which occurred in CEEC during the last decade. This period was accompanied by substantial labor shedding, against the background of industrial restructuring.

Table 8.1: Annual GDP growth rates in CEEC (% on previous year)

	1990	1991	1992	1993	1994	1995	1996	1997	1998	1999	2000	2001
Bulgaria	−9.10	−8.40	−7.25	−1.48	1.82	2.86	−10.14	−6.94	3.50	2.51	5.8	5.0
Czech R.	−1.22	−11.49	−3.29	0.57	3.21	6.36	3.91	0.98	−2.50	−0.21	3.1	3.5
Estonia	−8.10	−10.01	−14.15	−8.51	−2.00	4.29	3.98	10.53	4.06	−1.39	6.9	4.7
Hungary	−3.50	−11.90	−3.06	−0.58	2.95	1.50	1.34	4.57	5.07	4.27	5.2	3.8
Latvia	2.90	−10.41	−34.86	−14.87	0.65	−0.81	3.34	8.61	3.56	0.47	6.6	7.5
Lithuania	−3.30	−5.68	−21.26	−16.23	−9.77	3.29	4.71	7.28	5.15	−3.07	3.9	4.7
Poland	−11.60	−7.00	2.63	3.80	5.20	7.01	6.05	6.85	4.80	4.04	4.0	1.1
Romania	−5.58	−12.92	−8.77	1.53	3.93	7.14	3.95	−6.07	−5.43	−3.19	1.8	5.3
Slovakia	−2.47	−14.57	−6.45	−3.70	4.90	6.91	6.58	6.54	4.42	1.90	2.2	3.1
Slovenia	n/a	−9.0	−5.0	2.8	5.3	4.1	3.5	4.5	4.0	4.8	4.6	3.0

Source: Based on *Economic Survey of Europe 2000*, Vol. 2, UN-ECE, Geneva; *WIIW Research Report 283/2002.*

Table 8.2: CEEC – Labor productivity in industry (base year = 100)*

	1989	1990	1991	1992	1993	1994	1995	1996	1997	1998
Bulgaria	100.0	91.4	86.6	83.9	81.5	91.8	98.5	101.8	98.0	n/a
Czech Republic	100.0	99.6	78.7	76.6	75.2	78.9	87.6	96.0	106.7	112.7
Hungary	100.0	100.4	82.4	91.2	107.9	115.8	128.4	140.0	160.0	181.3
Poland	100.0	78.9	69.5	81.3	92.1	105.0	112.3	123.5	138.5	147.2
Romania	100.0	75.9	59.4	53.1	58.7	64.7	77.6	87.0	87.9	101.9
Slovak Republic	100.0	99.0	81.0	78.9	81.8	89.4	94.1	96.5	100.4	112.0
Estonia	n/a	n/a	n/a	100.0	101.1	107.9	108.3	112.3	141.9	145.1
Latvia	n/a	n/a	n/a	100.0	77.4	84.8	83.9	91.1	116.6	118.9
Lithuania	n/a	n/a	n/a	100.0	77.6	68.2	76.4	82.9	89.2	99.0
Slovenia	n/a	n/a	n/a	n/a	100.0	111.8	121.2	129.3	135.1	142.4

n/a – not applicable
* The indices have different base years because of differences in data availability for the different countries.

Source: World Bank calculations based on data from EBRD 'Transition Report', various issues (in Carmela, Martin, Velazquez, Fr. and Funck, B. op. cit., p. 24).

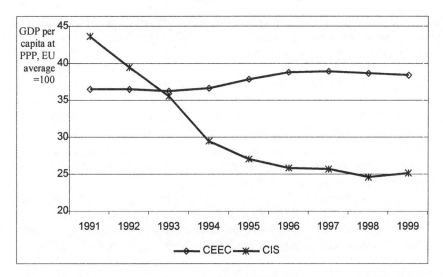

Figure 8.2: CEEC and CIS per capita GDP at PPP: 1991–9, percent of EU average

Source: World Bank calculations (in Martin, C., Velazquez and Funck, op. cit., p. 24).

The World Bank study mentioned above highlights four major lessons of transition, namely:

- the key role of the entry and growth of new firms (the strategy of encouragement and discipline);
- the need to develop and strengthen legal and regulatory institutions;
- the need for more aggressive use of the budget during a reform program, in order to protect the most vulnerable social groups;
- the recognition that initial winners may oppose later-stage reforms.

However, what seems to be underplayed in this enumeration, is the time-consuming nature of institutional development, which is at the root of various path dependencies. In this regard, one needs to highlight the relationship between precarious institutions (illustrated by endemic corruption, amongst others), and the persistence of bad equilibria, which hamper long-term economic growth.

But not the whole of the CEEC area has had similar macroeconomic dynamics. The most salient feature is the boom and bust dynamics of Romania and Bulgaria (see Table 8.1) and the persistence of high inflation in Romania. This evolution indicates more severe initial conditions and less consistent policy-making.

Over time, and in conjunction with reform consolidation, new concerns have emerged for the CEEC. Thus, economic growth has become of paramount importance in the quest to join the European Union, and also, as a means to solve increasingly sensitive social difficulties, at a time of rising unemployment. The main features of economic dynamics in the CEEC, which have relevance for the debate on catching-up, are summarized below:

1. Steady, high growth rates have proved to be quite an elusive goal for CEEC.
2. In all CEEC there have been substantial fluctuations of GDP growth rates, besides the impact of the first transformational recession. Poland, which was a champion of high growth rates in the late 1990s, returned to a much lower growth in the last couple of years. And Hungary's recent years of relatively higher growth still need to be validated in view of the ever closer link between its economy's business cycle and that in the EU.
3. The better performing CEEC seem to be characterized by moderate (rather than high) growth rates (see Table 8.1). Slovenia's record is telling in this respect, with a growth rate averaging 4–4.5 per cent in recent years. Actually, Slovenia is the only accession country whose income per capita is above 2/3 of the EU average.
4. Boom and bust cycles did appear in a few cases – notably in Bulgaria and Romania, and this type of dynamics may appear again (not only in those two countries) unless severe balance of payments crises are avoided.
5. Saving and investment ratios are not impressive, whereas the inflows of FDI have been concentrated in just a few countries.
6. All CEEC trade extensively with the EU. For all of them, the EU is by far the largest trading partner. Arguably, therefore, output dynamics in the CEEC has benefited from increased openness and integration with the EU.[31]
7. Substantial inflows of FDI foster growth, but they need favorable accompanying circumstances.
8. Persistent large current account deficits cause balance of payments crises and harm sustainable growth.

The features highlighted above cast doubt on the thesis that catching-up is looming at the horizon, or that it is very likely to occur as an outcome of current policies. This inference should sober us, particularly in view of the kind of growth rates that CEEC need in order to catch up with the EU area. It may well be that a realistic goal should involve more moderate growth rates of income per capita. However, even such moderate growth rates require heavy advances in structural and institutional reforms. Higher growth rates may occur if FDI flows are substantial (and profits are reinvested), and there is constant upgrading of production. But, at the same time, the CEEC would have to avoid, as much as possible, adverse external shocks.

Table 8.3: Years required to close per capita income gap (in PPP terms) with the EU

	Assuming 5% long-term growth rate average		
	EU average	75% of EU average	50% of EU average
Slovenia	13	3	–
Czech Republic	18	8	–
Hungary	24	14	0
Slovakia	31	16	2
Estonia	34	24	10
Poland	34	24	10
Latvia	40	30	16
Lithuania	40	30	16
Romania	45	35	21
Bulgaria	50	40	26

Source: *Progress towards the Unification of Europe*, World Bank Report (2000), p. 42.

Table 8.4: Per capita income levels in Europe (1998, in PPP terms as % of EU average)

Country	Per capita income level	Country	Per capita income level
Greece	66	Latvia	27
Ireland	101	Lithuania	31
Bulgaria	23	Poland	36
Czech Republic	59	Romania	27
Estonia	37	Slovakia	46
Hungary	49	Slovenia	68

Source: *Progress towards the Unification of Europe*, op. cit., p. 40

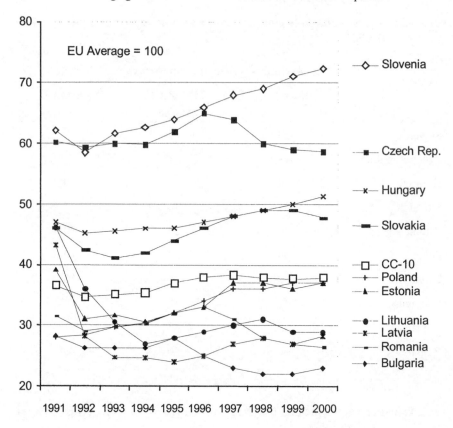

Figure 8.3:   CEEC – Per Capita GDP at PPS, 1990–2000, compared to EU average

Source: EUROSTAT; Figures for 1990–94, and for 2000 are extrapolated based on constant price data in local currency (cited by C. Martin, Velazquez and B, Funck, p. 25).

Table 8.3 resorts to some simple calculations. Assuming that the CEEC grow at an average per capita long-term rate of 5 per cent, and that the similar rate for the EU area is 2 per cent, it will take between 13 years (for Slovenia) and 50 years (for Bulgaria) to achieve convergence to the EU average.[32] Romania would need 45 years in order to do so.

EU Integration and Catching-up

Central and Eastern European societies do not look poor in important respects (e.g. the literacy rate of the population and general educational standards, behavioral patterns), but most of them face a set of challenges which are specific to poor countries: still fragile institutions, perturbing and growing inequality[33] (precarious *social cohesion*), incompetent governments (political elites), endemic corruption, which distorts and taxes business, etc. Therefore, these countries need to formulate policies which should tackle poor countries-type problems as well; they need development (catching-up) strategies.

Can integration into the EU be viewed as a Grand Strategy for economic catching-up (*beta*-convergence) and modernization – for the 'Big Push', which most of CEEC have been seeking during the last century?[34] It is worthwhile reminding what Paul Rosenstein-Rodan had in mind when he wrote his famous article in 1943. In that article, he referred to key inter-dependencies in an economy, which may preclude its development, unless there is effective coordination among its constituent parts (industries). Development asks for complementary changes of action and resources. And such simultaneous endeavors may not be possible in the absence of a strong stimulus, of a 'Big Push'. This is a fundamental question to be addressed by policy makers.

In this respect it should be underlined that the EU, as a phenomenon, is exceptional, in a historical perspective. It is unique both economically and politically in modern history. This is why, for example, one can hardly establish an analogy between NAFTA and the Europe agreements, which the accession countries have with the EU. As a matter of fact, the accession countries see in the EU enlargement a historical chance to speed up their economic development and modernization.

In the above context, a related question arises immediately: are the current negotiations and the efforts to adopt the *acquis communautaire* the equivalent of an effective strategy for economic catching-up? In many domains, it may well be so, to the extent that good institutions are smoothly 'imported' and function effectively, and to the extent that technology transfer and upgrading of production (via FDI) occur intensely, for the benefit of a majority of the citizens (and *social cohesion* is not impaired).

Empirical analyses show that the opening of the economy and integration with the outside world, have better chances to foster economic growth when there is an intense inflow of foreign direct investment, which upgrades the capital stock and human capital of the recipient countries. It is no surprise, therefore, that the frontrunner accession countries have received a disproportionate share of FDI.

Equally, a strategy for economic development (catching-up) requires policy ownership, which refers to domestic intellectual capabilities (expertise), as well as to the capacity to formulate policies. This is the lesson of the most impressive cases of catching-up of the last century (whether one thinks of Japan, South Korea, Singapore, or, more recently, Ireland).

It may be that the EU arrangements could partially supplant the need for domestic policy capabilities. But, as the reports of the European Commission consistently document, particularly in the case of the lower-performing accession countries, public administration reform is critical for development, which is a clear indication of the essential tasks of domestic policy. It is true, however, that, within the constraints of the institutional functioning of the EU, domestic policy formulation acquires a new connotation. But the problem as such remains, since Brussels cannot be a substitute for key decisions at the national level.

A caveat is needed at this point about the linkage between EU integration and convergence. Some of the CEEC premises for catching-up may clash with the strict conditionality of the Maastricht Treaty criteria, in case the accession countries intend to join the Exchange Rate Mechanism (ERM2) and, later on, the Monetary Union. A related situation is entailed by the implications of the *Balassa-Samuelson effect*, which threatens to make it impossible for accession countries to comply with the requirement of a low inflation rate in order to fit the EU (ERM) area.[35] And, should they try to attain a very low inflation rate, this may undermine growth and, therefore, catching-up. If this is the case, should some of the accession criteria be made more flexible? How would the EU member countries view such a weakening of criteria? To what extent can the logic of a 'variable geometry' play a role in this context? Would such a variable-geometry process of enlargement be manageable?

For the EU candidate countries, the low inflation criteria (and, further, the Maastricht Treaty provisions) and the negotiations with Brussels raise two main sets of questions. One regards trade links and, more specifically, the capacity of accession countries to withstand competitive pressures when trade asymmetries disappear. The other issue regards the possibility for the candidate countries to accommodate the stern exigencies of a very low inflation environment, even if they do not adopt the single currency.

It should also be highlighted that, against the backdrop of the vagaries of an increasingly uncertain world environment, the EU can provide a shelter, which should be seen in the context of a world tendency for the formation of economic and monetary blocks.

Final Remarks

If the line of reasoning suggested by this paper is accepted, it does make sense to ask the question: what are the basic premises for the EU accession countries to embark on rapid and sustained growth trajectories? The drastic decline of growth in Poland, lately, shows that such trajectories are hard to achieve and sustain.

One should not forget that substantial flows of FDI were attracted, in many cases, by large privatization deals. Once such deals come to an end (because the number of interesting state assets put on sale is limited), a drastic reduction of capital inflows can severely strain the balance of payments and may require painful adjustments, which would bring growth rates down.

What are the main differences among the clusters of accession countries, besides income per capita and economic performance (for instance, between the so-called Visegrad Group plus Slovenia, and Romania and Bulgaria)? Are there any particular traits pertaining to the Baltic countries – apart from the support that they receive from Nordic countries? Could Croatia (which is not yet a candidate country) move much faster than other Balkan countries? Arguably, in this regard, the quality of institutions plays a major role.

If growth trajectories are so hard to sustain, what would be the implications of this for the politics and the economics of EU *enlargement*? What are possible venues (prerequisites) for enhancing *convergence*, and for making it occur in the foreseeable future? The issue of convergence is relevant both for the countries which are likely to join the EU in 2004, and for the other candidate countries.

One should also keep in mind that it is the first time in its history when the EU is supposed to accept such a large number of countries, which are considerably less well off (in terms of income per capita, and not only) and have lower economic performance. Under the current rules of the game, a 'big-bang' enlargement could considerably strain the Union, both financially and functionally. Therefore, it is not clear that the enlargement will be a success, unless the institutional reform of the EU and other common market issues are solved in a timely fashion. But is it possible? And, if not, would that involve a less impressive enlargement (fewer countries), or a delay of the process?[36] The worsening conditions of world economy, which are increasingly felt in Europe as well, will certainly have an impact on the public debate about enlargement, and the conditions attached to it.

In this context, the political and economic mechanics of *enlargement* would have to be considered in conjunction with what the candidate countries need in order to achieve rapid and sustained economic growth.

Under the present circumstances, a more realistic goal for governments may be to foster sustainable growth, which will eventually allow convergence, rather than enforcing EU accession criteria at any costs. Whilst the former may be as difficult to achieve as the latter, it also is the only key to development.

Notes

1 Professor of Economics, Academy of Economic Studies, Bucharest, and Visiting Professor, UCLA; ddaianu@rnc.ro. I thank Radu Vranceanu for his observations.

2 By real convergence, I refer to the fundamental institutional set-up of a society, which fosters sustainable technological and economic progress (income per capita growth), without disruptive social effects.

3 For an interesting and broadly based explanation (including cultural) of economic growth, see Deepak Lal (1999).

4 Angus Maddison (1995).

5 Total factor productivity is meant to denote the rate of technological progress, or the so called 'Solow residual' (i.e. what remains in the neoclassical growth equation after the quantitative increase of capital and labor).

6 On a general upbeat tone, Grzegorz W. Kolodko examines the chances for catching-up in the context of globalization. In this regard, he underlines the need for 'correct

policies', which is an indisputable statement (2002). Nonetheless, I assume that Kolodko himself accepts the existence of controversial policy issues and venues.

7   *The Washington Consensus,* as a name, was concocted by the economist John Williamson, with reference to the essence of IMF and World Bank's policies pursued in the last couple of decades.

8   Easterly's results seem to contradict one of the main conclusions of the World Bank's Global Economic Prospects for Developing Countries 2001, which asserts that 'Developing countries as a group enjoyed accelerated economic growth over the past decade...' (World Bank Policy and Research Bulletin, April-June 2001, p. 1). It is fair to say, however, that Easterly refers to per capita income growth.

9   These countries achieved macroeconomic stabilization via low budget deficits and tight monetary policies, but did nor refrain from targeting potential 'winners', through industrial and trade polices. A natural question arises whether such policies can be effective under the pressure of globalization and when public administration is weak, or captured by vested interests, as is the case in many transition economies.

10   William Easterly, 2001, manuscript. See also his 'The Elusive Quest for Growth' (2001).

11   Op. cit., p. 291.

12   See The World Bank's Annual Conference on Development Economics, proceedings of the 1999 and 2000 meetings. As the World Bank economist P. Richard Agenor put it, 'the conventional neoclassical theory has proved incapable of explaining in a satisfactory manner the wide disparities in the rates of per capita output growth across countries' (2000, p. 392).

13   Pioneered by Paul Romer and Robert Lucas. Radu Vranceanu pointed to me that Lucas (1988, pp. 3–42) explains why divergence does happen, instead of convergence.

14   Dani Rodrik (2000), manuscript. Rodrik emphasizes five functions that public institutions must serve for markets to work properly: protection of property rights, market regulation, macroeconomic stabilization, social insurance, and conflict management. He also underlines that 'there is in principle a large variety of institutional setups that could fulfill these functions'(p. 3).

15   Mauro F. Guillen (2001).

16   *Variety* as a value was stressed, decades ago, by Kevin Lancaster; and it applies to institutional constructs as well as to product markets.

17   As the World Bank's Global Economic Prospects and the Developing Countries 2001 report says, 'trade barriers in industrial countries represent a major roadblock for developing countries' (ibid., p. 2).

18   The preparations for the Doha WTO conference were quite telling in this respect, with the USA, the EU and Japan having basically set the agenda.

19   This is the message of a recent report on globalization prepared by a group led by George Soros (forthcoming in February 2002). Lord Dahrendorf is also very critical of the way in which the existing international institutions address these issues (his lecture delivered at the New Europe College, Bucharest, October, 2001).

20   Larry Summers (2000), p. 1. See also Ulrich Beck (2001), p. 17.

21   Karla Hoff (2000), p. 170.

22 'Progress Toward the Unification of Europe', The World Bank, Washington DC (2000), p. 40.

23 Denis O'Hearn (2001), p. 80.

24 While foreign profit repatriations made up 3 per cent of GDP in 1983, by 1995 they climbed to 19 per cent and, by 1999, to a stunning 40 per cent of GDP (Denis O'Hearn, op. cit., p. 83).

25 Carmela Martin, Francisco J. Velazquez, and Bernard Funck (2001).

26 The Cohesion Fund was created in 1993 in the wake of the Maastricht Treaty to help poorer member countries cope with the demands of monetary union.

27 The purchasing power standard (PPS) is defined in such a way that, for each individual aggregate, the European Union total obtained from converting the values in national currency with the purchasing power parities is equal to the European Union total for that individual aggregate in euros. In a sense, the PPS can therefore be thought of as the euro in real terms (EUROSTAT definition).

28 Such as Mezzogiorno in Italy, parts of the United Kingdom, etc.

29 Concept used by Olivier Blanchard (1997).

30 Pradeep Mitra and Marcelo Selowsky (2001).

31 See Lucian Cernat and Radu Vranceanu (2001).

32 See 'Progress Toward the Unification of Europe', Washington DC, World Bank, 2000, p. 42.

33 It should be acknowledged, nonetheless, that much of this growing inequality is unavoidable, as a result of the change from a command (highly equalitarian) to a market-based economic system.

34 P. N. Rosenstein-Rodan (1943, 1961).

35 Dariusz Rosati (2001). See also Laszlo Halpern and Charles Wyplosz (2001).

36 It is noteworthy that some leading politicians talk about a possible 'big-bang' approach to EU enlargement. Ten countries would be eligible for admission in 2004.

References

Agenor, P. Richard (2000), *The Economic of Adjustment and Growth*, New York, Academic Press.

Beck, Ulrich (2001), 'Globalization's Chernobyl', *Financial Times*, 6 November.

Blanchard, Olivier (1997), *The Economics of Post-communism*, Clarendon Press, London.

Cernat, Lucian and Vranceanu, Radu 'Globalisation and Growth: New Evidence from Central and Eastern Europe', May 2001 (manuscript).

David, Ben (2000), 'Trade, Growth and Disparity Among Nations', in *Trade and Poverty*, WTA, Geneva.

Dauderstadt, Michael and Witte, Lothar (2001), *Cohesive Growth in the Enlarged Euroland*, Friedrich Ebert Stiftung, Bonn.

Ellis, H. S. (ed.) (1961), 'Economic Development for Latin America', St. Martin Press, New York.

Easterly, William (2001), 'The Lost Decades: Developing Countries' Stagnation in Spite of Policy Reform 1980–1998', February, (manuscript).

Easterly, William (2001), 'The Elusive Quest for Growth', MIT Press, Cambridge.

Halpern, Laszlo and Wiplosz, Charles (2001), 'Economic Transformation and Real Exchange Rates in the 2000s: The Balassa-Samuelson Connection', chapter 6 (pp. 227– 40) in *Economic Survey of Europe 2001*, UN/ECE, Geneva.

Hoff, Karla (2000), 'Beyond Rosenstein-Rodan: The Modern Theory of Coordination Problems in Development', in *Annual World Bank Conference on Development Economics. Proceedings*, World Bank, Washington, DC.

Guillen, Mauro F. (2001), *The Limits of Convergence. Globalization and Organizational Change in Argentina, South Korea and Spain*, Princeton University Press, Princeton.

Kolodko, Grzegorz W. (2002), *Globalization and Catching-up in Transition Economies*, University of Rochester Press, Rochester, NY, and Woodbridge, Suffolk, UK.

Deepak, Lal (1999), *Unintended Consequences. The Impact of Factor Endowments, Culture, and Politics on Long-Run Performance*, MIT Press, Cambridge.

Lucas, Robert (1988), 'On The Mechanics of Economic Development', *Journal of Monetary Economics*, Vol. 22 (July), pp. 3–42.

Maddison, Angus (1995), *Monitoring the World Economy: 1820–1992*, Development Centre Studies, OECD, Paris.

Martin, Carmela, Velazquez, Francisco J. and Funck, Bernard (2001), 'European Integration and Income Convergence. Lessons for Central and Eastern European Countries', May, (manuscript).

Mitra, Pradeep and Selowsky, Marcelo (2001), 'Transition: The First Ten Years' World Bank (manuscript).

O'Hearn, Denis, in Dauderstadt, Michael and Witte, Lothar (2001), *Cohesive Growth in the Enlarged Euroland*, Friedrich Ebert Stiftung, Bonn, pp. 80–90.

Rodrik, Dani (2000), 'Development Strategies for the Next Century', February, Harvard University (manuscript).

Rosati, Dariusz (2001), 'The Balassa-Samuelson Effect among the CEEC', paper presented at the Balassa Commemoration Conference, Budapest, 18–19 October.

Rosenstein-Rodam, Paul (1943), 'Problems of Industrialization of Eastern and South-Eastern Europe', *Economic Journal*, 1943, Vol. 53 (June–September), pp. 202–211.

Rosenstain-Rodan, Paul (1961), 'Notes on the Theory of the Big Push', in Ellis, H. S. (ed.) (1961), 'Economic Development for Latin America', St. Martin Press, New York, p. 57–81.

Summers, Larry (2000), 'International Financial Crises: Causes, Prevention and Cures', Richard T. Ely Lecture in the American Economic Review. Papers and Proceedings, May.

The World Bank (2000), 'Progress Toward the Unification of Europe', World Bank, Washington DC.

Chapter 9

Systemic Variety under the Conditions of Globalization and Integration[1]

Tadeusz Kowalik

Introduction

The purpose of this paper is to analyze the scope and depth of systemic differences between the national economies in the modern world, as well as to try to foresee future trends. Although variety can be regarded as the other side of globalization, this issue has not been studied at length, because almost all attention is focused on the processes of unification, standardization and universalization. Therefore, this paper contains more questions and problems than answers.

Of course, the authors adopting an extreme globalist perspective, such as K. Ohme, who believe that the world is fast heading towards a borderless global economic order, give a simple answer: variety disappears with the progress of globalization. Extreme 'integrists' within the European Union, who support a single socio-economic and political system, share a similar opinion. Variety is for them a question of different levels of maturity, but the ultimate goal is the same for all. However, such 'end of history' views seem more and more a thing of the past. The anti-globalist movement, although it has not proposed a clear theoretical alternative, has made the world of politics and international corporations aware of the fact that globalization is a social process whose final outcome is unknown.

Furthermore, the European politicians now express much more cautious views on the future shape of the European Union. Even if federation is proposed, its form is much more moderate than e.g. the system of the Federal Republic of Germany or, in particular, the older idea of the United States of Europe. Obviously, hypocrisy is quite widespread here. Particularly in countries facing the difficult task of obtaining social approval for accession in a referendum, politicians may stress an absence of threat for their national independence, cultural identity and sovereignty, if this fits their purpose.

In the second half of the previous century, the idea of homogeneity of the market economy or capitalism, as a concept which does not require any further definition, was given up. It was a time of great systemic innovations, both successful and dreadful. One of such dreadful experiments was fascism – an aberrant outcome of extreme irrationalism. Communism lasted several times longer, so it had time for evolution, adaptation and transformation. However, if, for example, communism had ended with the death of Stalin, it would be viewed from a historical perspective as nothing more than a totalitarian nightmare.

However, even those systems taught us a lesson. They simply created a new point of reference, new competitive challenges. We know now that the Soviet challenge for the West was to a large extent magnified by false statistics. Nevertheless, it triggered reforms. Let me just mention the post-sputnik shock in the United States, which forced a deep reform of the education system. Even Khrushchev's bluff of 'catching up with and leaving behind [the West]' was treated as a quite serious threat to the West by a considerable part of the Western public opinion (the American scholar who formulated two likely (!) scenarios of the Soviet Union catching up with the USA in terms of income per capita is probably still alive. According to the optimistic scenario (from the Soviet point of view), the USSR needed 14 years to achieve that aim and according to the pessimistic one – 34 years!). History likes to play tricks: approximately 34 years later, the Soviet Union collapsed. Furthermore, it is very likely that the innovative character of the socio-economic systems of Japan and Western Germany is a result of the communist threat. It is the simplest explanation of the fact that the authorities occupying those two countries after World War II promoted (in Japan, actually forced) systems which were very different from the free market economies prevailing in their own countries.

The origin of the systems known as Scandinavian or Nordic was more autonomous. However, they were also described as the third or middle way (*Middle way*, Childs, 1936). Therefore, they found reflection in the two competing systems. The communist legacy (not quite clear yet), as well as the shape of the newly forming systems of China, Vietnam and Russia, can be explained in a similar way. So, it is very likely that the period of systemic innovation is not over yet and we are witnessing the establishment of new systems, although such phenomena are usually accounted for theoretically *post festum*.

The experience of the previous over half-century as well as the present time seems to indicate that we are going through a period of intensive system innovation. Therefore, it is hard to believe that the acceleration of the globalization processes will put an end to the variety of socio-economic systems or that the European integration will eliminate the possibility of institutional experiments. Theoretical and historical arguments suggest a different conclusion: **the higher the level of social development, the stronger the tendency towards variety and differentiation, i.e. enrichment of the forms of social and economic life**.

At present, even egalitarians believe that equal opportunities, as well as equality in terms of income and property, should contribute to greater variety rather than uniformity among people. This is the sense of the theory of equality of Amartya Sen and John Rawls. Is it not applicable to societies, countries and nations as well? Does it not seem realistic that we are integrating in order to create a better platform for co-operation of different cultures, to make the community of nations richer not only in terms of money, but also in terms of culture, i.e. to promote variety? The word 'culture' is used in a broad meaning here, comprising also socio-economic systems based on different sets of values.

Even within the European Union the processes of convergence are very slow. The fact that there still exist significant differences between the systems of the six 'veterans' of European integration is meaningful.

A homogeneous economic model does not exist in Europe. The British model is closer to the US one than to German one. The Italian model, dominated by family capitalism, weakness of the state, enormous deficit of public finances and surprising vitality of small and medium companies, cannot be compared with anything, except perhaps the model of the Chinese Diaspora [i.e. Taiwan – TK] (Albert, 1994, p. 24).

On other occasions, Albert points to the differences between the French 'model' (similar to the Spanish one) and the German model.

It is enough to look at the indices regularly published by London's *The Economist* to see that big differences are not restricted to the above-mentioned countries. The unemployment rates in the EU countries vary from 2 to 13 per cent, the child poverty rate varies from over 2 per cent to approximately 20 per cent. These differences do not seem to have decreased over the last 15 or 20 years. In addition, significant differences in tax rates and tax systems, pension systems and social security in general should be mentioned. Furthermore, the systems of ownership, employee participation etc. are different, too.

One of the tasks of the EU is the convergence of the economic development level of its member states. However, at present this seems to be a distant perspective. The South of Europe is catching up with the European leaders very slowly and the differences between the regions do not shrink. On the contrary, many regions experience the process of polarization (Boldrin and Cavalio, 2001; Kolodko, 2001). Let us, however, assume optimistically that this goal will be achieved in a not-so-distant future. One cannot rule out the possibility that thereupon, under the conditions of general welfare, the tendencies towards decentralization would grow even stronger, as the individual regions and countries would seek on their own the best forms of co-operation and competition and the best institutional solutions to help people in their work and leisure.

Yes, there is a danger of uniformization introduced from Brussels,[2] so bureaucrats, who do not like variety by nature, should be controlled by society.

The Informative Example of Marxism

There is no room here for more detailed studies of globalization. Let me just point out that the contemporary globalization enthusiasts are unable to make use of past experiences. I refer here to their common tendency to shorten the historical perspective. A good lesson is taught by the Marxists, who suffered serious consequences of the same mistake. Let us take a look back.

Karl Marx and Friedrich Engels were among the first enthusiasts of capitalist globalization. The opening sentences of their *Communist Manifesto* sound like a great apology of the expansion of the market, money and capital and a projection of a global social order. Our contemporaries usually hear about Marx as a radical critic of capitalism and a prophet of its collapse, so let us recall his own, very different words.

> The bourgeoisie has through its exploitation of the world market given a cosmopolitan character to production and consumption in every country. To the great chagrin of reactionaries, it has drawn from under the feet of industry the national ground on which it stood. All old-established national industries have been destroyed or are daily being destroyed. They are dislodged by new industries, whose introduction becomes a life and death question for all civilized nations, by industries that no longer work up indigenous raw material, but raw material drawn from the remotest zones; industries whose products are consumed, not only at home, but in every quarter of the globe. In place of the old wants, satisfied by the production of the country, we find new wants requiring for their satisfaction the products of distant lands and climes place of the old local and national seclusion and self-sufficiency, we have intercourse in every direction, universal interdependence of nations. And as in material, so also in intellectual production. The intellectual creations of individual nations become common property. National one-sidedness and narrow-mindedness become more and more impossible, and from the numerous national and local literatures there arises a world literature. The bourgeoisie, by the rapid improvement of all instruments of production, by the immensely facilitated means of communication, draws all, even the most barbarian nations, into civilization. The cheap prices of its commodities are the heavy artillery with which it batters down all Chinese walls, with which it forces the barbarians' intensely obstinate hatred of foreigners to capitulate (Bottomore and Rubel, 1964, pp. 136–7).

This aspect of 'pre-globalist' thought was alive in the first half of the 20th century. A catastrophic vision of the establishment of global economy was developed by the Polish-German socialist Rosa Luxemburg. Her vision of the fall of capitalism was associated with the disappearance of the non-capitalist environment that allowed the accumulation of capital, creating a barrier to capitalism as a system. The ultra-imperialism of Karl Kautsky, the general cartel of Rudolf Hilferding, Vladimir Lenin's idea of imperialism as the ultimate form of capitalism, the idea, developed by Henryk Grossman, of profit margin disappearing as a result of the increase of organic capital composition – all these were different varieties of globalist concepts.

Rosa Luxemburg and her party, the Social Democracy of the Polish Kingdom and Lithuania, met with the condemnation of a significant part of the Polish public opinion, including socialists, because of her faith in global capitalism, which she expected to prepare ground for global socialism. On these grounds she believed national states to be a reactionary relict.

Unilateralism and Determinism – Continued

The Marxist adventure points to the common features of the past and present concepts of globalization. They are characterized by a radical reduction of the historical perspective. The Marxists noticed more than did the contemporary representatives of subjective economy: they described and analyzed the progressive concentration of production and capital. However, they failed to notice the strong counter-trends. They were also characterized by 'unilinear determinism', marked by the belief that these processes were spontaneous and could not be influenced by the societies within the limits of a given system.

For long decades, this necessity-based way of thinking (Roberto Unger called it 'false necessity') was also characteristic of academic thought. Even Joseph Schumpeter, who noticed the overwhelming tendency towards state control present both in capitalism and in socialism, considered that tendency on a very high level of abstraction, where there was no room for variety or choice. In his opinion, the emergence and expansion of shareholder ownership and management control in place of an individual entrepreneur-capitalist, and the expansion of the 'tax state' were factors weakening the dynamism of capitalism.

J. M. Keynes made a heroic attempt at awakening society from determinist lethargy. His fundamental message was: the capitalist market system cannot be left to its own devices and allowed to develop spontaneously. It not only can and should be reformed, but, in fact, it must be reformed under the threat of stagnation. The state policy can transform free market capitalism into capitalism with full employment. Lord Beveridge drew further conclusions from Keynes' activist theory – he prepared the concept of welfare state. However, as an unintended effect of both Keynes' *General Theory* and the welfare state concept, the capitalist world becomes more and more divided into countries which, to a varied extent and in different forms, have followed and still follow these concepts and those which reject them.

The concept of balance between antagonistic forces, put forward by K. Galbraith (1952) was the next step towards understanding the nature of capitalism. Its actual sense is reflected not by the main title of his book (*American capitalism*), but by the subtitle (*The concept of countervailing power*). In Europe, self-organization of social groups could have been taken for granted as a result of the historical past. North America was behind Europe in this respect. Galbraith derived this concept from his understanding of this fact and the current needs. He argued that economically weaker groups, such as manual workers and farmers, must become stronger for capitalism to function normally. He wrote:

> Steps to strengthen countervailing power are not, in principle, different from steps to strengthen competition. Given the existence of private market power in the economy, the growth of countervailing power strengthens the capacity of the economy for autonomous self-regulation and thereby lessens the amount of over-all government control or planning that is required or sought (Galbraith, 1952, p. 155).

Until the 1970s, such balance existed in the USA. The trade unions might even have gained an advantage as a result of full employment in the late 1970s. However, the alignment of power was reversed in the next years. The trade unions sustained a significant, if not complete, loss of their power, while inequality, poverty among workers and unemployment were on the increase. Also the British trade unions lost much of their power. The situation of trade unions is currently one of the factors that differentiate socio-economic systems. At present, there are countries with strong trade unions and co-operation based on social agreement (the Scandinavian countries, Austria, possibly Germany), countries with antagonistic relations in industry (Italy, Spain), countries where trade unions have lost the battle, countries where the power (membership) of trade unions is growing and those where it is shrinking (mainly the Anglo-Saxon countries) (*The Economist*, 2000a, p. 96). Therefore, it is not true that trade unions are a thing of the past which is disappearing from the economic scene, as is commonly argued in Poland (Gardawski, 2001).[3]

J. Schumpeter did not deny that he owed his understanding of capitalism to Marx. Indeed, thanks to the author of *Das Kapital*, he understood that capitalism was not market economy in general, nor even private market economy, but a new civilization – a civilization of inequality, i.e. an economy dominated by great fortunes and their logic. However, he assumed wrongly after Marx (his famous: 'Accumulate! Accumulate! That is Moses and the Prophets') that accumulation and investment follow from the very nature of a capitalist entrepreneur and are limited by nothing but supply, the amount of profit, or the availability of credit. Accordingly, he did not perceive any specific barriers to capitalist accumulation. This logic of operation of capitalists (rather than entrepreneurs in general) was discovered and analyzed by Keynes. He found a deep discrepancy between savings and investments. Contrary to the conventional wisdom of neoclassical economy, according to which savings must increase in order to increase investment, he put forward the opposite argument: savings depend on investments. He formulated the 'law' that the tendency towards consumption decreases as the income (profit) grows.

Without this law, it would now be impossible to understand Reagan's presidency or the latest American 'economic miracle' or the recent economic boom in France. As the condition of the American economy largely determines the condition of the global economy, one can imagine what would have happened in America (and the rest of the world), if Reagan had chosen to stick to his election rhetoric of 'sound finances' and had not fuelled the economy with unprecedented, save during a war, budget deficit and public debt.

If, subsequently, America had not expanded its (foreign) debt on an unprecedented scale, its 'economic miracle' of the 1990s would have been impossible. The relevant data must be shocking for the followers of neoclassical economy. During the peak of the economic boom in America, the level of savings of the private sector was more than five percent below zero. The same can be said about France – had Dominique Strauss Kahn continued the fiscal and monetary policy of his predecessors, the French economy would still be half-stagnant. On the other hand, the German economy of the 1990s, with its rather slow growth rate, had a much higher level of savings. Those who advocate an increase of savings even during recession should keep this in mind.

Strangely enough, the present situation of the countries of Central and Eastern Europe resembles in many respects the situation of America in the past, not because trade unions have never existed there, but because they are treated as relics of the previous system. Moreover, the politicians, still thinking in terms of planned economy, do not understand that the workers' fight for higher wages and for rights protecting them from various risks (unemployment, disability, old age, illness) increases the purchasing power of society and automatically gives rise to regulations preventing or alleviating recession. Polish renowned economists have moved backwards to the times when it was believed that savings were completely and without delay transformed in every cycle into investments. They disregard the barrier of demand in the capitalist economy. Individual capitalists do not understand it and reduce payroll costs, which works against economic prosperity. Thus, they collectively cut the branch on which they sit. If the workers did not fight for a pay rise, capitalism would suffocate because of its own logic of restricting demand.

Cyclic fluctuations of demand and its dependence on the accumulated pessimism or optimism have always been associated with a risk of instability. In the era of globalization of financial capital, mainly speculative, capitalism becomes a highly unstable system by nature. It was Keynes who first proposed the idea of 'casino capitalism'.[4] From the point of view of balanced growth, globalization brings about not only MacDonaldization and informatization, but also the elephantism of 'casino capitalism'. Therefore, on a global scale, a rational (praxeological) concept of balanced growth is contrasted with the casino logic.

Different Social Philosophies: Individualism versus Communitarism

Social Security

Apart from a small group of specialists in comparative economics, the fundamental division observed and discussed in non-communist world is that between Anglo-Saxon capitalism (system, model, version) and German and Japanese (sometimes German-Japanese) capitalism. This division arises from different social philosophies. The former model is individualistic, the latter one is communitarist. A more detailed analysis of these philosophies has recently been proposed by two American scholars (Morrison and Wolf, 1999/2000). Here are some of the major conclusions they arrived at after several years of research.

- For the Germans, the welfare state (*Wohlfahrtsstaat*) is an outcome of a kind of social agreement between the government and the citizens. Social aid is not only accepted, but expected. Most social services are provided as rights, regardless of their cost and the income of a particular family. The state is obliged to build a social network for the common good. Communitarism prevails over individualism. In contrast, in the United States people on welfare are seen as failures. There is a strong tendency to condemn losers. The state is perceived as an inevitable evil and the expenses on maintaining the state – as a threat to individual freedom. The authors quote one of the recurring themes of Bob Dole's pre-election speeches: 'The scariest words in the English language are "I'm from the federal government and I'm here to help you."' It is hard to imagine a European politician, even an extremely conservative one, who would use this sentence as his election slogan.

- Differences consist not only in the level of material aid aimed at reducing poverty and social pathologies, which is much higher in Germany than in the USA, but also in a different method of action. The German welfare state tries to eliminate the causes of social pathology (preventive action). By contrast, social workers in the United States mainly take care of people already affected by pathology. Therefore, by nature, the German approach is more sociological and the American approach – more psychological.
- Knowing the American love of individual freedom, the authors' claim that in the USA an individual dependent on social aid is controlled by the government to a greater extent than in Germany must seem surprising. The authors explain this fact not only in terms of a different concept of welfare state, but also by reference to the allergy of Germans to all-embracing state control, dating back to the times of fascism.

As a result of the difference in approaches, the number of social care clients is much smaller in Germany than in the USA, which in the authors' opinion is a direct proof of the effectiveness of preventive action.[5]

Different Characteristics of Firms

Unfortunately, a comparison of American and German firms is not available, but the Italian-British-American economist Ronald Dore has contrasted the fundamental characteristics of British and Japanese firms, which can indirectly be applied to the opposition discussed above (see Table 9.1).

Dore elaborates on the above contrast as follows:

> One can call this the Community View of the firm as opposed to the Property View; the Entity View as opposed to the Profit Instruments View; the Corporate Membership View as opposed to the Matrix of Contracts View; the Shareholder Firm versus the Stockholder Firm (Dore, 2000, p. 26).

However, Dore himself prefers a milder form of this opposition: 'the employee-favouring firm versus shareholder-favouring firm'.

Table 9.1. The characteristics of Japanese and Anglo-Saxon firms

United Kingdom	Japan
What is an enterprise (firm)?	
Market property	Community, collective body
Main task of management:	
Ensuring maximum profits for shareholders	Long-term development of the firm, i.e. all employees
Managers' success criteria	
Share price as an index of their pay	Growth of the firm's market strength
Means of maintaining discipline among managers	
Dismissal by shareholders, hostile takeover	Loss of prestige in the firm, rebellion of junior managers, subordination to the central bank
Main criteria determining effectiveness:	
Managers' decisions (agency/principal theory)	Productivity of principal and all employees
Employment contract:	
Labor purchase contract	(Lifetime) career contract
Earnings:	
Pay for work done determined by the market	Pay calculated on the basis of career path, depending on the number of years with the firm
Differentiation of earnings:	
Big	Small
Motivation	
a) individual:	
Earnings, short-term	Long-term increase of pay and influence
b) group:	
Minimal	Quite serious: identification with the firm

Firm behavior during recession:	
Cost reduction – mainly cost of employment	Acceptance of lower dividend, decrease of profits, high salaries (if any) are reduced
Firm behavior in the situation of decline of a given industry:	
Fast liquidation of deficit departments, activization in new industries	Internal diversification of production, transfer of employees to departments with prospects
Qualifications of employees:	
Market as the source of better qualified staff	High expenditure on internal training, the firm is responsible for qualifications

Source: Ronald Dore's presentation, Prague 1994, script

Is German Economy Adopting American Ways?

Many authors believe so. Even Michel Albert (1991/1994), a supporter of German social market economy, regrets that the 'Rhine model is losing ground', although in his opinion it was more just and effective than the 'neo-American model'.

Albert gave a dramatic description of the struggle between the 'Rhine' (i.e. West German) system and the neo-American system. Although he stressed that the ultimate outcome was uncertain, he was concerned about the successful progress of the latter model:

> It will be an underground war, violent, obstinate, but partly hidden or even full of hypocrisy, just as any internal struggle within any one Church is full of hypocrisy. A struggle between brothers armed with two models ... carrying two antagonistic kinds of logic within the same liberalism. And perhaps ... two systems of values ..." (Albert, op. cit., p. 26).

Albert wrote these words more than ten years ago, but the final outcome is still hard to foresee, because in the long run the more effective and at the same time fairer of the competing systems does not always win.

Suzan Berger seems to have captured the logic of the competition between systems aiming at short-term profit maximizing and systems whose goals and resources are more socially oriented. She wrote:

> Absent a political will to sustain institutions and values that transcend efficiency and growth, no national traditions, culture, or historical legacies by themselves can restrain market forces. Seen from this perspective, even if the Japanese and German systems do better in the long run, they are vulnerable. In a competition between the long term

calculations about the uses of labour, resources, and capital characteristic of the political economies of these two countries in the postwar period and the short-term profit maximizing of Anglo-American capitalism, economic opportunism will win. When deregulation or open borders give national capitalists the chance to escape constraints on wages, working conditions, layoffs, financial speculation, mergers, or environmental protection, they will – no matter their previous involvement in social democratic neocorporatist, or Japanese-like lifetime employment systems. Given the general decline of the left and indeed of all those political forces in Western advanced societies that might sustain collective action on behalf of values other than competition and efficiency, market forces confront little opposition (Berger, 1996, p. 12).

However, for CDU leaders, social market economy still is a value that is worth defending. Here is what the chairman of the CDU Parliamentary caucus, W. Scheuble, told a *Polityka* journalist when asked about his opinion on the opposition between Rhine capitalism and Anglo-Saxon capitalism:

I prefer the traditional concept of social market economy .... Germany was doing quite well within its model. Now we have some problems, because our model is too bureaucratic. However, we are starting reforms, trying not to move too close to pure market economy. We will always have social market economy, based on the elimination of differences by political means (Scheuble, 2000).

However, it is hard to predict whether the politicians' and trade unionists' will is strong enough to resist the invasion of Anglo-Saxon corporations. The political maneuvers of the German social democracy do not give a clear answer to this question, either. Before their coming to power in 1998, the pre-election declarations of German social democrats were ambivalent, based on a sort of dualism: some voted for the left-winger Oskar Lafontaine, others for the more centrist Gerhard Schroeder. As the new Minister of Finance, Oskar Lafontaine, tried to change the macroeconomic policy, his main idea was to increase global demand by increasing real wages and salaries and reducing tax burdens imposed on poorer groups. At the same time, he wanted to increase corporate income taxes, especially paid by the companies that destroy the natural environment. He also wanted to impose taxes on capital. He attacked the central bank, demanding that fighting unemployment and fighting inflation be treated on an equal basis.[6] Furthermore, new hopes were associated with the establishment (or, actually, restitution) of the Committee of Labor, Education and Competition – a body consisting of representatives of employers, employees and the government, responsible for negotiating and adopting the main directions of economic and social policy.

Undoubtedly, this concept was based on the analyses and ideas of Keynesian economists, in particular Heiner Flassbeck, Lafontaine's closest aide and economic advisor. In general, however, Lafontaine's attempts at changing the macroeconomic policy were unskillful, although he encouraged the governments of the other European Union states to co-ordinate their macroeconomic policy, which even *The Financial Times* regarded as a good idea.[7] However, without waiting for the results of any talks, he started actions that were badly received by the business circles and the more and more influential Labor Party leadership.

After Lafontaine's resignation (in March 1999), Schroeder in a way returned to a policy inspired by the Maastricht Treaty. Lafontaine's office was given to a determined monetarist Hans Eichel. He immediately took steps to cut business taxes and dramatically reduce government expenditure (mainly social spending) to balance the budget. His proposal for a pension reform involved the establishment of a mandatory capital pillar (as in the Polish pension reform). Eichel's policy and his proposals not only gave rise to domestic protests, but also were severely criticized by *The Financial Times*:

> Mr Eichel's package is a school-book example of what fiscal policy should not be like. At the time of high unemployment and slow economic growth, he chooses strict fiscal policy ... It would make much more sense to do exactly the opposite (Munchau, 1999).

The article ends with an ironic remark: 'Eichel's predecessor [Lafontaine – TK] was not a reformer, either. At least, he understood economy'.[8]

This policy (including the joint declaration of Blair and Schroeder, published in June 1999) resulted in over half a dozen failures of the German Social Democrats in local elections (to Länder authorities), some of them quite spectacular. Moreover, both the declaration and the policy of the government were severely criticized and the conflict with trade unions worsened. The joint manifesto was perceived as an assault on the fundamental institutions of social market economy and an indication of welfare state demolition.

In consequence, the authorities had to withdraw from a number of intended reforms, e.g. the pension reform. Since that time the socio-economic policy of the government has gone in two directions. Moderate labor market liberalization is accompanied by a much more daring policy of lowering business taxes, liberalization and deregulation of the financial market and far-reaching openness to foreign competition. Deregulation and privatization of a number of industries has already begun (power sector privatization, demonopolization of Deutsche Telekom, announced privatization of the post). *The Wall Street Journal* expressed an enthusiastic opinion about this policy. It particularly appreciated the government proposal to abolish tax on the sale of shares in blocks (to date, the main barrier to 'hostile takeovers' of German firms by foreign capital). Hans Eichel has repeatedly said that 'Germany is no longer a closed market'. *The Wall Street Journal*, seeing Schroeder's intervention to prevent the bankruptcy of a well-known construction company Holzmann as an exception, added:

> What happened since then is of crucial importance .... Schroeder and Eichel managed to launch free market mechanisms without attracting attention. Therefore, it seems that the

policy of the current government is better for entrepreneurs than the policy of the former Chancellor Helmut Kohl (Roth, 2000).

Schroeder's government is aware that it must act with caution in matters concerning labor market flexibility and the corporatist system of pay negotiations, taking into account the power of the trade unions backed by the left wing of the SPD. According to *The Economist*, 'There are no reasons to believe that he is ready to dismantle the system of negotiations with trade unions, which restricts competitiveness of companies so much' (*The Economist*, 2000). Therefore, the active and quite consistent policy of liberalization, deregulation and privatization is accompanied by caution in the relations with the powerful trade unions, particularly in the field of restricting social and employees entitlements. It seems that Schroeder has drawn the following conclusions from the 1999 failures: give up Blair-style free market rhetoric, give up the idea of stressing the 'uniqueness' of his policy and make no more straightforward declarations of policy directions.

Is it only tactics? The fate of the pension reform project mentioned above is an argument in favor of such an answer (after the protests of the unions it was revised and now has a much less radical form). It may happen to a number of other projects, too. One of the main reasons for this is the fact that in Germany, as well as in France, liberalization (as well as the popularity of free market capitalism), is limited.[9] For Germany, the very fact of close co-operation with France is a certain barrier.[10]

Due to the special role of Germany and the German economy in the European Union, the fundamental question of convergence refers to the process of convergence of the German economy with the American economy, or submission to what Ronald Dore calls 'American-led global capitalism' at the expense of 'a good society'. Ronald Dore has studied the problem of the possibilities of retaining specific features of the German and Japanese systems perhaps more thoroughly than anyone else. A considerable part of his latest book (2000) is devoted to this problem. He has a much more optimistic forecast for Japan than for Germany. In Germany, further expansion of market economy and the 'finance-centered economy' now seems inevitable. On the other hand, the deeper educational awareness of Japan, as well as certain common features shared by its society with the neighbors (not only Korea, but also China) and a much more developed and all-embracing system result in a lower probability of globalization of the Japanese society and economy (op. cit., 220–25).

Notes

1   I would like to thank Professor Grzegorz W. Kolodko for his valuable comments.
2   It seems that also the authors of *The Transition Scoreboard*, working for the European Bank of Reconstruction and Development, build their list of transforming countries on the basis of the assumption of a single socio-economic system.

3   'Richard Freeman of America's National Bureau of Economic Research compared the degree of unionisation and the extent of collective bargaining across a range of economies between 1980 and the mid 1990s. In general, he found not convergence but divergence. America, Britain, Japan, New Zealand and Australia all saw declines in unionisation and collective bargaining. But in many European countries the pattern was mixed. France, Germany and the Netherlands, for instance, all had falling unionisation but rising coverage of collective-bargaining arrangements. And in some European countries – Spain, Finland and Sweden – unionisation and coverage of collective-bargaining arrangements increased' (The Economist 2000a:96).

4   Although a systematic concept was first presented by Strange (Strange 1986).

5   It should be added that not only the German welfare state model has been maintained, with slight modifications. Also the particularly well-developed Swedish welfare state model is surviving and seems no less effective than the systems of most OECD countries. Sweden still has the highest proportion of state expenditure in GDP in the world (approx. 65 per cent in 1996). Earnings and income inequalities are still small and the position of trade unions is strong. The poor and the unemployed still enjoy so ample rights that even the high unemployment of the first half of the 1990s did not cause a considerable growth of inequality or poverty (Korpi and Palme 1997).

6   Lafontaine skillfully referred to the policy of the US Federal Reserve: 'The head of the Federal Reserve Alan Greenspan proved that both inflation-free growth and increase of employment are possible' (in: Barber 1998).

7   The paper's regular columnist wrote about it (Wolf 1998). The editor added the following heading: 'Martin Wolf believes that although many of the ideas of the German Minister of Finance should be evaluated as wrong, he should be given credit for starting a debate on this issue'.

8   Because of a similar policy, Franco Modigliani called the former minister of finance, Theo Weigel, an economic ignoramus (Grzybowska 1997).

9   *The Economist* (2000b) sees these limits particularly realistically: 'Nonetheless, the faith in excluding governmental control of the European social model has its limits. As it is rightly pointed out on the Continent, advertising the British solutions is not very convincing, as on average the Germans and French are still richer than the British. The Germans, even though they have absorbed 17 million of poor East Germans, still feel rich and do not see a need to reduce their expenses. Moreover, even if the restructuring of the British economy in 1980s was successful, the success was only partial, because the productivity, even after restructuring, is still lower than that recorded in France and Germany.'

10   Unfortunately, I am not aware of any studies of systemic convergence between France and Germany, although there is an in-depth analysis of the process of convergence of the French system with the German system (Boltho 1996). However, it presents the common process of liberalization of both economies mainly as a result of the establishment of the common market. As far as the labor market institutions and employee participation are concerned, both countries have retained their differences: the far-reaching system of labor market socialization in Germany is still much different from the French system. After the almost simultaneous rise to power of the SPD in

Germany and the socialists in France, the differences in tax policy rather increased, as I have mentioned above.

References

Albert, Michael (1994), *Kapitalizm kontra kapitalizm*, 'Znak', Kraków (Originally published as: *Capitalisme contre capitalisme*, Edition du Seuil, 1991).

Barber, T. (1998). 'Schroeder Clashes with Bundesbank over Growth', *Financial Times*, 2 November.

Berger, Susan (1996), 'Introduction', in Berger, S. and Dore, R., *National Diversity and Global Capitalism*, Cornell University Press, Ithaca – London.

Boltho, Andrea (1996), 'Has France Converged on Germany? Policies and Institutions since 1958', in Berger, S. and Dore, R., *National Diversity and Global Capitalism*, Cornell University Press, Ithaca -London.

Bottomore, Tom B. and Rubel, Maximilian (eds) (1964), *Karl Marx: Selected Writings in Sociology and Social Philosophy*, McGraw-Hill Company, New York-Toronto-London.

Childs, M. W. (1936), *Sweden. The Middle Way*, New Haven – London.

Dore, Ronald (1994), lecture outline, Prague, handout in the author's possession.

Dore, Ronald (2000), *Stock Market Capitalism: Welfare Capitalism*, Oxford University Press, Oxford.

Galbraith, J. K. (1953), *American Capitalism. The Concept of Countervailing Power*, Houghton Miflin Company, Boston.

Gardawski, Juliusz (2001), *Związki zawodowe na rozdrożu*, Instytut Spraw Publicznych, Warszawa.

Grzybowska, Krystyna (1997), 'Weigel jest ekonomicznym ignorantem. Bundestag wrogiem euro', *Rzeczpospolita*, 16 August.

Marks, Karol and Engels, Fryderyk (1949), *Manifest Komunistyczny*, in Marks, K. and Engels, F., *Dzieła wybrane*, Vol. 1, Książka i Wiedza, Warszawa.

Morrison, John D. and Wolf, Robert A. 1999/(2000), 'Social Works and Social Policy in Germany and the United States', *American Studies Journal*, No. 44.

Munchau, W. (1999), 'Taxing Problem', *Financial Times*, 6 July.

Rawls, John (1994), *Teoria sprawiedliwości*, Wydawnictwo Naukowe PWN, Warszawa (originally published as: *Theory of Justice*, Harvard University Press, Cambridge Mass, 1971).

Roth, T. (2000), 'Nowe oblicze gospodarki niemieckiej', *Wall Street Journal Europe*, quoted after *Forum* of 31 January.

Scheuble, Wolfgang (1998), 'Nie porównujmy jabłek i gruszek', *Polityka*, 6 June.

Sen, Amartya K. (1998), *Nierówności: Dalsze rozważania*, 'Znak' Kraków (originally published as: *Inequality Reexamined*, Harvard University Press, Cambridge, Mass., 1995).

Strange, Susan (1986), *Casino Capitalism*, London.

The Economist (2000a), 'One True Model? The World is not Converging on a Single Kind of Capitalism', *The Economist*, 8 April.

The Economist (2000b), 'Blaski i cienie lewicy', *The Economist*, quoted after *Forum*, 12–14 February.

Wolf, Martin (1998), 'Is Lafontaine Half-Backed?' *Financial Times*, 25 November.

PART IV
CATCHING-UP AND EXTERNAL
FACTORS OF DEVELOPMENT

Chapter 10

Japanese Approach to the Transition Economies

Masahiro Taguchi

This paper presents the economic policy of the Japanese government for the support of developing countries and transition economies. The Japanese government has kept to a pro-globalization approach in domestic economic policy. On the other hand, Japan has been criticizing international financial institutions and the United States for their pro-globalization approach in development assistance policy. Although Japan appears to maintain a similar stance in macroeconomic policy, it will often adopt a development assistance policy quite different from the international financial institutions and the United States, especially toward Asian nations. This is the reason why the economists and the policymakers in the world wonder whether Japan has a clear idea regarding its economic policy. In this paper, I try to describe the Japanese approach (the approach of the Japanese government) in relation to developing countries and transition economies and summarize the Japanese economic policy to assist development and transition (Section 1), while analyzing Japan's stance to democratization (Section 2) and chronologically introducing the efforts to establish an Asian Monetary Fund (AMF) (Section 3).

1. 'Washington Consensus' vs. 'Japanese Approach'

In the 1990s, the 'Washington Consensus' (see Appendix 1) became a synonym for 'neoliberalism' or 'market fundamentalism', regardless of the meaning with which the term was initially used by Williamson (Williamson, 1999). This interpretation was convenient for the politicians and economists at that time. As a matter of fact, even though the 'Washington Consensus' was not a full consensus even in Washington, it has had a huge influence on the economic policies of developing countries and transition economies in the last decade. Incontestably, the 'Washington Consensus' accelerated globalization (marketization, monetary liberalization, etc.).

The Asian currency crisis, which started in 1997, gave us a lot of suggestions. The recipe applied by international financial institutions exacerbated the crisis in Asia. In particular, the excessive monetary restraint based on the 'Washington

Consensus' and large structural reconstruction demand heavily encumbered the Asian economies.

Globalization isn't always favorable for developing countries. Therefore, support is required in order for developing countries to overcome their structural weaknesses. For example, supporting priority sectors, training employers and employees and transforming technology are very important issues needed to enhance competitiveness for these countries. Reducing unemployment and the building of a safety-net are also central tasks for the stabilization and development of these countries.

Japan has been gradually clarifying the differences in approach with regard to international financial institutions since the Asian crisis. As a matter of fact, there is neither a 'Japanese approach' that has been officially declared by the Japanese government, nor is there a widely accepted 'Japan program'. Moreover, there is no consensus on Japanese development support or on transition economy support within the government, between the government and private financial institutions, the think tanks, or among economists in Japan. However, there is something akin to a common term or a greatest common divisor. A certain kind of common recognition has arisen based on the experience gained in dealing with the Asian financial crisis after 1997. It can be summarized as follows (with main emphasis on Asian issues). It is of interest to compare this with the 'Washington Consensus'):

1. Role of government: In the high-growth period of Japan, the government greatly contributed to its economic development. Now, the government is struggling to create an efficient, competitive free-market system in Japan. However, Japan is not requesting the other countries in transition to stop intervention in the market at once. In the economically weak countries, the efficient concentration of resources becomes difficult when the government weakens; and when the government weakens, the dynamics of economic growth decline. Of course, it is necessary to create a free-market system in the long run; however, a strong government which is able to design and create the free market, supervise the rules of transactions and control the market performances is required for this.

2. 'Translational implementation' (Maekawa, 2000) of a global system: In each country, there is a so-called 'base society', with roots deeply grounded in the culture, tradition and history (Ohno, 1996, pp. 61–92). This 'base society' does not 'jump'.[1] Therefore 'translational implementation' is necessary for the introduction of an international system to a country in the first stage of adjustment, though it is necessary to move to a free-market economy in the future.

3. Limitation of the range of conditionality: The present IMF's conditionality constitutes too wide a sphere. It covers almost the whole economic system. In transition economies and developing economies, there is neither enough capital nor are there sufficient human resources to create a complete, advanced free-

market system within a short term. It is necessary to limit the range of conditionality.

4. 'Good governance': The Japanese government has officially declared that democratization is an element of great importance for development (see Section 2). In practice, the Japanese government is still very cautious about adding the democratization issue to economic assistance packages. This doesn't mean that the Japanese government neglects the significance of good governing practices. A lot of careful opinions are voiced in Japan concerning democratization. Therefore, the policy of the Japanese government is to provide 'technological support' in areas such as improvements in the judicial system, the system of central and local government, etc.

5. Structural reconstruction: The contents of the structural reconstruction (privatization etc.) roughly correspond to the policies of the IMF and the World Bank. However, it is necessary to pay close attention to the timing, so as to decide whether the structural reconstruction should be done during the monetary crisis or when the emergency has passed.

6. Micro-financing: Fiscal and financial restrain strike first of all small and medium scale enterprises. Starting a sustainable small loan program is important to support domestic production and to avoid acute depression.

7. Trade financing: If severe monetary restraint is maintained and trade liberalization is rapid, trade financing is reduced and exports, which are the engine of economic recovery, will decline. In such cases, trade financing must be supported.

8. Problem of sequencing: Both trade liberalization and the liberalization of capital movement improve the efficiency of the domestic market. Thus, the introduction of the regulation of capital movement and the control of foreign exchange impart a negative influence to trade, and lead to the poor performance of the entire economy. However, many have argued as to whether or not trade liberalization and the freeing of capital transactions need to be done simultaneously in cases such as the Asian currency crisis. The liberalization of capital transactions requires mid- and long-term preparation. It is necessary to create a solid domestic financial system and to establish a control system to manage the enormous amounts of short-term capital which rapidly flows into (or out of) a country in the nascent stage of transition.

9. System stabilizer: The systems peculiar to the high-growth period of Japan, which are thought to have caused economic stagnation (government intervention in industry and the financial system, main-bank system and the cross-shareholding of stocks) are being reformed. However, such systems are sometimes useful at a certain level of development in order to maintain stability and the sustainable growth of the domestic market.

10. Exchange system: A currency basket system provides for exchange rate flexibility, thereby preventing the overvaluation or undervaluation of the currency.

11. Improvement of the condition of financial institutions: It is necessary to improve the condition of the financial institutions to prevent a monetary crisis and to persist in risk management (see Section 3).

12. Improvement of the level of education: The important factors for the production of internationally competitive industrial goods are technology and quality control. Establishing an education system and a skill formation system are key factors for industry. Long-term development assistance must be concentrated on consolidating the general education system to offer a bottom-up social education level and on creating retraining institutions to avoid employment mismatches in transition economies.

13. Building infrastructure: The enhancement of the infrastructure (communication networks, traffic, etc.) becomes an important factor for foreign direct investment.

14. Creating a safety net: The transition process expands income differentials at the first stage (the Kuznetz curve). Globalization brings another shock. The lack of a safety net quickly destabilizes a society. Thus, the improvement of weak labor market institutions, the establishment of a formal safety net for workers and pensioners and the correction of income differences through budgetary and tax reform are necessary in order to ensure the stable development of the economy and society.

The guidance for and the criteria of the Japanese approach are expressed in 'Japan's Official Development Assistance Charter' (Cabinet Decisions: June 30, 1992). This Charter says that

> Japan attaches central importance to support for the self-help efforts of developing countries intended to lift their economies. Japan will therefore use the ODA to help ensure the efficient and fair distribution of resources and 'good governance' in developing countries by developing a wide range of human resources and socioeconomic infrastructure that will include domestic systems and by supporting basic human needs (BHN), thereby promoting the sound economic development of the recipient countries (Ministry of Finance, 1992).

Japan's ODA is extended on the basis of requests from recipient countries. It stresses the importance of cooperation for the improvement and dissemination of technologies, assistance to human resources development and infrastructure improvement. Japan's ODA will pay full attention 'to efforts for promoting democratization and introduction of a market-oriented economy, and the situation regarding the securing of basic human rights and freedoms in the recipient country', but 'will be provided in accordance with the principles of the United Nations Charter (especially those of sovereign equality and non-intervention in domestic matters)' (Ministry of Finance, 1992). Thus, on the one hand, the Japanese government recognizes the importance of market liberalization, but on the other hand, it carefully avoids involvement in political issues, and tries to concentrate on the 'technical' matters.

Supporting 'good governance' is the key effort of Japan's ODA. Japan has experience in legislation, the system of government and the parliamentary system. Japanese experts will use their experience, gained in Japan, in the training of personnel, who will then be able to create their own economic policies and national plans. This technical cooperation to establish 'good governance' is undertaken in the fields of management, administration control, financial policy, monetary policy, industrial policy, manpower development, protection of the environment, social security, farming policy and regional development. This form of assistance has been given in Poland (industrial policy), Vietnam (legal system), Uzbekistan (training of personnel), Jordan (industrial policy) and Cambodia (law maintenance). However, the advice is limited to 'technical content' and intervention in politics is carefully avoided.

2. Democracy and Development

One of the most characteristic approaches of the Japanese government is its stance with regard to democracy and development. Generally, there are two kinds of ideas. One is the idea that democratization promotes economic development. Another is the idea that economic development promotes democratization.

The former is an idea to assure fair competition through democratization, which promotes the creation of a healthy market. The major international financial institutions as well as those of the United States are mainly based on this idea. Democratization also promotes the entry of FDI to a transition country, which contributes to its economic development. In the latter approach, economic development causes an increase in the urban population, the improvement of the level of education, an increase in the number of professional workers and the size of the middle income group, which leads to the collapse or 'meltdown' of an authoritarian regime or a dictatorial system. In addition, in the case where the government fails to achieve economic development under an authoritarian regime, a popular protest movement opposed to the political power may emerge, which becomes a democratic movement. As a result, the authoritarianism leads to democratization, even if the authoritarian regime fails.

Both opinions have their adherents. There is a stereotype that the Japanese government supports the latter one. Japanese government often adopts a development aid policy different from that of the United States toward Asian nations, including China and Vietnam, which is sometimes incomprehensible to the Americans. It is said that Japan has two faces. It means that the Japanese have their traditional philosophy, which is quite different from the western philosophies, but after the Second World War, Japan had to play a role of a champion of 'western' democracy, hand in hand with the United States. Moreover, Japan has profited enormously from democracy, not only in social terms, but also economically.

Japan has suffered from the stance it presents to the world and its internal reality. Japan has shown a vague attitude and has been criticized for having no philosophy or ideas pertaining to the support of development and transition economies. However, in practice, the Japanese government does not always overemphasize development and neglect democracy. There are many cases where the Japanese government has held to a policy of promoting democratization. For instance, it is availing itself of every opportunity to press for democratization and human rights improvements under the present regime in Myanmar. The Japanese government does recognize the significance of democratization.

Then, when does the Japanese government give priority to a democratization policy and when to development aid? It is widely accepted in Japan that democracy is a very important value in social life, which greatly contributes to development. Amartya Sen describes clearly the importance of democracy (Sen, 1999b):[2]

1. Political and social participation has intrinsic value in the lives of the citizens. Exercising civil and political rights is a crucial part of a citizen's existence in society and influences living standards.
2. Democracy has an important instrumental value in enhancing the consideration that people get in expressing and supporting their claims to political attention (including claims of economic needs). This is a strong incentive for politicians to response in good faith to the people's requests.
3. Under the democratic system, the process of public discussions and exchange of information helps society to form its values and priorities.

Thus, Asia has a culture different from Western Europe and the United States and even in those cases where the modern democracy system cannot be accepted, democracy remains a value in itself which must be pursued. It seems that Sen's stance on democracy is not too far removed from the views of the Japanese government. The problem is not whether democracy is necessary or not, but how we can achieve democracy and by what means we can support democratization.

Yasuhiro Takeda, associate professor of International Relations at the National Defense Academy of Japan, describes clearly the difference of diplomatic approaches to the promotion of democracy between Japan and the United States. He points out that Japan places much more emphasis on an incentive approach, which provides benefits for promoting democracy. On the other hand, the United States tends to use the sanction approach, which deprives a country of benefits if that country does not democratize (Takeda, 1997). He stresses that

> Japan, in particular, does not automatically apply a uniform response to countries that act in ways that are undemocratic. Japan decides its response after considering the country's circumstances and the relationship between Japan and the country, being very cautious when it comes to applying sanctions. The United States, on the other hand, is quick to cut off support to any country guilty of suppressing human rights or democratization movements under the Foreign Assistance Act. In addition, Congress,

which is sensitive to issues of human rights and democratization, frequently presents bills for sanctions against countries considered guilty of violations of human rights and this limits the government's ability to apply its own diplomatic judgment (Takeda, 1997).

Takeda does not come out in favor of one or the other of these positions. Each approach has its merits and demerits. It is important to establish common rules, because the difference between the two countries could lead to a conflict. Japan may conduct an advantageous policy with respect to a country, using a carrot approach; at the same time, however, the United States cannot use its whip approach effectively precisely because Japan does not take a common stance. According to Takeda the rules should be as follows (Takeda, 1997):

1. If Japan has substantial interests in a country, combined with a strong intent and the ability to provide the benefits promised, the effectiveness of the incentive approach is high. On the other hand, if the US has interests in a country it has threatened with sanctions, the credibility of the threats of sanctions seems less effective (the China case). In this case, the incentive approach is more viable.
2. It is reasonable to choose the sanction approach when the probability of success in achieving democratization is high and to choose the incentive approach when it is low. It is very rare for a monolithic and unified ruling elite to yield to foreign pressure and accept democratization, especially in the case when democratization would seem to lead to the abandonment or weakening of the present regime. In this case (when the probability of success is low), the incentive approach is more effective for promoting democratization.
3. When an authoritarian regime is seriously fractured internally, it would be effective to use sanctions to prevent armed suppression or to control mass movements that may trigger armed suppression.
4. The sanction approach has a certain level of effectiveness in checking a significant retreat from democracy, but it is not so effective in promoting democracy. When sanctions are carried out after deterrence fails, it is not the ruling elite, but rather the public that suffers most. In this sense, the sanction approach mistakes the means for the end. Sanctions to punish a significant retreat from democracy should only be implemented after specifying the time limits of the sanctions period and the level of the sanctions.

Takeda's conclusions are not the official consensus between Japan and the United States. However, such an approach is not too distant from the current diplomatic practices of the Japanese government in the area of support for transition economies.

3. Asian Monetary Fund

Japan takes initiatives concerning the international monetary system. In August 1997, a Japanese plan was announced for a monetary fund of USD 100bn to prepare in case of a relapse of the monetary crisis. It was put forward as the 'Asian Monetary Fund' (AMF) plan. Each country of ASEAN and South Korea agreed with the AMF plan. However, the United States was critical of it. The IMF took the position that 'the support plan in an Asian region that does not correspond to the support plan of the IMF will create a moral hazard in the realization process of the monetary policy'. China also showed a passive attitude to the plan.

In August 1998, the devaluation of the ruble in Russia hit the world market. Stock prices fell sharply worldwide and the exchange rates simultaneously became unstable. The international monetary market was confused. People were beginning to realize that the prescriptions of the IMF were not cure-alls. In October 1998, the framework of the government fund assistance was announced. The Japanese government aimed to support the reconstruction of the economies of Asian nations that were suffering from the monetary crisis. This was called the 'New Miyazawa Initiative' (A New Initiative to Overcome the Asian Currency Crisis) (see Appendix 2). The total amount involved was USD 30bn. The Export-Import Bank of Japan's (now operating as The International Cooperation Bank) would provide the financing and yen loans under a medium- to long-term support plan (supporting corporate debt restructuring in the private sector, making financial systems sound and stable, strengthening the social safety net, stimulating the increase of employment, facilitating trade finance and assisting small and medium-sized enterprises) in South Korea, Thailand, Indonesia, the Philippines, and Malaysia. The AMF plan had been reversed by the United States. This time, the Japanese government proposed a plan based on bilateral support. In this way, the plan met with understanding on the part of the United States.

In May 2000, a Finance Ministers Meeting was held in Chiang Mai in Thailand, and 'ASEAN+3' (Japan, China, South Korea, and ASEAN nations) adopted the 'Agreement on currency swapping' which would accommodate foreign currency in case of foreign financing difficulties. This was called the 'Chiang Mai Initiative'. It aimed to ensure the smooth accommodation of foreign currency reserves – mainly in US dollars – and to prevent a financial crisis that would be triggered by rapid capital outflow from the country. This system lead to the AMF plan.

In January 2001, the Asian Currency Basket Plan, in which the base currencies were the US dollar, yen and the euro, was adopted at the 3rd Finance Ministers' Meeting held in Kobe within the framework of ASEM (Asia-Europe Meeting). The participants came to the conclusion that a possible solution for many emerging market economies would be a managed exchange rate whereby the currency would move within a fixed range whose center would be aligned to a basket of currencies.

4. Concluding Remarks

The IMF's reform measures for the Asian currency and financial crisis in 1997–8 were not fully satisfactory for Asian countries. This was one of the reasons why the Japanese government wanted to establish the AMF. There were critical opinions that this alternative approach, which was quite different from the widely recognized neo-classical approach, might serve to weaken the expected effects of a typical macro-stabilization policy because the Fund would fill up the monetary shortage caused by the restrictive policy.

However, the AMF plan was not proposed as a means to escape from IMF's severe financial restraints. Introduced simultaneously, the IMF's restraint policy and the AMF's financial support policy may cancel out each other's effects. However, financing debt restructuring in the private sector, strengthening the social safety net, stimulating the increase of employment and assisting small and medium-sized enterprises will also aid to restore macroeconomic balance. It is important to work out the cooperation guidelines to create multiplicative effects.

The Japanese government does not always overemphasize development and neglect democracy. Democratization is one of the most important issues in Japan's ODA. However, a sanction approach in achieving the democratization of a transition economy is not always enough. An effective combination involves a mix of a sanction approach and an incentive approach.

Notes

1   Ohno ironically expresses his idea in contrast to the title of Jeffrey Sachs' book, the *Polish Jump to the Market Economy* (Cambridge: MIT Press, 1993).

2   See also Sen (1999a).

Appendix 1: The 'Washington Consensus' (Williamson, 1994, pp. 26–28)

Fiscal Discipline: Budget deficits, properly measured to include those of provincial governments, state enterprises, and the central bank, should be small enough to be financed without recourse to the inflation tax. This typically implies a primary surplus (i.e., before adding debt service to expenditure) of several percent of GDP, and an operational deficit (i.e., disregarding that part of the interest bill that simply compensates for inflation) of no more than about 2 percent of GDP.

Public Expenditure Priorities: Policy reform consists in redirecting expenditure from politically sensitive areas, which typically receive more resources than their economic return can justify, such as administration, defense, indiscriminate subsidies, and white elephants, toward neglected fields with high economic returns and the potential to improve income distribution, such as primary health and education, and infrastructure.

Tax Reform: Tax reform involves broadening the tax base and cutting marginal tax rates. The aim is to sharpen incentives and improve horizontal equity without lowering realized progressivity. Improved tax administration (including subjecting interest income on assets held abroad – flight capital – to taxation) is an important aspect of broadening the base in the Latin context.

Financial Liberalization: The ultimate objective of financial liberalization is market-determined interest rates, but experience has shown that, under conditions of a chronic lack of confidence, market-determined rates can be so high as to threaten the financial solvency of productive enterprises and government. Under that circumstance a sensible interim objective is the abolition of preferential interest rates for privileged borrowers and achievement of a moderately positive real interest rate.

Exchange Rates: Countries need a unified (at least for trade transactions) exchange rate set at a level sufficiently competitive to induce a rapid growth in traditional exports, and managed so as to assure exporters that this competitiveness will be maintained in the future.

Trade Liberalization: Quantitative trade restrictions should be rapidly replaced by tariffs, and these should be progressively reduced until a uniform low tariff in the range of 10 percent (or at most around 20 percent) is achieved. There is, however, some disagreement about the speed with which tariffs should be reduced (with recommendations falling in a band between 3 and 1 years), and about whether it is advisable to slow down the liberalization process when macroeconomic conditions are adverse (recession and payments deficit).

Foreign Direct Investment: Barriers impeding the entry of foreign firms should be abolished; foreign and domestic firms should be allowed to compete on equal terms.

Privatization: State enterprises should be privatized.

Deregulation: Governments should abolish regulations that impede the entry of new firms or restrict competition, and ensure that all regulations are justified by such criteria as safety, environmental protection, or prudential supervision of financial institutions.

Property Rights: The legal system should provide secure property rights without excessive costs, and make these available to the informal sector.

Appendix 2:   A New Initiative to Overcome the Asian Currency Crisis ('New Miyazawa Initiative') (October, 1998; summary)

I.   **Medium- to Long-Term Financial Support to Asian Countries** (USD 15 billion)

1.   Need **for funds in Asian countries**: Asian countries affected by the currency crisis need medium to long-term capital to implement the various policy measures described below for economic recovery.

   (1)   Supporting corporate debt restructuring in the private sector and efforts to make financial systems sound and stable;

   (2)   Strengthening the social safety net;

   (3)   Stimulating the economy (implementation of public undertakings to increase employment);

   (4)   Addressing the credit crunch (facilitation of trade finance and assistance to small and medium-sized enterprises).

2.   Measures **for financial assistance**: To meet these medium- to long-term capital needs of Asian countries, Japan will extend financial assistance to those countries making use of the various measures listed below. In doing so, due consideration will be paid to the better use of the Tokyo market to mobilize Japanese funds.

   (1)   Providing direct official financial assistance

      i) Extending Export-Import Bank of Japan (JEXIM) loans to Asian countries

      ii) Acquisition of sovereign bonds issued by Asian countries by the JEXIM

      iii) Extending ODA yen loans to Asian countries

   (2)   Supporting Asian countries in raising funds from international financial markets

      i)   Use of guarantee mechanisms

         a)   Utilizing the guarantee functions of the JEXIM
            – The JEXIM will guarantee bank loans to Asian countries.
            – The JEXIM will guarantee sovereign bonds issued by Asian countries (legal amendment is necessary).

         b)   Providing export insurance to bank loans to Asian countries.

      c) Requesting the World Bank and the Asian Development Bank to step up their efforts to provide guarantees to bank loans and bond issuance by Asian countries.

      d) It is hoped that in the long run the establishment of an international guarantee institution with a prime focus on Asian countries will be seriously considered.

    ii) Interest subsidies: Japan will establish an Asian currency crisis support facility backed by our funding. This facility will be used to provide interest subsidies to Asian countries that borrow funds from JEXIM or private banks in conjunction with loans from the Asian Development Bank.

        This will be an open facility in which all countries are welcome to take part.

(3) Financial **support in the form of co-financing with multilateral development banks**: Japan will continue to provide co-financing with the World Bank and the Asian Development Bank to Asian countries. In particular, we will call for maximum financial assistance from the World Bank and the Asian Development Bank to support those Asian countries that are faced with huge capital needs in an effort to address the issue of corporate debt restructuring and the restoration of stability in the financial system. We are ready to provide co-financing with these two banks.

(4) **Technical assistance**: The World Bank and the Asian Development Bank will be requested to provide necessary technical assistance through Japanese special funds to Asian countries that are to implement a comprehensive approach to address the issue of corporate debt restructuring and the restoration of the financial system. Japan is prepared to contribute by means of providing technical assistance to these Asian countries, taking into account the respective situations in those countries.

II. Short-Term Financial Support to Asian Countries (USD 15 billion)

Asian countries may face some needs for short-term capital in the course of making progress in their economic reform. To be prepared to meet these needs such as facilitation of trade finance, Japan will set aside USD 15 billion in short-term funds which will take the form of swap arrangements.

    Japan intends to cooperate closely with the multilateral development banks and the related countries, especially Asia-Pacific countries and G-7 countries, in implementing the new initiative.

References

Sen, Amartya (1999a), *Development as Freedom*, Alfred A. Knopf, New York.

Sen, Amartya (1999b), 'Democracy and Socialism', *Sekai* (June, 1999), Tokyo.

Kolodko, Grzegorz W. (2000), *From Shock to Therapy. The Political Economy of Postsocialist Transformation*, Oxford University Press, Oxford – New York.

Maekawa, Keiji (2000), *Anthropology of development. From Cultural Zygosis to Translational Implementation*, Shinyosha, Tokyo.

Ministry of Finance (1992), 'Japan's Official Development Assistance Charter' (Cabinet Decisions, June 30, 1992).

Ohno, Kenichi (1996), *The Strategy of Transition to Market*, Yuhikaku, Tokyo.

Takeda, Yasuhiro (1997), 'Overcoming Japan-US Discord in Democracy Promotion Policies', Tokyo Conference on the Japan-US Alliance Project, (Jan. 1997), mimeo.

Tsukamoto, Hiroshi and Yonemura, Noriyuki (1992), *Japan's Postwar Experience: Its Meaning and Implication for the Economic Transformation of the Former Soviet Republics*, Research Institute of International Trade and Industry, Ministry of International Trade and Industry (MITI/RI), Tokyo.

Williamson, John (ed.) (1994), *The Political Economy of Policy Reform*, Institute of International Economics, Washington.

Williamson, John (1999), 'What Should the Bank Think about the Washington Consensus?', Institute for International Economics, Washington.

Chapter 11

Globalization and the Role of Foreign Banks in Economies in Transition

Michael Keren and Gur Ofer

1. Introduction

The main argument of this paper consists of three connected parts: First, there is a deep comparative (and absolute) disadvantage of transition economies (TEs) in the provision of financial services, including banking services, caused by the heritage of central planning and the particular roles of banks in that system. Second, in TEs there is a particularly large need for financial and banking services, both for short and long-term operations. This emanates from two related sources: first, the highly developed, 'modern' and complex production sector inherited from the old regime in most TEs, and the high level of urbanization; and second, the great need for restructuring and privatization, and for the adaptation of the economy to the new conditions of an open market economy. The third part of the main argument is that foreign banks are much better equipped to provide the needed services than domestic banks and that the recent development of global, multinational banking services, provides a great opportunity for TEs, by bringing them in to expedite the transition and to encourage higher levels of economic growth.

The debate in the literature regarding the advantages and disadvantages of the operation of foreign banks in developing economies (DEs) has not yet been fully settled. While the World Bank reports that 'recent studies have confirmed the economic benefits of admitting foreign-owned banks' (2001, Vol. II, Working Paper no. 11, p. 187), an opposite view is quoted by Abel and Siklos (2001, p. 5).[1] We claim that there is little doubt that the arguments in favor of banking FDI in TEs are much stronger than for DEs.[2]

At the very time that the transition started and the need for foreign banks emerged, technological changes followed by organizational changes made it possible to integrate financial and banking services across national borders. The global financial and banking community was developing the advanced infrastructure, tools and capabilities to move abroad with relative ease and efficiency. The trend of openness and liberalization policies, embodied in international trade agreements, as well as the rapid technological changes in transport communications and information technology led to the rapid expansion of trade in goods over the last generation or two, followed in recent years by FDI and trade in services. A significant share of the financial and banking activities of the individual developed countries became global. Transition came about just when the process of globalization of financial and other services was taking off.

There is little wonder, given the triple argument, that in quite a few TEs nearly the entire banking sector has been taken over by foreign banks (Table 11.1 below). This is true with respect to the Baltic states, the Czech Republic, Croatia, Hungary and Poland, and the process is advancing rapidly also in Slovakia, Romania and Bulgaria. What may be somewhat surprising is that it took nearly 10 years of transition for this process to be completed. We come back to the latter question below. However, the phenomenon of a virtual takeover of an entire sector by foreign owners in a number of countries is very unusual for any sector, but even more so for the banking sector. At the same time one cannot escape noticing the very small involvement of foreign banks in CIS countries, and especially Russia. If the need is so great and there is capability and interest on the supply side, what has held up the entry of foreign banks to TEs in Central and Eastern Europe for so long? What is still holding it from happening in Russia and most other CIS countries? The search for an answer to this question is one purpose of this paper. One possible answer is that it took that long to overcome the usual 'nationalist' sentiment against FDI in general and the 'penetration' of foreign banks in particular. The nationalist argument is in many cases also a cover for more material vested interests of the owners of the domestic 'banking' sector, those of their related corporate clients and close political interests. An alternative explanation is that it is the level of market and legal infrastructure in general, as well as the prudential and supervisory environment in particular, that hampered the improvement in the functioning of domestic banks and the entry of foreign banks. The main claim of the paper is that the socialist heritage made the domestic banking sector in TEs a big part of the problem rather than of the solution and that the two alternative explanations for the late introduction of foreign banks are actually two sides of one and the same explanation.

There is a vast literature on the development of the financial sector in TEs but only few studies are dealing directly with the role of foreign banks in this process. Among these is a paper by Derviz (1997), who advocates an intensive policy of attracting foreign banks to dominate and guide the banking sector in the Czech Republic and other TEs. De Pointbriand (2001) has a section on 'A key role of foreign banks in enhancing banking system performance [in TEs]'. In addition to theoretical arguments, the section also shows how foreign investment helped reduce interest spread, introduce modern services and give a hand in providing risk assessment and investment loans. He also reports on the development of a nationalist backlash against this trend. The World Bank has a working paper on the desirability of bringing foreign banks to participate in the restructuring of the banking sector in Russia (World Bank, 2001, chapter 11), whose authors are mildly favorable to the idea but emphasize strongly that the establishment of a credible and effective legal environment is a precondition for any such move. When these conditions are met, so it is implied, domestic banks can also improve their performance. Bonin and Wachtel (2001) show how, recently, during the late 1990s, following some failures to restructure their banking sector domestically, a number of TEs finally resorted to the selling of state banks to foreign banks. They list the advantages of such a move but state that this may be a proper solution to medium size countries but not to bigger ones like Russia and China. Finally, papers by Opiela (2001) on Poland; Abel and Siklos (2001), on Hungary; and Galac and Kraft (2000); and Vujcic and Jermic (2001), on Croatia, all show some advantages in the performance of foreign banks.[3] The particular message of this paper goes to some extent beyond the above: it envisages an innovative, future development of the global economy created by the particular economic situation that TEs found themselves in as they embarked on a transition to the market, and in conjunction with the global technological developments in banking and financial services.

The structure of the paper is as follows. We open with a theoretical framework, which explains the needs of transition for a modern banking sector and the potential of FDI to supply them (section 2). Section 3 is a stylized analysis of the history of the banking sector in TEs, before and during the transition. Section 4 examines the potential contribution of foreign banks in TEs and section 5 evaluates the advantage of banks compared to other instruments of the capital market in TEs. Section 6 follows empirically the process of penetration of foreign banks to TEs in the context of changes in ownership of banks in TEs, and analyzes the correlation between foreign bank penetration and the performance of the banking sectors. The concluding section discusses the potential connection between improvements in the legal environment of TEs and in their banking sectors and the involvement of foreign banks. Which is the egg and which is the chicken?

2. A Theoretical Background

The comparative perspective that we employ requires a brief theoretical overview of the economics of banking FDI as it relates to TEs. We base ourselves on the Diamond model (1984 and 1996), which solves the basic agency problem of the banking system in a market economy. We do, however, have to include a wider array of institutional elements of the financial system in the model, and lead down all the way to the firms in the so-called productive sphere. Our problem lies with the latter: their governance has to be improved if they are to restructure and adjust to competitive market conditions. Banks can force transparency and profit-seeking behavior on firms that are in need of financing, but to do so agency problems in banks have to be solved first. If they are not, banks may help perpetuate malfunctioning enterprises. This is the reason why we believe that the reform of the banking system as a whole is such a priority task.

Consider the firm first. It is sufficient for now to think of the firm as a manager, $m \in M$ who has a set of available projects, T^m at his command. Project $t \in T$ requires an investment of 1 unit today and produces a stochastic outcome of $\phi^t \in \left\{ \underline{\phi}^t, \overline{\phi}^t \right\}$,

where the probability of the good outcome $\overline{\phi}^t$ is p^t. The optimal loan agreement advances m a loan of 1 unit, requiring a fixed repayment of f, $\underline{\phi}^t < f < \overline{\phi}^t$, such that whenever $\phi < f$ the firm is bankrupt and is dissolved, and whenever $\phi \geq f$ the loan is repaid (Diamond, 1984 and 1996). Furthermore, there exists a large number of individual depositors who are ready to lend to banks at the interest rate r, so that

$$p^t \overline{\phi} \geq p^t f \geq r :$$
(1)

on average the bank's expected interest income covers its interest payments.

The banker faces several pitfalls that may make it impossible to cover its interest costs. Suppose the set M is composed of two subsets, M^h and M^d, of honest and dishonest managers. Honest managers repay their loans whenever they are able to, and dishonest ones do not. Banker b incurs a cost of c_a^b, where the subscript a refers to adverse selection, when she checks the honesty of a manager, but once the check is undertaken she can be sure that m is honest and belongs to M^h, or dishonest and belongs to M^d. The second threat lies in m's choice of projects. Assuming that m does not suffer any loss when he is bankrupt, which occurs whenever $\phi < f$, his maximand is

$$E[\phi - f] = p^t \left(\overline{\phi} - f \right).$$
(2)

Moral hazard may therefore lead him to select highly risky projects, which compensate for a low probability of success p^t with a very high $\overline{\phi}^t$. In this case the lender bears all the costs of failure, and the borrower pockets the gains of success. This is one of the reasons the price system, i.e., an interest rate, is not sufficient to allocate credit, and credit rationing is needed (Stiglitz and Weiss, 1981). In Diamond's model, to prevent such a choice, the banker b has to spend c_m^b in screening and monitoring m. Let $c^b = c_a^b + c_m^b$.

Diamond shows that a well-functioning competitive banking system leads to an equilibrium solution,

$$f^t = \frac{r + c^b}{p^t}.$$
(3)

As a result only projects profitable to both the firms and to the banks would be funded. Let the list of approved projects be designated T^{B*}, and let $\tau^* = | T^{B*} |$, i.e., τ^* is the number of all approved projects, which also equals their value. Observe that the expected value of non-performing loans is $(1-p^*)\tau^*$, where p^* is the average probability of success of the approved projects. Thus

$$\sum_{t\in T^{B_*}} p^t\bar{\phi} \geq \sum_{t\in T^{B_*}} p^t f \geq \left(r+c^b\right)\tau^*, \tag{4}$$

and the banks stay solvent. When the banking sector is competitive the last inequality on the right of (4) becomes an equality.

This model cannot be applied un-amended to banks in socialist economies, nor to their successors in transition countries. Socialist banks are used to serve as passive financiers of existing state firms. Ministries, not banks approve projects , and much of the financing is to cover current losses, i.e., projects where $\phi^t = \bar{\phi}^t = 0$. We, therefore, need another player, the government bureau, which may be a ministry or a department of the central bank. In particular, banks are not supposed to bankrupt enterprises, or to threaten them with bankruptcy. Thus enterprise m selects project t in consultation with the ministry, and the criterion of profitability plays a very minor role in this choice. Enterprise m tries to make the project as undemanding on its capacity, so that there will remain the possibility of consumption on the job. Symbolically, let us denote the list of approved projects by $\tilde{T}^B$, where the wiggle denotes selection by the bureau. The bureau exercises adverse selection, since it gives priority to loss-making firms whose projects are sure to fail, i.e., whose $p^t = 0$, and the quality of $\tilde{T}^B$ is inferior to that of T^{B_*}. Let the total number of approved projects and their total value be denoted $\tilde{\tau}$, and let $\tilde{p}$ denote the proportion of loans that are expected to be repaid and $(1 - \tilde{p})$ the proportion of non-performing loans. Clearly, $\tilde{p} < p^*$, and the proportion of non-performing loans is substantially higher in socialist economies than in market economies. Furthermore, we cannot expect solvency condition 1 or 4 to hold. It is probable that

$$\sum_{t\in \tilde{T}^B} p^t\bar{\phi}^t \geq \sum_{t\in \tilde{T}^B} p^t f^t < r\tilde{\tau}, \tag{5}$$

that is, that total receipts of the banking system will not cover interest outlays (even if the socialist interest rate should be lower than the market rate r, and socialist banks cannot be considered solvent).

For the socialist system that has been described above to be able to survive over time, it has to have a soft budget constraint (SBC). I.e., for banks to continue granting loans that do not conform to constraint (1) and that they do not expect to be repaid, they have to be kept in funds in spite of their outgoings exceeding their incomes, as in (5). The government bureau covers the banks' deficit of

$$\Delta^B \equiv r\tau - \sum_{t \in \hat{T}^B} p^t f^t .$$

The government bureau is used to supplying funds to banks as the need arises, i.e., whenever these are needed, given the instructions the banks have to follow when distributing funds. The banks then distribute the funds to firms in accordance to the needs of the physical production plan, and when needed, whenever firms are short of funds: in case of unplanned shortages, the need is used to signal to superordinates that the firm in question needs special monitoring.

Come transition, to adjust to the new environment, both bank and enterprise should change their routines: the enterprise or firm has to restructure itself, i.e., invest in profitable projects that may save it from bankruptcy. The bank's task becomes to pressure the firm by not advancing any funds, except when it is sure that these will be used for investment in projects that are profitable. But to do so it has to transform itself into a profit-seeking organization. It has to learn to monitor. The problem is that when transition starts, both the government bureau and the banks tend to continue their routines, unless forced to change their act.

The first requirement is to harden the budget constraint. That is, to eliminate the ability of the bureau to transfer funds to the banks, and of the banks to bail out sick firms. This obvious solution is not easy to enforce, since all banks are insolvent because of past non-performing loans, and its enforcement would mean that the whole banking system would cease to operate, threatening to bring economic life to a standstill. Furthermore, even if this solution was adopted, and some of the banks would stay alive, they totally lack monitoring skills. Both c_a^b and c_m^b would be extremely high and we could not assume that once monitored, banks would be sure that adverse selection and moral hazard of borrowers have really been averted. Suppose c^b of equation (3) were replaced by $\hat{c}^b > c^b$, and p^t by $\hat{p}^t > p^t$. Then

$$\hat{f}^t = \frac{r + \hat{c}^b}{\hat{p}^t} > \frac{r + c^b}{p^t} = f^t .$$

Consequently f, the fixed repayment rate of (2), would be extremely high, and the advantages of monitoring are seriously diminished. We thus have two obstacles on the way to turning the banking system from a protector of the old system into a force for restructuring: the first is incentives, which are stuck because of the difficulties of getting rid of the SBC. The second is the lack of skills.

The basic reason state banks are insolvent lies in the legacy of loans extended during the old regime. It may therefore seem that the solution to SBC is simple: relieve the banks' balance sheet of the burden of the old debts by taking them over in return for government bonds (Portes and Begg, 1993). Once this is done, the banks would know that the rules of the game have changed and that the budget constraint has hardened, and would henceforth lend only to deserving customers and projects. The problem is that any such one-time-only relief of non-performing loans is a signal that a repeat will come when necessary.[4]

Another way would be to privatize the banks. The banks can be sold net of the non-performing loans, leaving the private owners with a solvent portfolio of loans to firms that have to be monitored, but that on average are expected to repay their loans. But this route is risky: if a bank is to be a catalyst of restructuring, it is essential that it should aim at its own profitability. It may have different aims: if it is sold to a producing firm, the latter may be more interested in its own survivability than in that of the bank. If m acts in his own interests or that of a part of the bank's new owners, he may be involved in *tunneling*, i.e., siphoning out funds to other parties or to her own accounts in foreign banks (Glaeser, Johnson and Shleifer, 2000; Coffee, 1996; Bures, 2002; Weiss and Nikitin, 2001). Thus another change is also needed, that of an added bank supervision, i.e., turning the upper tier of the split mono-bank into the comptroller of the commercial banking system. This too is not free of problems: the central bank too has to spend resources to make sure that the commercial bank's funds are not being diverted, and that its lending is not concentrated on a narrow sector of risk-correlated borrowers – which is not simple, given the origin of these new banks in the specialized departments of the mono-bank – and in particular, not on its owners.

Foreign banks could be an essential part of the solution, were they to buy into the existing banking system and acquire some of the existing state banks. Lacking the old channels of influence in the bureau that used to assure the old banks of the SBC, their own budget constraints are hard. Once the budget constraints of local banks have hardened and foreign banks enter, the competition of the latter should force local banks to strive for profitability in order to survive. As a result, all banks tend to concentrate lending on borrowers who maintain transparency and good governance. They also import the monitoring skills which local banks lack, but these skills, once taught to local personnel, tend to flow to competitors and enrich the economy as a whole.

3. History: From the Socialist Mono-bank to Transitional Banks

The legacy of the banking sector during the old regime can be characterized as strictly orthogonal to the mission of banks in a market economy. The sole similarity between the two institutions is their common name, and this in itself was an obstacle for reform during the first years of the transition. During the socialist period the government-owned mono-bank operated strictly under government instructions to clear transactions among firms and government agencies, to collect taxes and to provide grants and loans to the production sector. It provided accounting services to enterprises and had some control authority in the name of the government. Very little decision-making power was endowed to banks in terms of project selection or risk assessment, and the accounting and auditing rules were those of a centrally-planned system. In many cases the bank failed to collect loans (which were later written off by the government). Departments of the mono-bank specialized in particular industries or functions, and did not accumulate economy-wide knowledge. The savings bank, a department of the mono-bank (*Sberbank* in Russia, for example) collected household savings but did not develop other services included under retail banking in a market economy, such as checking accounts, consumers' loans and mortgages. Corruption crept in between the banks and their clients and between the banks and their immediate superiors, especially when the discipline imposed by the government and the fear of its sanctions weakened during the last decades of the old regime. All the elements and functions of a banking sector in a market economy were absent.

Most of these deficiencies were gradually revealed in the early stages of the transition. It was generally recognized by both insiders and foreign advisers that an early reform of the banking sector is essential in order to move to a market economy. This reform was particularly important in order to facilitate privatization and restructuring, as well as for the opening of the economies (World Bank, 1993, quoted in World Bank, 2001, p. 9).[5] What was not recognized by most was that the so-called domestic banks left over from the old regime needed much more than 'reforms' and that they were incapable of self-transformation into real banks.[6]

During the early stages of transition, many TEs converted the mono-bank into a double-tier system, with a central bank at the top and the departments of the mono-bank now renamed commercial banks. At the start all these banks remained in state hands. At a later stage some banks were fully or partially privatized. In any case, most of the managers and personnel of the 'new' banks were the same people as under the old regime. Because of the specialized structure of the mono-bank, the portfolio of the new banks was highly correlated and risky.

In addition, a liberal policy regarding the establishing and licensing of new, private banks was followed, and many newly created private banks were allowed to enter. In most countries there were initially few restrictions on entry: capital and know-how requirements were relatively liberal and lax, and banking supervision was weak and ineffective. Although new legislation to adapt the system to the market environment was introduced, enforcement was scarce. Under such conditions, the performance of the banking sector further deteriorated.

This liberal approach to the development of the banking sector emanated from the general, naïve belief that prevailed in many TEs at the time, in free enterprise and competitive markets. It failed to consider the accepted view among economists that a preferred industrial organization for a banking sector is a more concentrated one with larger banks and with somewhat limited competition and higher profits. In this way banks can develop their own reputation that has to be preserved, thus limiting them from engaging in activities leading to negative selection and moral hazard (Stiglitz, 1994). The relationship between numbers and the supervising authorities should not be neglected either. A multitude of weak banks puts an extremely heavy supervisory burden on the new and inexperienced central bank and government agencies, working with yet-to-be-consolidated legal and enforcement tools. Many banks had to spread thinly the very small number of capable people who knew how to operate market-oriented banks. The counter argument against limiting the number of banks is that too large banks and too concentrated industry cause a moral hazard of a different kind – of a 'too large to fail' de-facto government guaranty against failure (WB Russian banks, Bonin and Wachtel, 2000). It is true that one has to strike a cleverly balanced concentration in order to minimize both dangers. In TEs, however, the main problem of a too high concentration is that of remaining state-owned banks rather than monopolistic private banks. In this case the moral hazard due to size is particularly risky to the health of the banking sector.

The main heritage of the past was the large stock of bad loans carried over from the last years of the old regime. But many of the banks continued to lend to enterprises pretty much as before, in some cases on instructions of and resources supplied by the central banks and the governments, and thus continued to accumulate more bad loans. These developments defeated the efforts to privatize the banks. Keeping the bad loans in the banks scared potential buyers, but shifting them away to various 'consolidation' banks (as in the Czech Republic) or other arrangements (as in Hungary) created a serious problem of moral hazard that perpetuated the problem. Other bad loans were accumulated due to the general absence of the needed knowledge of the domestic banks to assess risk and distinguish between good and bad projects and the weak corporate governance of enterprises. The complex economic environment during the early stages of the transition imposed exceptional demand on such skills. There was little effective supervision to prevent such developments. 'Hence, weak banks with no expertise in restructuring large companies wound up taking ownership stakes in their weak clients, bank credit was provided regularly, to ailing enterprises and no meaningful enterprise restructuring was promoted' (Gray and Holle, 1996). The expansion of risky loans under a regime of soft budget constraint led in a number of countries to financial crises in the banking sector, with damaging results not only to banks but also to macroeconomic stability and to the real growth of GDP (Bonin and Wachtel, 1999).

Second, in many cases the old-new specialized or sectoral banks continued to work with the enterprises belonging to the same sectors, a situation that encouraged internal deals, lack of effective risk assessment and prudent supervision, and absence of transparency. That in turn encouraged and facilitated discrimination against (private) minority shareholders, and scared away foreign investors. In Russia, many groups of enterprises formed *Financial Industrial Groups*, the so-called FIGs, with banks in their center serving as a source of finance and deals, getting most of their resources from the newly created central bank or the Ministry of Finance. The FIGs engaged in insider deals and to a large extent also in corrupt and unlawful transactions, among others also with government officials and agencies. In many cases such behavior helped both banks and enterprises to avoid 'biting the bullet' of restructuring. The sectoral organization of many banks also caused severe segmentation of the financial sector, making it difficult to transfer funds from industries with surplus resources and cash (like the energy sector in Russia) to sectors starving for funds for restructuring.[7]

Third, during the first years of transition most banks, old and new, refrained from servicing the production sector or the household sector and concentrated mostly on transactions in foreign exchange and in government bonds, activities which were much more lucrative and safe. In this manner they contributed in a number of countries to fiscal deficits and to inflation, raising doubts regarding the justification of their existence. Only a small number of banks developed modern retail services for the emerging small and medium business sector and for households, e.g., attractive savings and loan schemes.

Finally, in most of the TEs only a small segment of the banking sector was privatized during the early years (See Table 11.1) and most government banks continue to operate, following more or less their old routines and traditions.

It can be concluded that during the early and crucial years of the transition, the domestic banking sectors, even in their privatized part, failed to provide the production sector, the emerging sector of small and medium sized enterprises (SMEs) and the household sector, with the kind of services that a normally functioning market economy sector could probably offer to help the privatization and restructuring efforts and support the emerging new sector of SMEs. As a result countries found themselves busy trying to cure the ills of the banking sector. Instead of becoming part of the solution to problems of transition and transformation, the banking sector in most countries occupied a prominent position on the list of problems, an urgently needed bed in the emergency ward. Furthermore, in several countries the old-new domestic banking sector cemented its links with their industrial clients, and joined up with political allies, preferably those trumpeting nationalistic creeds, to fend off the entry of foreign banks. The potential aid of the latter, in serving as leaders in the reform of the banking sector and contributors to the process of transition, was thereby aborted, or at least delayed. Such a lobby, whose creation was catalyzed by the erroneous early steps of reform of the banking sector, was also not interested in effective and transparent bank supervision and in the prudent supervision of banks over the governance of the enterprises. This lobby thus became an obstacle to domestic reform, whose absence helped scare off foreign banks (Abel and Siklos, 2001).

4. The Potential Contribution of Foreign Banks

What can foreign banks offer to TEs? As mentioned above, it is now generally accepted that foreign banks can contribute to the efficiency and economic growth of emerging markets. A World Bank report states the following:

> Recent studies have confirmed the economic benefits from admitting foreign-owned banks. Introduction of foreign banks can provide a powerful means of stimulating both

operational efficiency and competition and eventually stabilizing the financial sector. The entry of foreign banks has generally been associated with improvements in the quality of both regulation and transparency, particularly if the entry of foreign banks is accompanied by the introduction of international standards of accounting and auditing. The pressure of competition from foreign banks may encourage local banks and less than reputable local banks to take higher risks thereby weakening the banking sector. This emphasizes the urgency in strengthening prudential regulation of the banking sector.[8]

In particular foreign banks can bring to TEs the entire package of services needed for restructuring:[9]

- a state-of-the-art economy-wide payment and transaction system;
- mobilization of household savings, and channeling resources;
- short and long term intermediary saving and credit services across the economy;
- proper risk assessment and evaluation, risk transformation and risk sharing;
- advice, training and assistance in financial management;
- supervising the proper corporate management of enterprises;
- guidance in the spheres of accounting and auditing;
- monitoring the performance of loans and repayment schedules;
- lobbying for and helping to introduce the proper regulatory regime for the entire banking sector;
- reducing transaction costs and improving information.

In addition to their knowledge and experience, foreign banks bring with them trust, of both households and businesses – trust that is based on their record and reputation in their home countries and in the global economy. Trust and reputation are gravely missing in the local financial sector and this severely hinders their ability to fulfill their mission, unlike foreign banks who bring with them their international reputation and can hardly afford to compromise it. The World Bank Study on the Russian Bank Sector is entitled 'Building Trust' (World Bank, 2001). Trust cannot be reborn without an intensive initial involvement of and setting the norms by foreign banks. All these can increase savings, or at least the willingness to trust them to the banks, raise the level of (proper) investment and will allocate investment funds in a more efficient way throughout the economy. Finally, foreign banks bring with them the lifeline of the global economy, investment resources, potential entrepreneurs and investors for other industries, and networking links for foreign trade.

The ability and willingness of foreign banks to step in depends to a large extent on the legal and law-enforcement environment prevailing in the target countries. There are several aspects to this general term. First, there is the general legal and law-enforcement infrastructure that makes it possible for an outsider to operate. Second, there is the more particular aspect of the financial and banking laws and regulations that set the capitalization requirements, the prudential regulations of risk management, the bank supervision structure, the accounting norms and credit protection and bankruptcy laws. A legal infrastructure is also the basis of an environment of equal opportunity, a 'level playing field' for foreign and local banks (World Bank, 2001, Vol. I. Chapter 2). Third, in order for foreign banks to be able to be productive, a sound regime of corporate governance of the potential client firms must be established. All these are the responsibilities of the government and in many TEs this process takes time.

The lack of such a universal and transparent environment gives a clear advantage to local banks that can rely much better on connections, insider networks, discretion and corruption. This is why most (honest) foreign banks considering moving into TEs are, or should be, interested in effective supervision on their operations as well. Delays in legislation and enforcement partially explain the relative late arrival of the foreign banks to most TEs. The obverse side of this picture has already been mentioned in section 3: the domestic banks and their patrons, allied to the many who believe that foreign banks harm the economy, worked against attempts at improving the legal environment of financial transactions in order to leave foreign banks out. Domestic banks and their political supporters, and foreign banks may thus have a completely orthogonal legal and law-enforcement agendas of merit vs. 'connections'. A decision to encourage foreign banks to step in thus forces the government to expedite the formation of a minimum necessary legal environment, which is, of course, an added bonus. Once in, foreign banks become a natural lobby in favor of continuous tightening the regulatory regime. This is definitely true with respect to the protection of creditors and the improvement of corporate governance in enterprises. It is, however, most likely also true with respect to an efficient legal environment and supervision for the banking sector itself. Only in this way they can hope to overcome the advantage of the domestic banks.

In summary, the dominance of the domestic banks may result in a vicious circle that leads, as it has in a number of countries, to financial crises. Bringing in foreign banks early may generate a virtuous circle of improving regulation that improves performance.[10]

5. Why Priority to (Foreign) Banks?

The literature on financial services in TEs usually discusses in parallel banks and other financial services, especially capital markets, as two equally appropriate tools for the needs of TEs. It is our claim that for TEs the use of (foreign) banks as the main operators and regulators in the financial market is a much better alternative.

The advantage of well functioning (foreign) banks is that they enable a relatively small number of intermediaries to navigate, guide, control and supervise a large number of restructuring enterprises. The main input in short supply in TEs is human capital, the skills needed to properly operate banks in the difficult environment of TEs, capable, among others, of screening investment projects and risk, guiding enterprises, imposing on them a proper corporate governance and supervising their activities. Large and experienced foreign banks can therefore provide the skills needed to direct the investment activities of the business sector. La Porta and colleagues in a series of papers on the issue of investor (and creditor) protection in emerging markets, including TEs, make two major arguments that support the above proposition, though they focus mostly on the capital market rather than on banks. First, that the new rules to be created should not be the ideal but those that can realistically be enforced. Second, that the instruments used should be economical in their use of scarce skilled human resources and relatively easy to control. It is for these reasons that the authors prefer an administrative regulatory agency to a court system as the main supervisory authority to the capital market. Despite the danger of biased incentives to administrative regulators, they can do a better job than the judicial personnel trained and corrupted under the old system and the distorted and vast court system (La Porta et al., pp. 25–7; Glaeser, Johnson and Shleifer, 2000). The ability of foreign banks to supply the needed skills and to utilize them in the most economical way meets both these demands. A proper banking sector meets these demands much better than a capital (stock) market. The latter requires many more trained people, and a much more elaborate regulatory and supervision systems. This is clearly the lesson learned from advanced countries.

Another type of human capital, or institutional input in short supply in TEs that is required for the regulation and supervision of the corporate sector, banking included, comprises well functioning governments. Large and experienced foreign banks are the most convenient agents for the government regulator to supervise and control, in a manner that local banks cannot do. In a sense a well functioning banking sector described here can also replace some of the functions of the government, functions that most governments in TEs are not yet capable to perform.

A banking sector as suggested here is the most economical in the use of the needed skills and the best positioned to disseminate these and related skills downward to the enterprise level, sidewise to other banks, especially partner banks or in the framework of joint ventures, and upward, to the legislative, regulatory and supervisory agencies of the government. All these functions cannot be performed properly by a multitude of individual agents organized in networks of multi-level ownership structures.

6. Foreign Banks in TEs: the Empirical Record

Table 11.1 describes the penetration over time of foreign banks into the various TEs. The penetration is measured here by two variables, by the number of banks and by the asset share of banks with more than 50 per cent foreign ownership. We compare these two variables with the same measures for domestic banks, subdivided into state banks and private ones. Most TEs had very few foreign banks before 1993 or 1994, if any. The exception is Hungary, which already in 1989 had 7 foreign banks, in control of over 6 per cent of the assets of the banking sector. However, the process of the establishment of new private banks in most western TEs – and in some, also the privatization of state banks – had started by 1993 or 1994. Many small private banks were established in the Czech Republic, in Hungary, Poland, in the Baltic States, and the former European CIS countries.

As we said in section 3, the breakdown of the socialist mono-bank into a system of two-tier banking created in most TEs a sector of state banks divided along industrial, sectoral or regional lines. Usually they were large banks and thus limited in numbers. By 1993 or 1994, state banks controlled 70 per cent or more of banking-sector assets in Hungary, Poland, Slovakia, Albania, Bulgaria, Romania and Russia. In Lithuania and Slovenia, state banks' share was lower, around half of the assets. Only in the Czech Republic and Estonia, state banks were reduced to less than 20 per cent and 30 per cent, respectively, of the assets of the banking sector, through privatization and the entry of private banks, including foreign ones. The proliferation of private banks and some amount of privatization also reduced the share of state banks in Russia, Ukraine and other CIS countries, although there is no precise information for the early 1990s in their case.[11]

Within a few years of the transition, private banks became the owners of the greater part of banks in most TEs and gained control of more than 50 per cent of the banking sector in a number of them (again, measured by the share of assets with more than 50 per cent private control). The interesting exception to the first observation is Hungary (and Slovakia and Latvia) who brought in a significant number of foreign banks and restricted the establishment of new domestic banks. Among the TEs with clear majority ownership of private domestic banks we find the Czech Republic, Estonia and Latvia, and possibly also Ukraine and Russia, the latter with more than 2000 private banks as early as 1993.

Since the mid-1990s the transformation of the banking sector in TEs had some common features, but the pace and in some cases the strategies diverged. The main common trend was that of an increase in the number of foreign banks and a decline in the number of domestic private banks. The data show that more and more governments realized the beneficial potential of foreign banks and reduced barriers to their operation. The decline in the number of domestic banks resulted from failures in a number of countries following general financial crises of the banking sector,[12] consolidations and mergers, and purchase by foreign banks. In this way the ill effects of the initial naïve approach of a free-for-all type were somewhat corrected. These two trends made relatively small changes in the ownership composition of the banking sector. The crucial change was caused by a process of privatization of the large state banks, sold to foreign banks. This process started in Hungary in 1995, was followed in 1995/96 by the Baltic States,[13] and later, sometimes in the aftermath of a crisis, by the Czech Republic, Romania, Croatia, Poland and Bulgaria. By 2000, there were six TEs with more than two-thirds of the banking assets under foreign control. In Estonia almost the entire sector, and in

Croatia 85 per cent were foreign-owned, but in Lithuania, Slovakia and Romania, foreign control amounted to only about 50 per cent. The foreign takeover continued into 2001,[14] at the same time state ownership declined. By 2000, the state was still in control of nearly half of the banking sector in Romania and Slovakia, of more than a third in Lithuania, and between 20 and 25 per cent in the Czech Republic, Poland and Bulgaria.

In Eastern Europe, the glaring exception to this trend is Slovenia, with, by 2002, only 15 per cent of foreign-owned bank assets, and government ownership of over 40 per cent. Russia and other CIS States did not join this trend, either. There was a decline in the number of domestic privately-owned banks and an increase in the number of foreign banks in both Russia and Ukraine, but there was no privatization of major state banks to foreign owners. Indeed, following the crisis of 1998, the stake of the state in the banking sector in Russia even increased (World Bank, 2001, Vol. II. Working papers 2 and 4; Iskyan and Besedin, 2001; Ivanov, 2001).

The sale of state banks to foreign owners helped a number of TEs to stop the cycle of accumulation of bad loans, re-capitalization of banks, and further accumulation. In Hungary and the Czech Republic, banks were sold to foreigners after cleaning them from bad loans, while in Poland the banks were asked to take care of their non-performing loans by themselves, and when Poland decided to sell state banks to foreign ones, it insisted on selling them with their bad loans as a condition for entry.[15] The same motivation probably played a role in other TEs (Pointbriand, 2001 pp. 409–10).

The trend in Eastern Europe was beneficial to the economies in a number of ways: first, the consolidation of the private banking sector eliminated weak and 'non-bank' banks, improved the concentration (section 3) and the conduct of the sector and also – even though it may sound contradictory – the competitiveness of the sector, and, what is no less important, made control more feasible and more effective. Second, the decline of the share of state banks helped create a more even playing field for competition and reduced the incidence of internal deals and of soft loans directed by the government. The relative weight of these two trends differed between TEs: while the Czech Republic and the Baltic States suffered mostly from the proliferation of weak private banks, Poland and to a lesser extent Hungary avoided most of that problem but suffered, and this is especially true for Poland, from the monopolistic position of the archaic state banks. Third, the introduction of foreign banks enhanced competition, expertise and know-how, assured better lending to the production sector, and improved banking conduct and standards. Russia and the other CIS members, with the possible exception of Tajikistan, did not follow this process and lagged behind, not only in banking reform but also in the ability of the banking sector to contribute to restructuring and growth (see more on this below).

The significance of this trend of wholesale transfer of the banking sector to foreign banks can be even better appreciated when compared to the much smaller presence of foreign banks in other emerging markets. Among all DEs, only in

Argentina one finds nearly half of the banking sector in foreign hands. Otherwise, there is no emerging country – or a developed one for that matter (New Zealand is an exception) – with more than 30 per cent foreign control (WB 2001, p. 196; Abel and Siklos, p. 5). There is no reason to believe that TEs are more cosmopolitan by ideology or less averse to foreign 'control'. Nor is it likely that the legal infrastructure, widely defined, is better in emerging markets than in long-standing market economies, but this issue will be examined further below. Assuming that the above two statements are correct, this phenomenon can only be explained by the benefits that can accrue to both sides, the inviting countries and the incoming foreign banks.

As we showed above, with the exception of Hungary, the presence of large foreign banks at the expense of state banks is a relatively recent phenomenon. Most studies seem to show better performance of foreign banks as compared with local ones, in terms of efficiency, including labor productivity, profitability, the extent of financial products offered, etc. A number of studies also credit to foreign entry the decline of interest spreads, and through the increased competition, the improved performance of the domestic segment of the sector, as well as the increased financing of the production and household sectors and the increasing levels of monetization. A more prudent supervision of loans contributed to the decline of the shares of bad loans.[16]

We are able to support several of these statements with empirical data. It has to be recognized though that the causal connection between some of these developments and the share of foreign banks is only circumstantial. Furthermore, in some cases the recorded performance of foreign banks may formally look less encouraging than that of local banks. For example, foreign banks may direct a higher share of their portfolios to credit to the business sector and therefore encounter more bad loans, let alone the bad loans that they have to swallow in order to be allowed to operate. In addition, one of the main deficiencies in the performance of domestic banks during the first decade was that they refrained from making resources available to the production sector. Under such conditions, there are also fewer bad loans.

Table 11.2 traces the dynamics of bad loans during the 1990s. These dynamics are related to some extent to the policy implemented in order to minimize the phenomenon. Some countries, e.g., Hungary and the Czech Republic, followed the policy of repeatedly re-capitalizing the banks by removing their bad loans into special state entities. The fiscal costs of this strategy were significant, but lower in Hungary than in the Czech Republic, due possibly to the earlier involvement of foreign banks (Reininger et al., 2001, Tables 11.1 and 11.12), although the relatively high level of financing of the business sector in the Czech Republic may have contributed to this outcome, alongside the mode of privatization that linked banks with enterprises and encouraged internal deals and *tunneling*. In Slovakia, which had been moving much more slowly to sell banks and state banks to foreigners, the level of bad loans is the highest in Central Europe, and their slow decline started only in the late 1990s. Poland fought bad loans by pressuring state banks into collecting them themselves from the original debtors. This minimized the fiscal costs of re-capitalization and apparently helped to reduce bad loans since 1994 to moderate levels. However, bad loans have been picking up since 1997, and this may have been a factor in tilting the state toward foreign privatization of state banks. The decline of bad loans in Latvia and Lithuania – in Estonia they had been low all along – coincided more or less with the process of bringing in foreign banks. Slovenia had all along a moderate level of bad loans but with no improvement over time, and almost no foreign banks. In Russia and the CIS bad loans actually rose until they peeked in the 1998 crisis. Russia has managed to halve their level since.

Data in Table 11.3 present a picture of economic changes in TEs that can be credited to the improved banking sector, in some cases with added international comparisons. Most of the observations are for a recent year (mostly 1999 or 2000). The main observations are as follows:

1. The level of monetization (M2/GDP) in the countries of CEE is not significantly lower than that of developed countries (Table 11.3, column 1). The range for all countries is between one half and more than total GDP. In Russia, however, it is only 22 per cent.
2. The relative size of the banking sector, as measured by the ratio of total assets to GDP, assumes in CEE similar magnitudes as above, much lower than those in Western Europe (in the US, the banking sector is notoriously small). In Russia, at just 16 per cent of GDP, this ratio is extremely small (Table 11.3, column 2).
3. Claims of the banking sector on the private sector, or 'credits' to the private sector, represent between a quarter and half of GDP in CEE, as compared with three quarters to 1.3 of GDP in Western Europe (ca. 90 per cent as average for OECD) and 35 per cent in a group of lower-middle income DEs (LMIs). The same ratio stands at just around 12 per cent in Russia and is the same or lower in other Western CIS (Table 11.3, Column 3). It has to be emphasized that the differences between the more advanced CEEs and Russia (and between well functioning banks and less well functioning banks everywhere) are not only quantitative. Many loans to the private sector in Russia are still made without proper risk assessment and in the framework of insider deals between banks and enterprises belonging to the same financing industrial group (FIG). Indeed, there is very little cross-sector or cross-FIG transfer of funds. These circumstances lead to gross misallocation of resources (World Bank 2001, Vol. II. Working Paper no. 2, pp. 17–18).
4. The weight of deposits in banks in GDP stood at 40–60 per cent in CEEs, at less than 20 per cent in Russia, and half that amount in Ukraine. The average OECD level was about 80 per cent and that of lower-to-middle income countries was around 40 per cent (Table 11.3, Column 4).
5. The interest rate spread was lowest in 2000 in the Czech Republic, Hungary and Estonia (at 3–4 per cent) and somewhat higher in other CEEs, between

6–8 per cent. These rates are compared with 18 per cent in Russia and 28 per cent in Ukraine (Table 11.3, Column 5). Many countries report on significant narrowing of the spread during recent years and credit much of the decline to the entrance of foreign banks (Galac and Kraft, 2000; Opiela, 2001; Reininger et. al., 2001).

7. Conclusions: Foreign Banks and the Legal Infrastructure – the Chicken or the Egg?

In this paper we have argued that in order to achieve transformation, there is no escape from an early and intensive use of a reformed banking sector. Unreformed, or superficially reformed, the old banks will in effect continue to maintain the firms' soft budget constraint, thereby hampering rather than enhancing restructuring. The enormous restructuring task of a complex production sector inherited from the old regime singles out the TEs among all emerging markets as being in need for modern and efficient banking services. Recent development and expansion of global banking, just when the needs for transition emerged, provided a golden opportunity for a strategy of using foreign banks to facilitate this reform. The takeover of almost entire banking sectors in a number of advanced TEs is a new phenomenon, unique among both emerging and developed economies, an innovative and exciting aspect of globalization.

Banking services have an advantage over other financial services due to their ability to economize on the particular human capital skills required that are in short supply in TEs; they provide a simpler and better institutional structure, amenable to more efficient regulation and supervision, and they are a better tool to oversee and guide corporate governance of enterprises. Given the typical weakness of governments and of the judicial system in many TEs, a well organized banking system working on the basis of Western patterns and with the reputation and resource support of Western mother banks, can substitute and improve on some government functions. The early entry of foreign banks into TEs is the best method of achieving banking reform and of harnessing the financial sector to the transition effort.

Having said this, we have seen in the paper that most foreign banks came into CEE relatively late and, with a partial exception of Hungary and a few other limited cases, the purchase of large state banks came even later, during the last two to four years. Furthermore, there are very few important foreign banks present in Russia and other CIS countries. Given the general recognition of the importance of banks to the transition to the market, to privatization and to restructuring, this must be considered strange.

There could be a number of explanations. First, there may have been the perception that domestic banks – whether new, state or privatized – can do the job once a newly installed legal system is in place. Until this had been proven at least partially wrong, there was a resistance to let foreign banks in, for the normal economic reasons and nationalistic views common throughout the world. The opening-up of the banking sector to liberal entrance, in the name of a free market and the reluctance, or inability, to privatize large state banks, added new difficulties on top of the inherited ones.

The second explanation of the delay in the entry of foreign banks is by a combination of the strong vested interests of the domestic banking sector and by the partial nature of the legal reform in general and that of the financial sector in particular. The incompleteness of the reform is due to the lack of political pressure and skills, but also results from counter pressures of the domestic banking sector, which is concerned with the pursuit of inside deals and tunneling activities, and with the maintenance of protection by personal networks in a corrupt political system. These banks thus avoid serving the production sector. Such a situation prevents the advance of proper legal and banking reform as well as the entry of foreign banks. This is how the domestic banking sector becomes an obstacle to rather than a facilitator of growth and restructuring.

An alternative, third explanation for the delay, the most straightforward one, which also complements the others above, is that it takes time to create and effectively enforce the legal, regulatory and supervisory institutional environment needed for either domestic or foreign banks to operate properly. This process takes longer time in some countries than in others.

All TEs experienced a dose of problems related to the first explanation. Russia and other CIS economies were particularly affected by the friction involved in the second. In Central and Eastern Europe, all three occurred in varying doses, but by the mid- or later part of the 1990s, the danger of the third scenario materializing was realized by the governments, which moved to admit foreign banks.

The last explanation above tells us that foreign banks will move in only when the proper legal infrastructure has been put into place. However, the negative influence of the delay raises an interesting question: was there an alternative policy option available, of inviting foreign banks at an earlier stage in order to be part of the reform process of the banking system, including an earlier privatization of state banks? The only case where such a policy was tried relatively early is Hungary. In all the other cases the empirical question that can be raised is a double one. First, was the quality of the legal infrastructure required for the operation of a sound banking system attained by the time the critical mass of foreign banks moved in? Did any substantial part of the improvement in this infrastructure take place subsequent to the foreign entry? A related empirical question is what were the dynamics of formal and informal barriers to the entrance of foreign banks up to and beyond the date of entry for each country.

Most of the available information on the legal status and strength of the banking sector in Eastern Europe indicates a very high correlation between indexes of law and governance and the performance of the banking sector, including the involvement of foreign banks. This is true with respect to the transition indexes compiled by the EBRD for the financial sector (see for example TR 2001, pp. 14, 38), and to the quality and preparedness of the financial and banking sector as compiled in the *World Competitiveness Yearbook* (2000) of the International Institute for Management Development (IMD), and shown for TEs in Table 11.3 of Keren and Ofer, 2002.[17] This evidence however does not solve the chicken-and-egg puzzle posed above, of the sequencing, of the dynamics of foreign bank entrance and of the improvement in the legal environment for the operation of banks. This will have to be left for future research.

Notes

1   Abel and Siklos claim that only Chile, among the DEs, welcomes foreign banks in a big way.

2   Our 2002 paper focuses on the comparison between the TEs and the DEs with regard to FDI in banking and commerce.

3   There are additional references on the topic in the papers listed above.

4   See the relevant Israeli experience, reported in Kislev (1993) and Keren and Levhari (1993).

5   'Transformation of the financial sector ahead of the enterprise sector is a unique feature of the Russian reforms and entails both considerable opportunities as well as risks. In the absence of a functioning capital market the commercial banks are likely to play a key role in the transformation and restructuring of the Russian economy' (World Bank, 2001a, p. 9).

6   The next sentence in the above mentioned report did recognize risks, but did not go far enough: 'The central role of the banks in the transition process also entails considerable risks: poor lending decisions and inadequate monitoring of borrowers could expose banks to substantial losses and could lead to systemic instability' (World Bank, 2001a, p. 9).

7   The historical verdict is not out yet on whether industrial financial groupings enhance or retard growth, and we come back to this issue below. It is quite clear, however, that in the case of Tes, whenever old-fashioned banks played a role, many such groups enhanced survival of old practices, prevented investment by outside investors and inhibited restructuring. FIGs lead by foreign, prudent banks may be a different story altogether.

8   World Bank. 2001b, *Finance for Growth: Policy Choices in a Volatile World*, World Bank Policy Research Report. Washington, D.C.

9   Based, among others, on Reininger et. al. (2001) and World Bank, 2001a, Introduction.

10 La Porta, Lopes-de-Silvanes, Shleifer, Vishny (2001). With respect to the capital market in general, the authors write as follows: 'With the legal reform slow and halting in most countries "functional convergence" (with foreign countries) may play a role in improving investor protection. The liberalization of capital markets in many countries increased… but also the economic and political pressure to create financial instruments acceptable to foreign investors' (p. 28).

11 By 1997 state banks controlled 37 per cent of all bank assets in Russia and only 13.5 per cent in Ukraine, but some privatization took place during the mid 1990s (EBRD data base).

12 Croatia, the Czech Republic, Latvia, Russia, and others.

13 Some of the foreign banks in Latvia and Lithuania were Russian, and therefore didn't really fulfill the role of market oriented foreign banks.

14 Privatization of state banks to foreign banks continued during 2001 in Albania, Croatia, The Czech Republic, Lithuania, Romania, The Slovak Republic, and Slovenia, *Transition Report 2001*, individual country survey.

15 'Foreign banks have been required, in most cases, to take over existing troubled Polish banks in order to obtain licenses. However, remaining restrictions on the entry of foreign banks will be lifted in 1999' (*TR* 1998, p. 183).

16 See, among others, World Bank, 2001; Galac and Kraft, 2000; Opiela, 2001; Reininger et. al., 2001.

17 Glaeser et. al. (2000, p. 37) says that '... the evidence corroborates recent research arguing that financial markets are helped by the legal protection of outside investors – both shareholders and creditors'.

Tables

Table 11.1: Banks by ownership type

Part a: Banks with foreign ownership of more than 50 per cent

	1993		1997		2000	
	No. of banks	Assets %	No. of banks	Assets %	No. of banks	Assets %
EU accession countries						
Czech Republic	12	4.7	15	23.7	16	66.5
Estonia	1	0.4	3	28.8	4	97.4
Hungary	15	12.0	30	59.7	30	67.4
Latvia	n/a	n/a	15	70.6	12	74.4
Lithuania	0	n/a	4	40.6	6	54.7
Poland	10	2.8	29	16.0	47	72.5
Slovak Republic	13	n/a	13	19.3	13	42.7
Slovenia	5	n/a	4	5.4	n/a	15.6
Other Eastern Europe						
Albania	n/a	n/a	3	n/a	12	35.2
Bulgaria	0	n/a	7	n/a	25	75.3
Croatia	n/a	n/a	7	3.0	20	84.1
Romania	n/a	n/a	13	11.5	21	46.7
Former SU						
Belarus	n/a	n/a	2	1.4	6	4.3
Moldova	n/a	n/a	4	n/a	11	39.8
Russia	n/a	n/a	26	6.7	33	n/a
Ukraine	n/a	n/a	12	8.2	14	11.1

continued on opposite page

Table 11.1 – continued

Part b: Banks with government ownership of more than 50 per cent

	1993		1997		2000	
	No. of banks	Assets %	No. of banks	Assets %	No. of banks	Assets %
EU accession countries (first round)						
Czech Republic	2	11.9	4	17.5	5	28.2
Estonia	3	25.7	0	0.0	0	0.0
Hungary	16	74.9	8	10.8	6	8.6
Latvia	4	n/a	2	6.8	1	2.9
Lithuania	n/a	53.6	3	48.8	2	38.9
Poland	29	86.2	15	51.6	7	24.0
Slovak Republic	4	70.7	5	48.7	6	49.1
Slovenia	n/a	47.8	3	40.1	3	42.2
Other Eastern Europe						
Albania	n/a	n/a	n/a	89.9	1	64.8
Bulgaria	n/a	n/a	n/a	66.0	4	19.8
Croatia	n/a	58.9	7	32.6	3	5.7
Romania	n/a	n/a	7	80.0	4	50.0
Former SU						
Belarus	n/a	n/a	n/a	55.2	7	66.0
Moldova	n/a	1.0	n/a	n/a	2	9.8
Russia	n/a	n/a	n/a	37.0	n/a	n/a
Ukraine	n/a	n/a	2	13.5	2	11.9

continued overleaf

Table 11.1 – continued

Part c: Banks with more than 50 percent domestic non-government ownership

	1993		1997		2000	
	No. of banks	Assets %	No. of banks	Assets %	No. of banks	Assets %
EU accession countries (first round)						
Czech Republic	38	83.4	31	58.9	19	5.3
Estonia	17	73.9	9	71.2	3	2.6
Hungary	9	13.1	3	29.5	2	24.0
Latvia	n/a	n/a	14	22.6	14	22.7
Lithuania	n/a	n/a	5	10.6	5	6.4
Poland	48	11.0	39	32.4	20	3.5
Slovak Republic	11	n/a	11	32.0	4	8.3
Slovenia	n/a	n/a	27	54.5	n/a	42.3
Other Eastern Europe						
Albania	n/a	n/a	n/a	n/a	12	0.0
Bulgaria	n/a	n/a	n/a	n/a	31	4.9
Croatia	n/a	n/a	54	64.5	41	10.2
Romania	n/a	n/a	26	8.5	29	3.3
Former SU						
Belarus	n/a	n/a	n/a	43.5	18	29.7
Moldova	n/a	n/a	n/a	n/a	7	50.4
Russia	n/a	n/a	n/a	56.3	n/a	n/a
Ukraine	n/a	n/a	213	78.3	138	77.0

Source: EBRD data base.

Table 11.2: Non-performing loans of banks (% of total loans)

	1993	1995	1998	2000
EU accession countries (first round)				
Czech Republic	n/a	26.6	20	19
Estonia	n/a	2.4	4	2
Hungary	29.6	12.1	7	3
Latvia	n/a	19.0	7	5
Lithuania	n/a	17.3	12	11
Poland	36.4	23.9	12	16
Slovak Republic	12.2	41.3	44	26
Slovenia	n/a	9.3	9	9
Other Eastern Europe				
Albania	n/a	34.9	35	43
Bulgaria	6.7	12.5	12	11
Croatia	n/a	12.9	13	20
Romania	n/a	37.9	59	4
Former SU				
Belarus	n/a	11.8	17	15
Moldova	n/a	39.1	32	21
Russia	n/a	12.3	31	15
Ukraine	n/a	n/a	35	33

Source: EBRD data base.

Table 11.3: Banking sector's effects on economy

	M2 (Money & Quasi-Money)	Tot. bank assets / GDP (%)	Credit to Private Sector	Tot. Deposits	Interest Rate Spread, 2000
	% GDP	% GDP	% GDP	% GDP	% p.a.
	(1)	(2)	(3)	(4)	(5)
EU accession countries (first wave)					
Czech Republic	76	125	51	65	3.74
Estonia	–	59	27	–	3.86
Hungary	44	–	29	–	2.97
Latvia	–	–	19	–	7.49
Lithuania	–	–	12	–	8.29
Poland	41	54	25	36	5.83
Slovak Republic	94	n/a	31	–	6.44
Slovenia	–	66	–	–	–
Eastern Europe Avg.	–	–	22	36.8	–
Other Eastern Europe					
Bulgaria	–	–	16	–	8.42
Romania	–	25	–	–	–
Former SU					
Azerbaijan	–	–	8	–	17.6
Belarus	–	–	7	11	–
Moldova	–	25	13	–	8.91
Russia	22	16	12	17	17.92
Ukraine	–	n/a	10	11	27.81

continued on opposite page

Table 11.3 – continued

	M2 (Money & Quasi-Money)	Tot. bank assets / GDP (%)	Credit to Private Sector	Tot. Deposits	Interest Rate Spread, 2000
	% GDP	% GDP	% GDP	% GDP	% p.a.
	(1)	(2)	(3)	(4)	(5)
For comparison					
France	51	–	73	–	–
Germany	63	313	122	–	–
Italy	56	358	72	–	–
Netherlands	89	66	137	–	–
United Kingdom	111	–	134	–	–
United States	61	–	49	–	–
Lower middle income countries	–	–	37	38	–

Sources: Column 1: World Bank, 2001, Vol. I, 'Executive Summary', Table 1. Column 2: Barth, Caprio and Levine, 2001, Table 2. Column 3: World Bank, 2001, Vol. I, 'Executive Summary', Table 1, Vol. II. 'Introduction', Table 1.1, 'Working Paper no. 2', Table 2.6, 'Working Paper no. 10', Table 10.2. Column 4: World Bank 2001, Vol. II. 'Introduction', Table 1.1, 'Working Paper no. 2', Table 2.6. Column 5: World Bank, 2001, Vol. II. 'Working Paper no. 10', Table 10.3.

References

Abel, Istvan and Siklos, Pierre L. (2001), 'Privatizing a Banking System: A Case Study of Hungary', mimeo.

Barth, James R., Caprio, Gerard, Jr. and Levine, Ross (2001), 'The Regulation and Supervision of Banks Around the World. A New Database'.

Bases, Daniel (2002), 'Slow Banking Reform Said Hindering Russian Economy', Reuters, 14.3.2002, New York.

Bonin, John and Wachtel, Paul (1999), 'Toward Market-Oriented Banking in the Economies in Transition', in Blejer, M. and Skreb, M. (eds), *Financial Sector Transformation: Lessons for the Economies in Transition*, Cambridge University Press.

Bonin, John and Wachtel, Paul (2002), 'Financial Sector Development in Transition Economies: The First Ten Years', mimeo.

Bures, Oldrich (2001), 'Czech Banking Reform – Biggest Free Lunch Ever?', in Carter, Dave (ed.), *International Student Conference. Future in the Making: Opportunities... Choices... Consequences...* (Dec).

Derviz, Alexis (1997), 'Financial Sector Performance and Removing Barriers to International Competition', WP 81, Czech National Bank.

Diamond, Douglas W. (1984), 'Financial Intermediation and Delegated Monitoring', *Journal of Political Economy*, 99(4), August 1991, pp. 689–721.

Diamond, Douglas W. (1996), 'Financial Intermediation as Delegated Monitoring: A Simple Example', *Federal Reserve Bank of Richmond Economic Quarterly*, 82(3) (Summer), pp. 51–66.

EBRD, *Transition Reports 1996–2001*, London.

European Central Bank (2001), 'Financial Sector Developments and Convergence in Accession Countries: An Overview', Directorate General, mimeo.

Galac, Tomislav and Kraft, Evan (2000), 'What has been the Impact of Foreign Banks in Croatia?' Croatian National Bank, mimeo.

Glaeser, E., Johnson, Simon and Shleifer, Andrei (2000), 'Coase vs. the Coasians', mimeo.

Gray, Cheryl W. and Holle, Arnold (1997), 'Bank-Led Restructuring in Poland (II): Bankruptcy and Its Alternatives', *Economics of Transition* 5,1 (May), 25–44.

International Institute for Management Development (IMD). *World Competitiveness Yearbook*, Lauzanne, Switzerland, 2000.

Iskyan, Kim and Besedin, Andrei (2001), 'Russian Banking Sector: A Desert of Reform – But Hope Persists', Renaissance Capital, mimeo.

Ivanov, Andrei (2000), 'Russian Banking Reform', Troika Dialog, mimeo.

Johnson, Simon, La Porta, Rafael, Lopez-De-Silanes, Florencio and Shleifer, Andrei (2000), 'Tunneling', *American Economic Review* 90,2 (May), pp. 22–27.

Keren, Michael and Ofer, Gur (2001), 'The Restructuring of Trade and Supply Networks in Transition Economies and the Role of FDI', ACES, New Orleans, January 4–7, 2001.

Keren, Michael and Ofer, Gur (2002), 'The Role of FDI in Trade and Financial Services in Transition: What Distinguishes Transition Economies from Developing Economies?' *Comparative Economic Studies*, 40, 1 (Spring).

Keren, Michael and Levhari, David (1993), 'The Israeli Moshav as a Credit Union: Adverse Selection and Moral Hazard', in Cask, C. and Kislev, Y. (eds), *Agricultural Cooperatives in Transition*. Boulder, CO: Westview Press, pp. 125–141.

Kislev, Yoav (1993), 'Experience with Collective Action and Cooperation in Agriculture in Israel', in Cask, C. and Kislev, Y. (eds), *Agricultural Cooperatives in Transition*, Westview Press, Boulder, CO, pp. 269–90.

La Porta, Rafael, Lopez-de-Silanes, Florencio, Shleifer, Andrei and Vishny, Robert (2001), 'Investor Protection and Corporate Governance', mimeo.

National Bank of Poland (2001), 'Summary evaluation of the financial Situation of Polish Banks: First Half 2001', Warsaw.

Ofer, Gur (2001), 'Development and Transition: Emerging but Merging?' *Revue d'Economie Financiere.*

Ofer, Gur (1973), *The Service Sector in Soviet Economic Growth: A Comparative Study*, Harvard University Press, Cambridge, MA.

Opiela, Timothy P. (2001), 'Assessing the Efficiency of Polish Commercial Banks', NBP, Research Department, Paper No. 18.

Pointbriand, Gael de (2001), 'Banking System in East Europe and the CIS', *Revue D'economie Financier,.* special issue.

Portes, Richard D. and Begg, David (1993), 'Enterprise debt and financial restructuring in Central and Eastern Europe', *European Economic Review* 37, (Mar), pp. 396–407.

Reininger, Thomas, Schardax, Franz and Summer, Martin (2001), 'The Financial System in the Czech Republic, Hungary and Poland after the first Decade of Transition', Bank of Austria, mimeo.

Stiglitz, Joseph E. (1994), *Whither Socialism*, The MIT Press, Cambridge, MA.

Stiglitz, Joseph and Weiss, Andrew (1981), 'Credit Rationing in Markets with Imperfect Information', *American Economic Review* 71,3 (June), pp. 393–410.

Szapary, Gyorgy (2002), 'Banking Sector Reform in Hungary: What have we Learned and What are the Prospects?' *Comparative Economic Studies*, 40,2 (Spring).

Vucic, Boris and Jermic, Igor (2001), 'Efficiency of Banks in Transition: A DEA Approach', Croatian National Bank, mimeo.

World Bank (1993), *Russia: The Banking System in Transition*, Washington DC.

World Bank (2001a), 'Russia. Building Trust Developing the Russian Financial Sector', Volume I, 'Executive Summary and Discussion Paper' and Volume II, Working Papers 1–15.

World Bank (2001b), *Finance for Growth: Policy Choices in a Volatile World*, World Bank Policy Research Report, Washington, DC.

Chapter 12

Implementing Global Best Practice Standards: The Fiduciary Role of the Private Sector

George Vojta

Following on the financial crises of the late 1990s, the international community considered numerous concepts of how risk, transparency, and crisis prevention/management processes in the global financial system could be improved. Suggestions ranged from radical proposals (e.g. establish a global bankruptcy court) to modest initiatives (e.g. countries ought to adopt a policy of confining short-term foreign currency borrowings to a level not exceeding available free foreign exchange reserves). Most suggestions were rejected or at best, unevenly adopted, but finally a consensus developed to the effect that a feasible path to improve the financial system involved country adoption and implementation of best practice standards in what came to be termed 12 key policy areas.[1]

There is general agreement that deficiencies in these policy areas magnified, complicated and extended crises, which initially were caused by macro-economic imbalances, event or contagion risk. Most would endorse the belief that countries which adopt and implement these standards will become better, with more transparent risks over time for domestic and foreign lenders and investors. It is expected that implementation of these standards will also improve the community's ability to prevent and/or manage crises. After a period of discussion, most if not all countries now agree that it is in their interest to give priority to adopting the core standards in more or less universal form.

The standards movement was initiated by the G7 countries, working with the principal IFI's and various standard-setting bodies. In the early stages, non G7 countries and the private sector had no involvement or input into this effort. With the formation of the G20 and increased outreach programs by the main IFI's, more countries are now participating in this process. To date, there has been some outreach activity by the IFI's to the private sector to develop support for global standards. However the private sector has only modest understanding of the standards initiative and little working knowledge of on-going events related to the issue.

This discussion argues that the time has come for the private sector to become more significantly involved in promoting acceptance of global standards. Countries must become incentivized by the private markets to implement standards and to view this effort as a principal path to achieving a positive climate for financial stability, investment and growth. Without powerful market incentives which reward adoption and implementation of standards, there is little chance that the standards movement will be effective in achieving the desired improvement of the financial system. The private sector, which controls the preponderance of resources necessary to sustain global growth, should support standards implementation in its own interest. Now, however, it can be fairly argued that the private sector has a fiduciary duty to embrace and promote standards compliance. The rationale for this proposition is as follows:

Basic Propositions

1. Management and directors of private enterprises (both financial and corporate) have the fiduciary responsibility of investing the resources (capital, credit, people, technology etc.) entrusted to them prudently to make acceptable returns without compromising or destroying the principal value of these resources.
2. In making decisions to deploy these resources, the management/board are *obligated* as fiduciaries to act on the basis of the most fulsome, accurate, timely information available to assess the risks to be taken and the rewards expected.
3. In determining countries (and related institutions) with which to do business, assessment of macro-economic policies continues to be essential (as noted, unsound macro policies or event and contagion risks can trigger a financial crisis.) As stated above, experience shows that deficiencies in country practices in the 12 key policy areas magnify, extend and complicate crises. Consequently, failure to consider the position of a country (institution) on standards implementation in initial due diligence analyses, produces incomplete, less than fulsome conclusions about the risks and rewards of doing business in particular countries and with their institutions.
4. Countries which become compliant over time with the core standards, while maintaining reasonably adequate macro policies, will become better investment/credit risks.
5. Countries not in compliance with standards and which declare unwillingness to comply or take no public position on standards compliance *warrant caution* in investing/lending in that country. Negative or neutral positions on standards taken by a country signals a negative *intent* relative to actions they might take to improve risks for potential lenders and investors.
6. If the foregoing are true, it is correct to conclude that a proper analysis of country risk (and related institutions) requires analysis of macro-economic

policies *together with the country's position on the core standards*; failure to consider both dimensions of country risk will result in inaccurate assessments.[2]

7. There is significant, growing empirical evidence that countries which comply with the core standards are rewarded with better performance, which in turn can result in further benefits such as a lower cost of capital, higher stock price etc. The research also is demonstrating that the converse proposition is true.

8. To date systematic assessment of country/institutional compliance with the core standards is not an integral dimension of private sector risk management and rating agency processes. The reasons for this state of affairs are:

   a. Lack of useable current information about country compliance with standards;

   b. Lack of conviction by the private sector that standards compliance is essential to risk assessments;

   c. Some concern that adding standards compliance to risk management assessments could result in loss of business to competitors who do not do so;

   d. Lack of systematic use of standards information by rating agencies.

9. But, if in fact standards compliance is material to a proper assessment of country/institutional risk, private sector management/boards of directors have the *obligation* to obtain, utilize, and reasonably contribute to the *development of standards information in private sector decision making*. Failure to obtain, utilize and encourage the dissemination of this information will increasingly be construed as a *breach of fiduciary responsibilities* by private sector constituencies.

10. The private sector also has a fiduciary responsibility to *explicitly* encourage countries/institutions to adopt and implement these standards, reward successful compliance and sanction poor or no compliance. Private sector liability for failure to use and disclose standards information – to clients, to shareholders, to employees, and to regulators – is rising; increasing recourse to litigation to obtain reimbursement for losses incurred by investors/lenders because of failure to utilize or disclose available standards information is beginning to occur.

11. Countries are open, in an unprecedented manner, to supporting standards adoption/compliance; but it is important that they receive a *strong continuing* signal from the private market place that standards compliance is important and will be rewarded appropriately. Strong signals from the market place will cause standards compliance to improve and information about standards to become a strong source of market discipline on behalf of standards adoption. The signals will act like a self-fulfilling prophecy.

The Pragmatic Significance of Compliance with Standards

The risks associated with compliance or lack thereof with core standards can be summarized briefly:

Non-compliance with data dissemination, fiscal and monetary policy transparency standards indicates that national statistics may not be accurate and may not disclose the correct view of economic policy. There may be hidden liabilities, excessive money creation and deficit financing etc. Consequently, such information as is available may not be reliable and truly portray the country risk. Non-compliance with accounting and auditing standards may mean that enterprise values and profit and loss performance are obscured and/or inaccurate. Lack of good corporate governance can involve risks of mismanagement or worse. Absence of an effective bankruptcy regime may mean that it is impossible to restructure troubled or failing enterprises efficiently and equitably to parties at interest. An unsatisfactory money laundering condition connotes an unethical, corrupt business environment. Poor standards of regulation of the payment mechanism, banks, securities and insurance companies can indicate a dysfunctional financial system with unrecognized asset and capital impairment which jeopardizes growth and stability in the economy.

All of the foregoing, importantly, materially modify the macro-economic profile of a country. This information must be assessed in initial due diligence analyses and appropriately weighed and disclosed e.g. by underwriters, syndicate managers, fund managers, traders, and equity investors to clients, shareholders, the boards of directors, regulators and employees *before risks are assumed and while risks are in portfolio*. The fiduciary responsibility to manage standards-related risks in this fashion is inescapable.

The Current Context

Currently, the prospects for sustained global development are mixed. As yet, there is no agreed upon mechanism to resolve financial crises; the World Bank and IMF are under criticism for failed policies, wasted resources, and ineffective results. Capital flows to emerging market countries have not only slowed to a trickle but in many countries have reversed to net outflows.

The only feasible path to rekindled global growth and sustainable development involves countries adopting sound macro policies and commitments to implement global standards, and in so doing create national conditions favorable to higher levels of domestic and foreign equity investment in wealth creating enterprises. The international community and particularly the private sector *must* support the successful execution of appropriate policies and practices and strongly link terms and degrees of access to the global markets to good performance relative to these policies, practices and values.

A future which involves further regression of low income and emerging market countries is unacceptable; reversing this dangerous trend must be given highest priority.

This question has become more visibly urgent in the aftermath of the September 11 tragedy. The recently concluded UN conference in Monterrey, which focused on the issues of financing development, highlighted the issue of poverty and re-affirmed a goal of reducing by one-half the global population below the poverty line by 2015. The World Bank projection of global population increase to 8 billion (from 6 billion) and the increase in the population below the poverty line from 4.8 to 6.8 billion, if present trends continue, is a grim prospect. Currently, 20 per cent of the global population earns 80 per cent of the world's income. No one can predict the trend of this number in the future because of uncertainty about global investment, assistance flows and developmental outcomes in specific countries.

Optimistically, official developmental assistance may rise to an annual level of USD 50bn in the next few years; private capital flows (direct investment, portfolio investment and bank lending) are normally in the USD 300bn range. Obviously, these levels must be maintained and increased; equally obvious is the fact that official assistance cannot come close to achieving the levels necessary to support required global growth. A conclusion reached over and over is that private investment, domestic and foreign, in wealth creating activities is the best, and only, hope to achieve the desired level of economic progress and such private investment cannot occur unless country conditions are hospitable to such investment. In turn, success in attracting private investment requires sound policies, good practices and wholesome values at the country level.

The discussion has come full circle – visible acceptance and implementation of global best practice standards must be strongly embraced by countries in the global system and continuously encouraged, promoted and rewarded by global lenders and investors.

Notes

1　The 12 areas are: Standards for national data dissemination, fiscal and monetary policy transparency, accounting, auditing, corporate governance, bankruptcy regimes, money laundering, and regulation and supervision of payment mechanisms, banks, securities and insurance firms.

2　For a further examination of this point see the writer's article 'Global Standards: The Path To An Improved Global Financial System' in *Central Banking*, Vol. XII, No. 1 – August 2001.

Index